WANTED

A Spiritual Pursuit
Through Jail, Among Outlaws,
and Across Borders

WANTED

CHRIS HOKE

HarperOne
An Imprint of HarperCollins*Publishers*

HarperOne

WANTED: *A Spiritual Pursuit Through Jail, Among Outlaws, and Across Borders.* Copyright © 2015 by Christopher Hoke. All rights reserved. Printed in the United States of America. No part of this book may be used or reproduced in any manner whatsoever without written permission except in the case of brief quotations embodied in critical articles and reviews. For information address HarperCollins Publishers, 195 Broadway, New York, NY 10007.

HarperCollins books may be purchased for educational, business, or sales promotional use. For information please e-mail the Special Markets Department at SPsales@harpercollins.com.

HarperCollins website: http://www.harpercollins.com

HarperCollins®, ▰®, and HarperOne™ are trademarks of HarperCollins Publishers.

FIRST EDITION

Library of Congress Cataloging-in-Publication Data
Hoke, Chris.
    Wanted : a spiritual pursuit through jail, among outlaws, and across borders / Chris Hoke.
        pages   cm
    ISBN 978-0-06-232136-7
    1. Hoke, Chris (Prison chaplain)   2. Prison chaplains—United States—Biography.   3. Church work with prisoners—United States.   4. Prisoners—Religious life—United States.   I. Title.
BV4340.H65   2015
259'.50973—dc23   2014021655
15 16 17 18 19   RRD(H)   10 9 8 7 6 5 4 3 2 1

For Richard.
I hope this does you justice.

And for Bob.
Thank you for welcoming me into a new world.

We have an altar from which those who officiate
in the tent have no right to eat. . . .
Let us then go to him outside the camp . . .

—*Letter to the Hebrews 13:10, 13*

CONTENTS

INTRODUCTION   1

WANTED I   5

NIGHT SHIFTS   13

WANTED II   47

BIRDS OF THE AIR   53

NO CONTACT   75

WANTED III   87

IN SEARCH OF SACRED SPACE   91

THE ANGLE OF DESCENT   103

WANTED IV   127

FLY FISHING WITH THE DAMMED   133

WANTED V 153

FUCK THE WORLD 165

HEARTS LIKE RADIOS 191

STRANGER ON THE EDGE OF TOWN 229

WANTED VI 251

CALIMERO 255

WANTED VII 273

SAINT CHRISTOPHER ON A KAWASAKI 279

DONACIO'S TABLE 301

FIRE IN THE HOLE 317

WANTED VIII 349

EPILOGUE 357

Appendix: Tierra Nueva 359
Acknowledgments 361

WANTED

INTRODUCTION

THIS IS WHERE I TELL YOU WHAT TO EXPECT, why I wrote this book you hold in your hands.

I'll begin with a story.

During the darkest days of my early twenties, when I wanted to dispose of myself, I hid from my despair and demons one afternoon by slipping into a museum of modern art. High on the top floor in San Francisco, in what felt like an attic, I came across an ominous, nine-foot-tall work by Mark Rothko. (Look him up online if you don't know the artist. *No. 14, 1960,* to be exact.) I forgot about the rest of the museum. This one drew me close. It held me. I found myself leaning into it, nearly.

Like most of Rothko's works, this painting was only two fields of color, hung like frayed and glowing curtains, one atop the other, Dutch-door-style, as if between us and the world we were made to seek. I stood and stared. There was a familiar fire beneath all those layers of midnight blue and bloodlike paint.

It looked like when you close your eyes while facing a light. Or what you might see if you had a window into a living heart. It seemed to swell, breathe. I wanted to step through the frame. I might have tried, even—given my condition those days, reaching my fingertips to the canvas—if there weren't security cameras, alarms, and uniformed guards. But I kept coming back.

One visit, I read on the discreet placard beside this portal on the wall that when the artist was asked what he was trying to do with these heavy veils of pigment, canvas after immense canvas, he answered, *I am trying to paint God.*

This claim charged what hung on the wall with a danger, as well as a stranger beauty.

Since reading that, I've seen his paintings differently. Just the shapes—two rectangles, one large, one a narrow banner above or below—no longer resemble doors in my imagination, but something else: the old "WANTED" posters of outlaws still loose in the world. In this sense, Rothko's WANTED portraits are blurry for a good reason. It is difficult to capture so elusive a subject.

I am trying to do something similar with this book. With these stories of wanted men, my relationships with criminals in various states of transformation, I am really trying to capture a greater subject—a divine presence that has yet to be held very long in any official custody.

The pages you hold in your hands—a mix of true crime and spiritual adventure—can be read as a story, the story of my ongoing pursuit of this presence among the unwanted characters I've met in the small county jail where I moonlight as a chaplain now. The story is mostly about my friendships with young gang members, set in a misty agricultural valley in the far Northwest, with one particular thief running through it all, ducking in and out of the chapters. And yet, I have resisted the temptation to force my memories into a seamless narrative arc, putting a narrator—me—too squarely in the center as the main actor. I'd rather think of these chapters as forensic sketches, a kind of mystical portraiture across time, varying in color, material, tone, and size. That is, after nine years moving in and out of the jail as an uncredentialed minister, learning to pray in a cathedral of tattoos and temporary release orders, these stories are my versions of Rothko's answer. I am trying to paint God.

Like Rothko's paintings, these chapters may look, at first, nothing at all like God, full of unsavory criminals, profanity, violence, death, and drugs. But I invite you to look more closely, to lean in and allow an image of God to surprise you, and maybe a presence to embrace you.

As with all WANTED posters, I have sketched these portraits because this presence has escaped me in recent years. Whatever broke into my heart in these dark places, it has left my life altered, and there's no undoing that. The purpose of WANTED posters, then, is to alert the public. My hope is that these portraits might raise your awareness of what could be just outside your door, still alive, slipping through the shadows on the edge of your county or your heart.

WANTED posters are created from the testimony of eyewitnesses on the basis of events remembered. The same is true of this book. And these sketches are colored by my own subjective experience of the events. Firsthand witnesses can be overwhelmed with the trauma of a murder, or the wonder of a snow leopard, so close at hand. It shapes their reports. I am no different.

Also, I have had to disguise the names of many people and a few places, to protect both the innocent and the guilty, including myself.

But all the events I describe happened. Dialogue is rendered as best I can remember it, significant portions often scribbled in my journals soon after conversations. Overall, though, I confess that these portraits are shaped less by a journalist's sensibility and more by the images that continue to haunt me throughout the day and sometimes into the night.

I haven't gotten it right. But I keep trying to find a shape for this presence that is still at large.

I leave my doors unlocked.

WANTED I

S OMEONE CALLED THE COPS ON RICARDO MEJIA AS soon as he was born. As soon as his fifteen-year-old mother had finished ridding him from her body, she slipped out of the Skagit Valley Hospital and left him there. When the nurse came in and saw the squirming newborn on his own in the clear plastic bin, she made no move to pick him up or cradle him. Instead, she picked up the phone and called the police.

Richard—as family called him—could remember sitting in court when the state tried to force his mother to claim him. Many children suffer through watching their parents fight, and many others endure the anxiety of knowing those fights are the result of custody battles. Seated on a wooden bench behind the lawyers, his small feet not yet reaching the floor, Richard looked on as representatives of the state fought with his mother for the opposite reason: neither party wanted him. Sometimes the state won, and her begrudging hand would lead him out the courtroom door. But just as often, the small boy watched his mother walk out of court without him, her eyes avoiding his.

So, years later, Richard could hardly contain his delight when a helicopter and multiple squad cars chased him at high speeds through neighborhoods and down farm roads: the thrill of so many people laboring to keep him in their sights, sparing no cost to get their hands on him. As he swung the stolen sedan around corners of potato fields and long rows of beets, Richard shot his twitching, open-jawed gaze past one young woman in his front seat and another in the back and saw, through the rear window, how the squad cars would not give up on him. Richard had been burglarizing a house with these new partners when the police spotted them, and the hunt began. Richard managed to prolong this waking dream—search parties in hot pursuit of *him*—for three days, disappearing each evening. Being invisible was, after all, the state he knew best. The afternoon of his first escape from the chase, Richard veered the small Honda into tall fields of corn, plowing his own harvest maze of sorts. On hands and knees and alone, he disappeared into the field like a treasure to be hunted.

When a young woman flipped on the hanging light bulb in her small laundry basement that night, she saw a skinny, half-white, half-Mexican–looking young man with a shaved head crouched in the corner smiling back at her, holding a tattooed finger to his lips. Methamphetamines had sucked his face into a near skull, but the gleam in his deep-set eyes above his high cheekbones still had the effect of a child's disarming grin. Each night he was at large, Richard made new friends this way.

Immigration and Customs Enforcement (ICE) joined the pursuit on day two, their canine units sniffing through torn-down trailer parks where he was believed to be hiding. The photos of these perplexed officers and German shepherds on long leashes covered the front page of the following morning's *Skagit Valley Herald,* right next to Richard's mug shot from a past arrest. The article stated that Richard, at age twenty-three, had joined the official list of Washington State's Most Wanted.

———————

The officers found Richard hiding atop a storage container behind the Walmart in Mount Vernon, between the dumpsters. They did not immediately lay hands on him. Instead, they tazered him. Fourteen times he remembered. Later press accounts said only six. Richard said that, after cuffing him to a bedpost hours later, the exhausted lead investigator confessed to him, scraped and bruised, that he'd never had such difficulty tracking down a suspect on these streets. Normally, the detective told him, he could get any drug addict to rat out another by offering a small fold of cash. The search would be over in hours. This time, he told Richard, he went to all the usual houses, offered hundreds of dollars, but no one would say a word. All denied knowing Richard.

"I gotta hand it to you, Mr. Mejia," Richard remembered the man with a badge on his belt saying to him, wiping his forehead. "You've got a lot of respect out there on the streets." This made Richard smile, but it did not surprise him. Unlike most thieves and addicts, whenever Richard scored some drugs, he called everyone he knew to share the cache with them. Richard liked being surrounded. He often threw the only kind of feast he knew in order to gather a willing fellowship. Those who came, who accepted his invitation, were, of course, other unhealthy, drug-addicted souls in the criminal shadows. While the motives in these affairs are as mixed and deceptive as the baggies of various white powders they exchange, an addict goes with what's available. There is, in these desperate relationships, as with cut drugs, enough of the pure to get one through the night.

Early in his thieving career, Richard gained the attention of local gangs. The alienated children of migrant farmworkers adrift in rural, white counties band together in this way (maybe this was why Richard, like so many other Mexican youth, never went by his birth name, Ricardo). And so agricultural valleys like ours become ganglands that can rival those of the biggest cities. These gangs wanted Richard. So he joined them. They liked his pluck and gave him a new name: Lil' Jokes. When he was in need in the middle of the night, they would pick him up. They would never call the cops on him. He tattooed the barrio's name and symbols on his chest, neck, and behind his ear, next to the names of women who were able to love him for short periods of time. He gave his gang everything he had. He did what they told him to do, and more.

But what the detective confessed to Richard, who sat handcuffed to the bed, was evidence of something that transcended normal street allegiances. It was proof that Richard was special. Whether or not those people standing behind cracked-open front doors lying to police officers loved him in the truest sense or not, it was certain that they at least felt a tenderness, a protectiveness, something like respect, for this wounded, flailing, and uniquely unguarded young man tearing through their blurred lives.

———

The night I first met Richard in jail, I was losing the attention of the men in the circle of chairs at bible study. "Hey guys, check this out." I tried to pull us together. "Guys . . . check this out. . . ."

Richard, new to our group, sat just to my left. He spun on me from his laughter with two other inmates and pointed his finger right at my face, his head cocked. "No, bro," he said. "How 'bout you check *this* out." What he then began to aggressively throw at me—from his life, his opinions—was so good, I started taking notes. He monologued about the streets, about being slave to a needle, about misery, betrayal, being hated, being tazered on the ground while multiple officers stood around him with dogs. It didn't feel like he was trying to show defiance or silence me for cheap attention. Instead, in that first jail meeting, he countered my flailing bible study by filling the remaining time with a generous and more robust offering from his own story. When he saw me taking notes, asking him to slow down and repeat a few phrases, Richard smiled.

The multipurpose room door clanged open and a guard stepped in to announce, "It's time." All the inmates stood up to go back to their cells. But Richard leaned in close and looked me in the eye: "Hey, come visit me this week. I'm serious."

When I visited Richard one-on-one a week later, in a cramped cinder-block cell, sitting on a hard chair facing him across a bare table, he said he wanted to offer me something. "If you're gonna know me," he began, "I don't wanna hide shit." Richard told me about a home video he had taken of himself. This was his most treasured possession, he said, and he wanted me to have it. I was confused as to why I deserved such a gift, so suddenly. "I was high out of my mind a few weeks ago when I made it, I'm not gonna lie. But one night I almost cried over how fucked up my life is. And I decided, I'm gonna videotape this: *A Day in My Fucked-Up Life*. It turned into *three* days. It's full of shit I don't want just anyone seeing, you know? But I want you to go to my mom's house and tell her I sent you. She knows where I hid the camera and tape. Her name's April. She's not my real mom, you know. She's the only mom I've ever had. To me, she's my mom. But watch that video. I'm *telling* you, Chris."

I never saw the raw footage of those days in Richard's uncensored life. When I called the number he wrote down in large, cartoonish numerals in my journal, I learned that whatever passed for the record of his existence had already been thrown away—burned and buried in the backyard. Too much evidence against him, April told me.

So I tried to imagine Richard carrying around his stolen camcorder, pointing it at himself, the blinking red dot proof of its steady gaze, the undivided attention it paid him. It would follow him. It would listen. It would not interrupt nor scold nor judge. It would be there. It would remember him, everything he said. He would put on no performance, feign no smiling introductions before this lens. Richard didn't want that. He took the electronic witness along with him into his places of shame, his hours of boredom, his hibernating-then-running routine of addiction and theft, the camera capturing all the unhappy people with unhappy words in unhappy homes where he crashed.

I knew the portrait had been destroyed. But still, I wanted it.

———————

To be continued . . .

NIGHT SHIFTS

Growing up, I often heard my father say that nothing meaningful could happen past ten at night. That's when arguments could pick up in the house, he knew. That's when reason lost its control. That's when the mind's grasp grew sleepy and passions ran freely, like drunks on the highway. It is the hour when you lock your doors. It was around that hour when my father couldn't understand what his family was suddenly yelling at him or each other about. Just before shutting it down, he'd look at his watch and see that it affirmed his suspicion. It was time.

I found as I grew up that this was the very time I came most alive.

After ten P.M., I heard music inside me where before there had been only noise or silence. I would pour a bowl of sugar cereal and try to capture these songs on my guitar—quietly, of course, while others slept. If you walked the dark hall and pressed your ear to my childhood bedroom door, you'd have heard the faintest of melodies. I was trying to find the sound for a desire that awoke at this hour, one I could not yet name.

Boredom disappeared with the sunset. Now I wanted to step out the door and walk the warm suburban sidewalks and look at the desert stars. I wanted to read more books, then write some myself. In this hour, I suddenly knew what I wanted to do with the rest of my life. I wanted to pray.

I don't think this was a religious impulse. I had no sense for tradition or ritual, the bowing of heads or folding of hands, no interest in robes or prayer books. Nor was I longing for something transcendent—in the sense of looking outside or above our mildly troubled suburban existence. Rather, I sensed there was a sweeter world hidden under the thin skin of this one. And I could rarely see it under the glare of the Southern California sunshine. Around this time of night, however, it was—and still is—as if a fire were kindled inside my head. And in its interior light I saw more of what was hidden. I bought journals and tried to write down in erratic cursive everything that was suddenly, beautifully clear in these hushed hours. I wrote as fast as I could before the threat of morning's empty malaise sent me to bed, lest it overtake me and catch me at dawn. The next day I would review my notes from the evening before, and they read like nonsense. All the stories of carriages magically dissolving into pumpkins at a certain hour, stories of men transformed into werewolves under the moonlight, then back again at dawn— these made sense to me.

Contemplatives of every tradition describe carrying on a romance with this while-the-world-is-sleeping hour: entering the silence of the mind like a lake before dawn, its surface still undisturbed by the day to come. I tried. I crawled out of bed when the windows were predawn blue and knelt in the groggy silence, wandering, lost. I never found that lake in my mind.

One of the earliest monks, John Cassian, spoke in the fourth century of some prayer as "that fire known to so few." During my high school years, it's possible that this yet-unidentified flame within me got channeled, like fuel, into a more familiar set of teenage nocturnal practices. Like nighttime phone conversations with pretty girls, staring at the underside of my top bunk and whispering with the phone tucked against my ear for a duration of hours only monks could sustain in hushed prayer. Then it powered long drives with my first girlfriend when I got my driver's license and a very old, midnight blue Mustang with a narrow backseat. Her father's firm curfew made those brief hours burn all the hotter. Then with ten other teenage boys, we'd buy discounted boxes of one dozen jelly-filled donuts and chase each other through town in separate cars, screeching through empty parking lots under flickering orange lights while leaning out the tops of sunroofs, hurling the gooey confections at moving windshields and into each other's open windows, laughing till four A.M.

In the morning I'd stagger out of my bedroom in pajamas, passing my dad in the hallway. He'd be dripping with sweat and exhilaration, already back from his five-mile run along the bright morning orange groves. If it was Sunday, I sat in church and took notes during the sermon just as I would in any other class. I'd sing on tune and bow my head earnestly. But there was no fire.

"The Word enters our dreams and images more easily at the time before the sun's light," a contemporary Trappist monk, Francis Kline, has written. "Only in the darkness are certain, more choice intuitions of God received." I have wondered whether these Trappists, an extreme order of monastics, rise for vigils at three in the morning when it is still dark for the same reason I have stayed up so late. Maybe we were just coming at it from different sides of the clock.

———

My senior year of high school I heard about a program where young people live together like monks in one of America's four most violent inner-city neighborhoods. The program's recruiter asked in his pitch—as I would read in Kierkegaard's yellowed pages years later—*If Jesus were our contemporary, somewhere out there, among us, where would we find him? And if we found him, would we join him or be offended by him?* I pictured the manicured evangelical liberal arts colleges where I'd applied for fall entrance. Was this where I wanted to continue my search? Then I pictured myself walking through torn-down neighborhoods, not having to drive back to the suburbs come nightfall, free to walk through bad parts of town and hunt what the gospel stories had taught me to seek, wondering whether I'd recognize the presence. I pictured myself playing guitar with homeless guys on the corner till all hours, sleeping under bridges, a reeking sleeping bag all my own among them. I signed up, deferring my acceptances to the private colleges. The program sent me north, to East Oakland.

Against the program's house rules, I often stayed out past curfew. During the day I served food and filled out social security applications at a homeless shelter, ate at long tables with folks dying of AIDS. I met drag queens with stubble, platinum blond wigs, sometimes with a nasal cannula and oxygen tank in tow. I witnessed laughter and communion at these tables that I knew to be rooted in a pain I had not experienced. But I was on the outside of this fellowship, serving their paper plate meals, then wiping the tables after them when the room emptied.

It was in the nighttime hours, though, when a form of such communion opened to me: I stayed late at my neighbor Leno's house, a Salvadoran gang member hiding from his San Francisco enemies with his girlfriend Crystal and their two daughters in the East Bay. He laughed at my bleached hair from Southern California's surf culture, invited me to his Corona-and-carne-asada parties on his side of the chain-link fence with other guys in huge pants and white tank tops, and he tried to hotbox me most nights in his garage. This garage was a realm of swirling marijuana smoke and guys with names like Sniper and glossy posters on the walls of naked women reclining on the polished hoods of lowriders. Sniper and the others found my presence in their realm unnatural, to say the least. But Leno introduced me like I was just another homeboy on the block.

He took me with him to a big barbecue his friends threw at a public lake, Santana's "Black Magic Woman" blasting on a large boombox. He knew how to throw a feast. When I stepped on a bee in my bare feet and Leno saw me drop to the grass in pain, he told his laughing friends to "shut the fuck up" while he got on his knees and worked to pull out the stinger from my pale foot. It was the closest—and most authentic—thing I'd experienced to having someone wash my feet, that is, in the way Jesus's disciples were instructed.

The year came to an end. I wasn't sure whether I'd caught up with Jesus on those streets. But Leno called me his friend, confessed more of his darkest secrets in our lengthening conversations, and even had me teach him guitar. I gave him mine, in exchange for all he'd taught me. He said he wanted to sing, late at night, when his homeboys went home and left his garage quiet and still. "You know," he looked over his shoulder cautiously in the garage, shut the door to the kitchen, licked his lips, and said more softly, "like, to praise the Lord." Such a stale phrase that I'd heard endlessly in churches sounded profound from Leno, especially with a Scarface movie poster stenciled on the comforter across the couch behind him. "I'm not a Sunday morning church kinda guy. But I been wantin' to sing my own kinda prayers, here, at night, you know? That's when I feel it."

I saw changes in both of us. He married his girlfriend, moved out of the hood, and became a paramedic. I cancelled my acceptances to the evangelical colleges and applied to UC Berkeley, a ten-minute drive north of there. Whether I'd found Jesus or not, I didn't want to stray too far from what I'd found on those streets.

———————

As a college student, I pushed through the sweaty frat parties and tried to catch up with some classmates on our way out of

lecture, but I could not find a friend like Leno. I poured most of
my time into my girlfriend, but after a year it became clear that
while I wanted to get back to the streets after graduation, she
had different plans, like medical school. I wanted to pursue this
penniless call. But I didn't want to be alone. That was my bind.
She finally had to cut me off. So after two years I invited another
friend from the Oakland program, Troy, to move back to the
East Bay from his hometown up in northwest Washington and
share my apartment with me. He, like me, preferred balancing
glasses of wine with opened copies of used books to keg stands.
We preferred dancing on my apartment's coffee table to shoving
through sticky frat-house hallways. We read J. D. Salinger and
Kierkegaard, Wendell Berry, Annie Dillard, and Dostoevsky—
often aloud, while drinking, sometimes to the point where we
ended up embracing in embarrassingly sentimental outpour-
ings, even trying to pray, on our knees, hands open or on the
other's forehead, there amidst the empty bottles, loaded ashtrays, and loud indie rock music well past two in the morning.
Maybe it was because the passages we read from these books,
through the tipsy blur, always pointed us toward the life Jesus
described to us long ago, when we listened as kids in Sunday
school—that is, giving our lives over completely to holy love, a
mystery much larger than us, serving others whom the world
despises, maybe touching another world hidden within this one,
university ambitions and careers be damned. But who would
help us follow these promptings when inspiration struck? The
rest of the responsible world was at home with their families.
Church and classroom doors were locked for the night. Only

drunks and thieves were out at this hour. Sometimes we could hear them in the alleys below, their bottles clinking eerily faint echoes of our own.

Church was not a place to find the exploring partners I sought. I'd been to dozens growing up, an over-churched up-bringing, and had visited a handful more in my first two years of college. I knew the routine: a crowd of showered people, mostly families with good homes and decent jobs, in our Sunday best sit facing a stage or an altar, sing songs, hear a sermon, nibble a tiny piece of bread we are told is something more, wander back to our seats, chat over coffee in the lobby, go home or out to a nice lunch. But the cross hanging behind most preachers haunted me. The first-century electric chair. Cosmic redemption, the story told us, happened in the seat of criminality, out on the edge of town, between two dying thieves—and when the land had grown curiously dark. The world's execution seat had been transformed into a portal: Christ had invited the thief dying beside him to come to paradise with him, as if they could slip out and be there in moments, together. Hymns and revamped old spirituals had us croon about a "Wondrous Cross," and I came to believe them: a sense of wonder was paired with such a place in my imagination. But I wasn't sure how to access that unwanted place in our own time.

I visited professors during their office hours in the religious studies department. They found my thrill at the New Testament to be a sentimental relic from the Dark Ages. They tried to en-lighten me by exposing the mysteries with critical theory and the social sciences. Their explanations felt as bright and sterile as a surgical lamp. So I tried to meet up with the pastors of those churches I'd visited, but on weekdays, outside the service, in cafés or bars in the evenings. Maybe they could speak more candidly outside of the sermon—about the frightening darkness within us, the nastiness we are capable of, the mystery of God lurking outside those neat theories that give us comfort on Sunday mornings. But the pastors seemed concerned by the type of stuff I was pulling out of my backpack and reading. And besides, they had to get home to their families for dinner and bedtimes. Mornings are better, they said, as they stood and finished their lattes.

———————

"Sorrow may last through the night," I had sung in many churches, a famous passage from the psalms, "but joy comes in the morning." I had experienced the opposite to be true. For me, anxiety and panic came in the morning. Around this time, I was so lonely and unsure of what I was going to do with my life after college that I woke morning after morning with my heart pounding in the bedroom's bright silence. I felt useless to the world. In an upward-bound university, surrounded by innovative young activists and poets and scientists and future shapers of global policy, all with promising career trajectories, I had nowhere to go with my dead weight. The only image in my mind as I lay there an hour before my alarm went off? Stepping off the tallest building on campus, as soon as possible. Dawn was the witching hour.

Some of those mornings, I made it to the upper exhibition floor of the Museum of Modern Art in San Francisco where, for a short time, the night-filled paintings of Marc Chagall covered the plain white walls. When the Chagall exhibit was taken away, I climbed the steps even higher. That's when I found that nine-foot-tall Rothko in the back corner of the museum's loft. I stood many bleak mornings before that massive and ominous portal like a kind of threshold.

Within the next few years, though, I would discover a real portal, one that opened to another society that inhabited the night. Though I found it in the farthest northwest corner of the country, every county has one. I would go through the jail.

––––––––

In the rainy farmlands north of Seattle, one of my professors told me, there lived a theologian who was neither dead nor in Europe, but whose pages, I soon discovered, had that same dark fire I'd met in the Gospels. This man and his wife—Bob and Gracie Ekblad—had been soil conservation activists and radical theologians among landless peasant farmers in the mountains of Latin America and started an organization called Tierra Nueva. They were inspired by the prophet Isaiah's vision of God making not just a new heaven, but a "new earth." These were texts they read together with the straw-hatted campesinos under the shade of mango trees, with heavy hoes in their hands and pistols in their belts. It was a lawless, wild west during those years when paramilitary troops haunted the tropical mountain villages. But now Bob was in the States, teaching not in a seminary, but in a crowded county detention facility. He was leaking online excerpts from a book he was writing, conversations with inmates under the title *Reading the Bible with the Damned*. Just hearing the title, I pictured a scene I'd underlined heavily in Dostoevsky's *Crime and Punishment:* Raskolnikov and Sonya, murderer and prostitute, together reading a Bible in a dark tenement cell, one candle burning between them.

In Bob's rough book excerpts from the jail, there was a hint of storybook magic that I love. For example, I read a story about two inmates locked in separate solitary cells whispering the psalms to each other through the rims of their toilets and the sewage pipes connecting them. They synchronized their flushes to open a window of thirty seconds between them. This form of communion—what Bob called "the word of God spoken through the filthy lips of toilets"—was one inmate's response to reading the first words of Genesis. Bob was talking about the Bible's opening passage, how the Spirit hovered over the waters, over the darkness and chaos at the dawn of time. Creation begins, so Bob the jail scholar affirmed, not in a clean vacuum, but in the place of darkness and chaos. "Where do you see the darkness and chaos in *your* lives?" Bob had asked the circles of inmates during these unique bible studies. Then he wrote down everything they said.

This was the faith community, the vocation, I was looking for.

As I read, I was already packing my bags in my mind.

I drove to the far northwest.

———

The first time I stepped into that jail with Bob, the land was already dark. As in all Washington winters, the sun was down before the earliest of suppers. The jail parking lot was empty, streetlights flickering. The double doors were locked. Chaplains can visit only at night.

Mornings belong to the busy shuffling of papers and chained bodies of inmates through corridors and courtrooms. After-noons are when public defenders flood the small visitation chambers to discuss the business of the law with underprepared inmates. But after dinner, after meds are distributed, when the day is done, a tired swing shift guard hears a beeping in the control booth and he looks at his small security camera screen: he spies Bob and me standing outside the locked entrance and he buzzes us into the building.

That first night, I followed my new teacher—gangly and white like me, with glasses too—up the dim stairwell, past the janitor wringing black water from his mop, through automated, bulletproof doors and into a realm most people hope to avoid.

We signed our names in a worn green book and handed over our keys. I followed Bob past the front desk, past the row of empty visiting booths, past the small holding rooms where I saw new intakes inside slouching over small tables. One man pressed his forehead to the small window and waved to Bob as we walked by. I followed him down the narrow hall toward the concrete multipurpose room where we would meet with four separate groups of inmates for bible studies. An officer in his starched uniform led the way. His head was shaved. The keys attached to his thick belt clinked as we walked, his black boots squeaking under the pressure of each step. The three of us stood at the last door and waited. The officer's glare shot past us to the surveillance camera, and he gave a nod to his unseen coworker watching us through it. Then the door opened all on its own with a loud clang.

Inside the cold room with its tall ceiling, Bob showed me how to rearrange the plastic chairs from their rigid rows into a simple circle, as was his custom. There was a hulking pulpit used by some visiting preachers, and Bob smiled at me as he asked for help pushing it against the wall, facing the corner. "Where it belongs." He winked. We pulled a stack of deteriorating New Testaments from the bottom shelf of the donated library's messily stacked selection. Extra bed mats were piled high against a tall wall, just beneath a massive mirror. Through it, the guards would watch us. Another door clanged open and twelve men shuffled in. They wore oversized red scrubs that exposed pale chests at the neck and read SAMISH COUNTY JAIL in white stencil letters across their backs. Bruised-looking toes stuck out from their thin rubber sandals. Each man wore on his wrist a plastic bracelet with his name and mug shot—bleary-eyed or angry snapshots of some of the worst nights of their lives. We shook their hands as they entered the circle, and some of the younger Chicano gangsters who regularly attended these studies pulled us closer with a handshake and hugged us. And they'd never met me before.

Together, we read. We flipped to a few selected passages from the paperback New Testaments peeled off the stack. Halfway through our group discussion, I watched in fascination as Bob abandoned the study and put his arm around one of our reading partners. This man in his red scrubs was in the middle of tearily confessing to having stolen from Bob when Bob let him sleep on the couch at Tierra Nueva's ministry offices months earlier. I thought of how my friend Troy and I would embrace sometimes after reading in our apartment in college. Only now, the late-night friendship included the kinds of characters we'd heard lurking in the alleys below.

When Bob wrapped up the first half-hour group that night, he set his attention on one of the inmates, a hard-faced man with pockmarked cheeks and slippery eyes. "I'm sure you've been cursed plenty in your life," Bob said to him. "But has anyone ever blessed you before?" I watched this man change before my eyes, slowly, as Bob spoke simple words of blessing, his hand gently pressed against the man's chest, where we aim for the heart. The man in red scrubs began to cry, losing his composure and control. The Holy Spirit was invoked. Reason was losing its grip. The man opened clearer eyes. He smiled and wiped his face, looking shyly at his lap. I later learned this was one of the Skagit Valley's top meth cooks—being blessed. Law and order was losing its hold on the facility, at least in this room. And during this hour when I normally came alive, I saw a local dead man coming back to life as well.

The Gospel pages had finally opened into another world.

I could enter now. I was not alone.

Bob was the professor I needed, the jail his seminary, inmates my fellow seminary students.

On another night that first month, Bob said something that struck me: that the Bible offers a series of mug shots of God's presence. "We study these testimonies, these stories," he said, leaning forward in his chair among the circle of men, "so maybe we can recognize God's presence among us, breaking in and out of our lives. That's why we study. *How does God move? Where? What does God sound like? What's his style when he commits his acts?*" I looked down at the cheap Bible in my hands, feeling I was holding something suddenly new. I noticed other men in the circle looking at what they held with similar reconsideration. "I suspect," Bob continued, "you've come across this God before, and didn't know it. Maybe he's broken into your life before, spoken to you, rescued you, touched you. Maybe God didn't finish with the folks in these pages. Maybe he's after you, too." This was not a pious nor a skeptical theology. It was a pursuit. Or, a sense that we were being pursued, with a love we did not understand nor expect. Prayer was how Bob imagined we might surrender to, or confront, our pursuer.

———

A tall man in red inmate scrubs approached me the following week after our bible study, after the doors back to their cells had popped open. He had wide eyes, red hair shorn close against his scalp, wild runelike tattoos from his elbow to his wrist. "Some night, can you come and, like, visit me? There's so much shit running through my head, I—I really need to talk with someone." The guard waiting at the door for this last straggler finally cleared his throat loudly. "So can you meet with me? Like, right now?"

I asked Bob whether I could. He told me he used to spend years doing just that, visiting guys after the groups until lights-out, then coming back other evenings throughout the week. But now, he sighed, his kids were getting older and he was needed at home, so he could only stick to the group studies two evenings a week. "But you, on the other hand . . ."

I, on the other hand, was single, unemployed, newly friendless in a strange valley, and already prone to stay up until two A.M. These were slacker traits (the very traits that had so far disqualified me from most available options for a spiritually or socially helpful vocation). But when added to my awkward and undying desire to know God (which made me a failed hipster, no matter how much I looked the part), they now made me a perfect fit for this off-the-radar, dark and lockdown monastery.

My background check was clean, allowing me to return as a regular volunteer to the facility. The officer would unrestrain one of the men who'd asked for a visit and let him into the lawyer visiting cell with me and lock the door. In these tiny, sterile rooms, a world opened to me. They told me about running through the desert from immigration searchlights with their children in their arms; about demonic shadows prowling over them in a meth trailer's bed; about gunshots in the forests; about fathers' cracking belts or routine *leñazos* in their village back home; about pockets—or whole car trunks—full of cocaine; about rowing frigid boats over clam and oyster flats for twelve-hour night shifts; about girlfriends who'd walked out on them, leaving them overdosed in cold empty bathtubs; about orphanages in Mexico and juvenile halls and foster families in the United States; about rehabs, sometimes twelve of them in three years; about childhood churches and priests' groping hands and ensuing threats; about mothers' boyfriends in their beds; about drive-bys and stashes of guns and fistfights in alleyways; about mothers dying in the hospital and judges who denied them twenty-four-hour release orders to visit either the bedside or the graveside; about distant sons and daughters who wouldn't forgive them or reply to their letters. But against this dismal backdrop, a distinct light in their eyes, the spark of spiritual beginnings I had followed through so many nights myself, shone more fiercely than in most people I'd encountered outside those jail walls.

And through it all, as I had growing up, many of these men had also heard a faint music. They too tried to write their own songs in the night hours in their cell. They wanted to share them with me here—a cappella. Some of the songs had power and original charm. Some were simply bad and belonged only in that room. Our tight cinder-block chamber hummed like a bell with their melodies, seeping out into the jail's night shift corridors. They asked to hear my own songs, the not-so-disguised prayers that had been left in dusty CD sleeves after recording in my friends' after-hours studios. I faced their encouraging smiles across the bare table between us and began to sing my songs, without my guitar. Young gangsters beat-boxed along. Soon the jail became my constant venue for writing and singing new music, the high hard walls making each note sweeter than any reverb effect I'd channeled through recording studio headphones. Our laughter echoed out through the graveyard lobby in the same way.

Men who had felt closed and dead all day in court proceedings and over lunch trays now wept onto the dry table where their tattooed hands squeezed mine and we prayed. I came back three, then four, then sometimes five nights a week.

———————

This left me with a problem: I had no real job in the Skagit Valley to support this nocturnal adventure. Jail visits with Bob took place in the evenings, and only a few nights a week. I had read a lot of literature and agrarian essays in college, Wendell Berry kind of stuff, so I hoped to find a job on the scenic landscape and learn how to farm by day. Luckily, the smallest and reportedly finest organic farm in the valley was hiring. It was a model property lined with alders and poplars down where the Skagit River forks in two, on the delta of mineral-rich soil between the waters emptying into Puget Sound. "It's right along the water," a friend told me, "you cross a small bridge, and there's reeds lining the sloughs and river channels bordering the crops." The husband and wife who had farmed the place for years are some of the most knowledgeable in the valley, he said, but he warned that they were also known to be difficult to work with. My concerns were erased with his next saving description: "Trumpeter swans fly just feet overhead there, and storms of snow geese blow through the fields in winter."

It was winter. It sounded, again, magical. The farm turned out to be a mix though: as I would find in the jail, a good amount of dysfunction and darkness was blended with the magic.

That was the charm, really, of this entire rain-shrouded place, the Skagit Valley, which had begun to enchant me. I was attracted to its contrasts of lush beauty with urban pain, island-dotted coastlines with low-income projects, farmland with gangland, mossy evergreens with drive-by shootings. I fell for these contrasts of sun and rain, open land and dense forest, mudflats and snowy peaks, rhododendrons and Mexican food trucks, trumpeter swans and tattoos, a chorus of birdsong and trainsong in the wet air, long-necked blue herons and meth trailers, hard Cascadian peaks and even greater floating mountains of white clouds hanging over the dark and warming soil come summertime. The open farmland marked with red barns and skinny poplars looked like the old Dutch landscape paintings I'd identified in art history exams. No wonder the Dutch settled here when they stepped into this valley only a century ago. They, with the Swedes, diked the shallow Skagit delta into an elegant curve of a river coursing through now-rich and loamy rows. I didn't know the history of the Swinomish and Skagit and Samish peoples, what the land was like before the pioneers' diking and clearing. I knew little of how the constant lumber saws and Indian reservations had labored to tame this place. But early in my time here, I saw on coffee shop walls some vintage silverplate photos of the lumberjacks around the turn of the twentieth century. In one of them, eighteen stone-faced whiteys were lined up inside a standing-room scar they'd sawed into an evergreen as wide as a house.

As Gabriel García Márquez said of Latin America, this was a valley of outsized realities. Acres of yellow and red tulips opened each April. The raptors and steelhead, evergreens and crimes, all seemed oversized in this valley. Flannery O'Connor said that the blind need exaggerated shapes and gestures to see the truth: "You have to make your vision apparent by shock . . . to the hard of hearing you shout, for the almost-blind you draw large and startling figures." In this valley, in this jail and the lives I met there, a fuller reality was being communicated to me through startling shapes and outsized gestures. Here, all life-forms and their pathologies had enough space and rainfall to grow large.

———

On my first morning at the farm that winter, the husband and main farmer Harold squatted with me in the fog far from the house and pulled a melon-sized beet from its leafy row. He slit his knife across the beet's belly. It bled sweet blood, he wanted me to see. It oozed down the blade, over his wrists, and he fed himself the red morsel off the knife, right there, raw.

I spent hours alone out in the winter broccoli rows with a long harvesting knife of my own. Only the sound of snow geese spiraling by the thousands over nearby fields kept me company between the passing showers. I avoided my boss; his moods—tender, comic, volatile—made a microclimate that moved across the farm's rows of kohlrabi, kale, and carrots. He'd stomp on his tools in the greenhouse in spitting rage. I was more afraid of him and his brightly colored wool beanie cornering me by their house or against the alders than I was of any of the men in the jail I faced most evenings. I sensed him when he was working closer to me, through the bamboo stands and reedy sloughs where red-winged blackbirds warred for position.

That first frigid February, he found me in one of the long, humid greenhouses after he'd seen the crooked lines of spinach starts I'd transplanted beyond the raspberry bushes. Or maybe it was the shovel I'd left in the wrong place. He screamed at me and threw down his wool hat, his eyes pressing out from under the whites of his bushy brows, and through the curve of his thick lenses, with an eruption of hatred I did not understand. "I'm the Michael Fucking Jordan of farming and everyone knows it!" he shook his fist at me. "You give me the ball, you better *believe* I'm gonna drain the three every goddamn time!" He squatted and dribbled an imaginary ball right there by the steamy and tangled tomato vines, only to post up and fire what I assume to have been an impressive jump shot to the back end of the hoop house. "But I get paid jack shit and have to deal with idiots like you!"

His wife Julia would glare at me and then slowly close her eyes when she realized I had not been seeding her radish flats on the correct day of the lunar cycle. The next morning she would apologize by sitting me down in the living room and doing a "free" tarot card reading on the coffee table over our muddy rubber boots.

One late afternoon in the greenhouse, after preparing soft soil in black plastic flats, tucking tiny lettuce seeds into each little pod, I flipped on the scratchy old radio hanging on a nail by the door and began to sweep out the excess dirt. There was a curious news story about a young man who had been found dead, sealed in a black bag and lodged in the bottom of a river beneath a bridge. He was bound hand and foot, duct tape over his mouth. The autopsy showed water in his lungs. He had still been alive when he was dropped over the railing. I couldn't help but wonder in horror, as I leaned against the broom listening, hoping Harold didn't catch me slacking on his home court, what it would have been like to be alive that whole time in the bag—voiceless and sealed in the darkness, carried over the bridge while kicking, thrown over the side, sinking through the current and unseen fish, dead to the world, still falling, and still fully alive. I spent the rest of the afternoon trying to imaginatively enter the horror of that black sack as it fell, unable to stop accompanying the young man in my mind as he sank between life and death.

I did not know it then, but my growing number of encounters at night inside the county jail had already become a way for me to enter that black sack with captive lives as they sank. Such lives heard on the news are thrown away daily, I would learn, lives sealed off from the world, lives falling fast through a darkness we drive over daily, lives who are so voiceless they might as well have duct tape over their mouths, lives so enslaved to drugs or circumstance or legal status or unknown trauma that their hands and feet might as well be bound.

None of this greenhouse contemplation, though, made me a better farmhand. I often gave farmer Harold good reason to stop cooing at the robins as he did—say, when I weed-whacked through the electrical line against their house and killed their internet, or transplanted the spinach into pitifully crooked rows. "You and your university education," he'd spit with beet-red dribbles dried at the corners of his mouth, "aren't worth shit to me here!" So I kept my head down.

But come four o'clock, I'd escape.

I drove north to the opposite end of the valley, to the migrant farmworker cabins hidden far beyond the acres of berries. Bob's work with Tierra Nueva maintained two points of contact with the marginalized lives of the valley: the jail and the undocumented migrant farmworker community. As part of my orientation as a new volunteer with Tierra Nueva, I tried to get to know the soft-spoken indigenous Mexican families that arrived from California every summer and lived in these stark colonies of thin-walled cabins miles from the freeway. In the late afternoon, my pants and hands still dirty from my morning in the greenhouse or kneeling in the strawberries, I drove across a sagging wooden bridge over a slough and into the labor camps.

Mainly I wandered through the cabins with a lame smile, trying to build trust, making small talk with men drinking beer between their vehicles or walking in a towel and flip-flops across the muddy common area from the public bathrooms to their cabins. I worked at remembering their names and the sounds of their home villages, in hopes that I might one day be helpful to them. They invited me in to their crowded cabins, offered me fresh berries from the white buckets that had swung from their necks all day. I offered them prayer and the comfort of a local stranger remembering their names, welcoming them as neighbors. We politely accepted each other's offers at small creaky tables in these muggy cabins, or leaning against their truck beds under the evening summer sky. In this awkward twilight I most doubted what I was doing in the valley, so far from anything familiar.

I wasn't a farmer. And, I was finding, I wasn't a migrant advocate either.

But each evening, just around this time, when the sun would eventually set below the clouds that stop at the coast and cast a wild firelight against the cabins, I looked forward to pulling out my soil-crusted cell phone and dialing the jail.

"Come on in, sir."

I aimed my white '80s Volvo sedan, curled farmer hat, and beard toward the lockdown facility in the heart of the valley. The jail is downtown, across from the courthouse, where the river swings back from the tilled fields toward the county seat, against the foothills. I sped down long farm roads away from the farmworker camps. Deep shadows set in between the endless raspberry rows. Owls' wings flapped over the twilight fields.

It was time.

Once they buzzed me into the facility, I often bounded up the after-hours stairs.

"Who're you seeing tonight?" the deputy would ask. I'd give them four names, then step inside the six-by-eight-foot cell just down the hall, take a seat at the table inside, and wait in the stillness.

The crisp new Bible I'd bought that first summer, and took to the jail, soon became worn. As the men told me about their lives, all the scripture I'd absorbed from my years growing up in churches and summer camps, reading yellowed spiritual classics and theology books, these verses and stories and parables in the Old and New Testaments all began to rise in my memory. They came to new life in the presence of these men's stories. So night after night we pushed my pocket Bible's thin pages eagerly to find them.

When we leaned over these ancient stories from opposite sides of the table, we saw ourselves and our lives reflected back. Men born blind. Guys who'd lied and screwed over their brothers, like Jacob. Self-pitying prophets like Elijah on the run from governments they'd assaulted, hiding and suicidal in the desert. Violent persecutors like Saul having mystical encounters with the risen Christ out on the roads. These flawed characters always came up against a presence, a voice, sometimes an angel, a vision, and received the unexpected: new sight with mud and spit in their eyes, a felt presence that wrestled with him till dawn, a fresh cake and jar of cold water in the desert, forgiveness and a calling to tell the nations about this experience. As we leaned from opposite sides of the lawyer tables, leaning over these stories, and took turns reading, we saw ourselves reflected back in a new way, cast in a new role, filling out our incomplete images.

I used the prison-issued golf pencils the guards gave me at the front desk to fill the pages of my small notebook. It was the same hasty cursive as my teenage night journal entries. The men looked thrilled that I was writing down what they said. They had never heard such confessions of their conditions cross their lips before, they told me, and they knew they might never see things this clearly again. The space inside the front cover of my notebook where I kept a list of names of inmates to visit became crammed. The guys would often surprise me with an earnest embrace after each meeting while the guard stood waiting to take them back. Over my companion's shoulder, I gave the waiting officer the name of the next person I'd like to visit. I whistled in the cell while I waited. It felt like I'd brushed up against a holiness I'd only read about.

Inevitably, somewhere close to ten o'clock, came the knock on the cell's thick window and a guard pointing to his watch. It was time.

The last member of the jail staff would nod a farewell to me from his seat in the front control booth. One automated door shuddered shut behind me, and another groaned open before me. But I was not going home. Hidden in my journal's pages were new phone numbers, names, addresses, and hand-drawn maps for me to now follow deeper into the night.

"Go tonight, if you can," a young man with a gang tattoo darkening most of his throat and neck had said. He scribbled a rough map of the low-income projects so I could find his strung-out friend who, he said, also needed prayer. Another man on trial for murder gave me the phone number of an aunt at a cousin's house from whom he now wanted to ask forgiveness for letting her down. "They'll be up, don't worry," he'd smiled. "But you won't find them in the morning."

So I nodded back to the officer in the booth and stepped through the jail doors a second time, like a portal, now into the other side of my valley. I was in pursuit of a population that emerged only when the rest of the town turned off their lights.

One night I'd walk around the back of an apparently abandoned house, knock on a garage's side door, and be welcomed into a hazy cave of marijuana smoke by a few faces I recognized from jail bible studies. I'd quickly pass the message from the inmate I'd just left—that he loved him, the downcast one over in the corner, or that he wanted him to be at his next court date. Then these strangers nodding through their highs invited me to stay. They too, they explained, wanted prayer.

Another night I'd creep through an eerie drive-in-movie lot out by the refinery, between the reservation and the bay, filled with molding repossessed trailers. I avoided the security cameras, ducked under the chain, slipped through the shadowy rows, and, when I couldn't read the padlock combination written in my notebook without a light, I climbed through the trailer window. Inside the musty darkness I uncovered what I was sent for: the only mementos a gang member had of his deported mother and dead brother. Inside an orange shoebox under the bed, and buried under its contents of pornographic magazines and a blue paisley rag, I found pictures of the inmate as a boy in his mother's lap at Christmas long ago, and one prison letter written by his now-deceased brother, signed "Love" in cursive at the end.

———————

During my worst months back in college, when I was listless and morbid, my dad had wondered whether I was going through a "dark night of the soul" experience. I'd heard the phrase used like this before, usually as a way to spiritualize depression. Years later I would finally read Saint John of the Cross's classic *Dark Night of the Soul* and discover that the dark night he was describing was not a mystical passage of despair but of delight. "Once in the dark of night, when love burned bright with yearning," the poem begins, "I arose—O windfall of delight!" The Spanish mystic composed the verses while jailed in a cramped cell, stripped of all recognizable symbols and familiar religious structures to guide him. For John, the dark night was a happy leaving-behind of all that is familiar—"dead to the world, my house," "no sign for me to mark, no other light, no guide, except for my heart—the fire, the fire inside!" He was following a romance of total trust into the unknown.

———

Soon the unknown started looking for *me,* crawling through *my* windows. Bob had given me one of the upstairs rooms at the Tierra Nueva ministry headquarters, a massive, creaking, Victorian-style building that used to be a bank, a huge vault still at its core, peeling white paint outside, looming in the middle of the Little Mexico part of town. The pipes groaned from the furnace below, and I couldn't stand up straight in my half-story loft room. One night that summer, the fire escape rattled outside this almost-second-story bedroom window, waking me at three A.M. A shaved-head young man named Nate whom the gangs no longer wanted collapsed through my open window— maybe the way I'd once imagined leaning through the Rothko painting—and into the shadowy room, whispering my name. He was out of breath and afraid. He'd been chased through empty parking lots and down alleys, running from the police or demons or both, he stammered. Either way, he said he thought if he aimed for my window, he'd be safe.

Nate became one of my many new friends who similarly found themselves alive and in great need when others slept. I pulled out my studio headphones that night and opened a new audio file on my laptop. We recorded his desperate and impro- vised raps punctuated by his impressive humility, hilarious con- fessions, and beat-boxing skills, laughing till four A.M.

———

The theology books on my bed stand began to buzz. My cell phone charging on top of them would light up and vibrate, usually past midnight, and increasingly often. I'd pick it up, and in the darkness, I'd hear my name whispered again.

I got up and followed the call.

One night it was Neaners, the skinny, charismatic leader of one of the Mexican gangs I'd come to know, one by one. Neaners was the owner of the orange shoebox I'd hunted in the padlocked trailer. I could hear he was drunk and with all the homies, who were shouting in the background. He wanted me to see firsthand, he said, "how we get down, what we've only told you about in jail visits." When I arrived at the back room downtown, more than a dozen teenagers, some with firearms or knives, half-empty beer bottles, and bandanas pulled low over their brows, were trying to sit alert while Neaners, the shaved-headed captain in a tight white tank top, shouted orders and another disputed who was calling the shots. When I stepped in, I realized I had been called not because they wanted to show off, but because they wanted to be stopped. I saw it in the eyes of the youngest member, who peeled off his dark bandana in relief when he saw me at the back door. He smiled the same smile I'd seen across our jail visiting cell table months before.

"Ey everybody!" Neaners bellowed when he saw me, the only white guy, in my dark-rimmed glasses and beat-up Converse, standing in the back door. "This is our *pastor.*"

The word startled me more than anything else.

"We're not going out to do *shit* tonight. I wanted everyone together so he could meet all your asses. You can trust this dude."

There, in his enormous pants, his skinny white tank top, his lips swollen from drinking and eyes red, he opened his arms toward the whole group and looked at me as if I knew what to do next. As if to say, *They're all yours.* He nodded again, like, *It's time.*

I was confused.

"Come on," the youngest in the corner sitting next to me said in a soft voice, through a beer-soaked sorrow, "we need it." Two other heads with dark paisley bandanas slightly nodded, disclosing the desire in the room. Against the wall, the stereo they'd turned down still emitted a faint music, and blue vertical bars still rose and fell on the console screen like a small, waiting pilot flame.

They wanted to pray.

———

The next morning, and many mornings after, whenever I wasn't on the farm and the sun was bright and it was close to lunchtime, I went downstairs and stepped through Tierra Nueva's advocacy offices in my pajamas. I'd rarely gotten to bed before three A.M. As I shuffled sleepily through the waiting area, to get to the photocopy machine, gentlemen from southern Mexico who were waiting for legal assistance stared at me in my striped pants, my hair sticking straight up. Their knees were muddy, their shirts were sweaty, and their hands were stained red from picking strawberries in the dirt since dawn.

One of the gangsters the night before had told me about his court date this afternoon. He was afraid, he'd admitted, because he had no one to go with him. The nine-to-five world of offices and authorities was an unsafe and strange realm for him and his friends. It was a maze of rituals and regulations that no one explained to them. Eyes peered out from desks, across sidewalks, through surveillance cameras during these bright hours, always watching them. There were few shadows into which they could safely slip. So I agreed to drive him to court. And make photocopies of all original documents, first, of course, as I did now.

I learned how the system worked. I took notes as I would in any other class. I already knew how to navigate the morning cultures: I knew how to set my alarm, tuck in my shirt, pull into jammed parking lots with coffee in a mug between my legs, pass through metal detectors, accompany them through many-doored hallways. It was second nature to carefully and confidently answer the lawyers and parole officers, just as I had carefully and confidently answered teachers and professors my whole life. I could guide them through this world, just as they were guiding me into theirs. Useless and unwanted as I felt myself to be to the world just months earlier, now I was useful—wanted.

Sometimes, the morning brought too much terror for these young men. I banged on a locked trailer door in the eight A.M. chill while adjusting the silk tie I'd selected for the formal immigration hearing. No one answered the door. With my dress shoes digging for traction into the doublewide's siding, I squeezed through the small window and fell into the bedroom, finding the young man buried beneath blankets, heavy and airless as despair.

I had experience in battling the morning. I could fight for these men if only they would follow me and keep alert, keep walking. An hour later, this young man's lawyer would look at me suspiciously as we entered his office just before court.

"Excuse me—you are . . . ?" the public defender wanted to know.

"Um," the young man would say, tucking in his oversized shirt as the office door closed behind us, "this is my pastor."

I winced at the word. At first, I thought these young men were mocking me when they said it. To me, a pastor was a CEO of an established religious social club. I'd shake my head each time the guys called me this and try to explain how the titles *pastor* and *priest* are reserved for those who have been ordained, and I was not. I preferred words like *grassroots activist, jail chaplain, theologian, advocate,* even *young community organizer.* But those words meant nothing to these guys.

"Naw," Neaners corrected me once, "you're our *pastor,* dawg. We've never had a pastor. Now we got you." He said it like it was a good thing. "When we wanna connect with God, when we're in a bad spot late at night, where we gonna go? We call you."

The only way I came to terms with this label was rediscovering its root in the pages we read in the jail, in the Spanish-language New Testaments. The *buen pastor* is the good shepherd. Shepherds were never respected professionals. They were esteemed just about as highly as graveyard shift laborers or struggling musicians today. Often, they were both—singing to keep themselves awake through the night, singing softly to their anxious companions, watching for predators that lurked in the late hours. Shepherds gathered the scattered and accompanied them through remote places, hidden places, both hauntingly beautiful, I imagine, and dangerous. They were mobile, coming and going, not the ranch managers. Shepherds straggled into town with their charges, marked visibly by their odd life. They spoke differently, sometimes crudely. The apparent tenderness and camaraderie between the shepherds and the lives they cared for made them suspect to civil folk. Their instinct was to defend, and fight if need be, against predatory forces. But I imagine what made the shepherd's call sustainable were the quiet hours, when the many breaths rising around the shepherd in the darkness made the night pulse with dreams as he stoked the fire.

Someone, both then and now, has to tend the fire in the night.

In this way, I slowly came to embrace my call: an unofficial ordination that came not from higher-ups, but from below. The *good* shepherd, Jesus said, goes out into the night looking for the one sheep that got away. "That's us," one round young man with devil horns tattooed on his scalp said in a jail bible study about this passage. "The black sheep. The bad ones." I was learning how to become a good shepherd to the black sheep.

At least the schedule worked for me.

In the years to come, when I'd get up from the supper table, wipe my mouth, say my good-byes to my apartment mates at Tierra Nueva, including the former gang members I'd begun to bring home with me, when I'd grab my old nylon-stringed guitar and drive across the sunset-lit river to the jail, I was finally at peace with the sense that I belonged to the night.

The officer in the control booth would salute me when I entered, and again when I exited two hours later with more people to go find, out in the darkening valley. Sometimes I whistled and strummed the small guitar as I descended the jail's echoing stairwell. The janitor squeezed more black water into the bucket. Just before I stepped out through the jail's front doors and into the streetlamps' light, I sometimes passed an officer in crisp uniform. He was on his way up the steps to clock in with fresh coffee in his mug. We'd smile and nod. We were the night shifts.

WANTED II

I N THE JAIL MULTIPURPOSE ROOM WHERE WE MEET with groups of men like Richard Mejia, there are book-shelves along two walls crammed tight with the kinds of literature that bookstores leave outside in milk crates. Giveaways. The ones nobody wants from these piles end up in the county jail: trashy romances, self-published memoirs, and dated political propaganda. Christian bookstores provide the rest: a wealth of sentimental and less-than-inspiring religious paperbacks full of the kinds of stories and theology that don't even stick in the homes and hearths of the faithful. This is the last stop. More keep arriving, and they are stuffed horizontally across each other until no space is left. It is where books come to die. They are passed around, pulled apart, and eventually destroyed in the various cells.

Sometimes I recognize a rare gem that would go unread and unappreciated in there, and I am tempted to tuck it under my shirt, or pair it square with my small Bible, and sneak it out. Though clearly unwanted, it is still jail property. So this would be my small version of dumpster diving—a practice familiar to both homeless and hipster enclaves: breaking into dumpsters behind big stores for rare treasures in produce, less-than-fresh pastries, late-season electronics, off-pattern clothing, anything else cast off by the world but now championed with hunger or subversive values or both. I've asked the shift sergeants for permission to take some of these paperbacks, but the system makes no exceptions. So I have to decide. Some stories might be worth the risk.

The only new books given to the jail are glossy stacks of New Testaments, and they begin their lives among the discarded and dead volumes. Since free and blank stationery is hard to come by, their cardstock covers and crisp white insides are often torn off and harvested for drawings, love letters, covert gang messages putting hits on other inmates, or the occasional (and always rhyming) poetry. So when we begin our small group gatherings, men grab from the lowest shelf and pass around these thin testaments that are as stripped as the men are, equally misused and misunderstood, sharing criminal records, and full of as much hope and suffering.

Richard would never take one for himself. He preferred to lean back, cross his rubber-slippered feet out in front of him, fold his arms across his chest, and just listen. He liked the stories where Jesus walked among the kinds of characters he could relate to: thieves, prostitutes, people with problems like the untouchable sick who had to announce their presence when entering a neighborhood, old widows bleeding between their legs, madmen in graveyards cutting themselves and breaking their chains. Richard started to pay attention to this protagonist who spent much of his time among lives gathered in the cracks of towns and all around the edges, the outside, like trash. Jesus enjoyed them, it seemed. Even loved them, valued them. He touched them, restored them, and spoke of a kingdom where they belonged, a kingdom that was both here and hidden. He talked as if God were like this as well.

"That's sick," Richard said once, like an *Amen,* after another inmate finished reading the Gospel selection. He'd been listening with his eyes closed. On the streets, "sick" means good. Out there, as in the Gospels, many words and their values are turned on their heads.

A month later, Richard leaned sideways to read over the shoulder of a man in the circle whose copy was folded back to Luke's Gospel. A woman described as an infamous sinner breaks into a home where she is not invited. It is a dinner party of respectable community leaders who clearly do not want her there. She has not come to steal anything but seems desperate to make her way toward one of the guests, hijacking the gathering and forcing an audience with one man. She wipes his feet with her hair and tears, dripping scented oil all over his toes. This is Jesus's response: *Those who are forgiven much . . . love much.* And vice versa. It's directed at the hosts who sit silently, politely containing their disgust. The respectable folk in attendance, Jesus suggests, had not given nearly as much as this woman at his feet, who was clearly guilty of breaking and entering.

"Whaaat?" Richard looked up from his neighbor's page at me with surprise. He'd found himself in the story.

This whore's perfumed oil, I considered, was like the *Day in My Fucked-Up Life* video he'd wanted me to have: it was all she had, and she gave what she had, immediately. In this story of a dinner party so scandalously crashed, Richard saw that Jesus accepted such questionable things from questionable people, and that he recognized these profane contributions as gifts of love.

"Hella gangsta," Richard added, and turned to smile at his fellow inmates.

On our second one-on-one visit, Richard interrupted a story I was telling him. He was looking at my coat.

"That coat's sick."

He eyed it with a calm smile, like he approved. It was an old herringbone coat with oversized vintage lapels I'd found in a Goodwill store for a few dollars. The sleeves were too short, so I'd slit the hems at the cuffs, letting out extra fabric to cover my long arms; the frayed white liner extended two more inches over my wrists. I think its ragged alteration caught his attention. Often uncomfortable wearing full wardrobes with inmates who have only red scrubs, I was eager to balance the garment scale.

"You wanna try it on?" I asked.

"Hell yeah," Richard beamed and slid his shorter tattooed arms into the unlikely East Coast attic attire. His shaved head, with faint stubble cropping out of the ornate tattoo lettering there, now tilted down to examine the fit, and it nodded at what he'd just acquired. "Hella gangsta."

He knew he couldn't keep it. Jail rules. He'd have to take it off when the visit was over. Neither of us had to say it.

"Even for right now, though," he said, "it feels good. I can pretend it's mine. I know if we were on the outs, you'd give it to me if I asked you—huh?"

He was right, especially with something as easy to part with as that. Visibly enjoying the feel of a heavy coat on his shoulders, across his back, around his chest, sliding softly against the skin on his forearms—places we usually experience physical expressions of approval, protection, and affection—Richard continued: "You wanna know why I was so good at robbing houses?"

I did.

"I'd just pretend it was my house. Other shady-ass thieves sneak around, keep their heads low, move around the back. Me, I just pretend I'm coming home. Middle of the day. I walk right up the front steps, open the door. If it's locked, I go to the next house. No one notices. That's why I like doing this so much, not just for the stuff, really. Honestly, my favorite part is just sitting down in the living room, looking around, and telling myself: *All this is mine. This is my home.* See, I never had *shit* growing up. I mean nothing. No one ever gave me anything that was mine. I never had a home. I'd crash in all sorts of places, but not a *home,* you know? I'm not asking for sympathy, I'm just saying."

Many men during these visits stare down at the peeling wood façade of the cheap table as they recount and revisit chapters of their lives with me. But Richard would look right at me, his head slightly tilted to the side, as if he were not just the speaker, but the listener as well, as curious and intent on hearing what he would say next as an audience member. As if he were deeply moved by what he heard. Such was the hyperpresence that pulled us into his story together.

"So, just standing in that living room, for a few minutes, with the TV, couches, lamps, chairs, books, just pretending—that's what hooked me. The feeling, even for a few minutes, that I was in my own home. Sure, I'd steal all that shit when I had to bounce. Load it into a truck I'd have pulled up the driveway. But that was a lot of *work,* dawg, like a job, just to get rid of it and sell it all for cash. I became so good at stealing, really, mainly so I could get a shitload of drugs with the money and throw a big-ass party and call up everyone I knew—and they'd come." He paused, listening to what he'd just said. "That's all I wanted, anyway. Does this make any sense, or what?"

I think I just smiled, scratched away in my small, lined notebook. Guards in their dark brown uniforms occasionally passed the thick window to our visitation room. A frightened new inmate just booked and being escorted down the hall carrying his tub of linens, soap, and sandals looked in at us for a moment.

"Yeah, a lot of times, though, I wouldn't need anything, and I'd *still* go into houses, on my own. I wouldn't steal anything, only sit in the living room. Just to pretend."

BIRDS OF THE AIR

HERE IN THE SKAGIT VALLEY, IN THE FAR NORTH-west corner of the country, on this fertile pause of gla-cial soil between the snowy Cascade range and the cold blue Puget Sound with its wind-blown grassy islands, when the last red and yellow leaves have already fallen in October and line the gutters like wet trash and the encroaching chill is no longer colorful, when the final blueberries have been long picked off the end of the Indian summer and all that falls are days of rain in ever-earlier dark, for many people, there really is no reason to stay.

Around this time of year, the families from southern Mex-ico who inhabit the hidden fruit-picking camps all summer and move through the cabbage and raspberry fields under ten P.M. sunsets—neo-nomadic Oaxacan peoples—pack up and pull out. The used Chevy Astro minivans roar up one at a time. A modern tribal caravan, they file out onto Interstate 5 and disappear south for the winter. The song of high and low tonal languages—Triqui and Mixteco and Zapoteco—is gone and the camps are nearly silent. There's just the rain running off the cabins' corrugated tin roofs. It drips into gravel potholes where cars once parked each night, their open windows filling the fields and drab plywood encampments with the music of bouncing bass lines and bright accordions. But now the sky is gray and the wet air is without song. Not even the trumpeter swans have arrived yet.

But when they do, in the weeks ahead, the large white birds' honking and morphing Vs pass just overhead, heralds of winter's advent. When the rest of us are sealing up our windows, they descend from the northern arctic to fill our emptied skies and our muddy fields with their otherworldly beauty. They fly so low you can sometimes hear the air in their feathers, hear them breathing in labor.

Such migratory fowl have fascinated me since the first winter I moved here years ago. The old association between flight and faith is there in my imagination—especially with these white-robed trumpeters, who do not belong to this valley, who feed off of abundant provision hidden in the soil. *Look at the birds of the air,* Jesus said in his outdoor sermon on the life of faith. And so I do. But *which birds?* I see our valley's native raptors that perch high in the poplars and evergreens, surveying their territory, secure in their large nests lined with the collars of dogs and cats long gone missing—according to what a local farmer found when he chopped one of these trees down. Such predatory birds are a symbol of national pride. The Gospels' instructions, however, about trust, about not hoarding possessions, about venturing a life of vulnerability, about being cared for, are paired in my mind with the foreign swans that fill our dark winters, that sleep not in high places, but close to each other in the soft, low folds of the earth.

Sometimes, in the early dusk, I still drive out to the fields where they gather, just to be near them. I get out of my car, hop over the watery roadside ditch, and creep as close as I can before they honk at each other and open their heavy white wings. Any closer and their black webbed feet step into the sky, sometimes just over my head, with a thundering host of beating wings. I bend my neck back and follow their formations while my feet sink in the soft muck. I have often imagined rising into the air with them, caught up in their magic and flight, disappearing with their humble music into the night.

———

On one of these wet nights seven years ago, I pulled up to the last farmworker cabin that was still lit in Camp #5. I was finishing my second season at Tierra Nueva, back when part of my role was still visiting and accompanying migrant families in the valley. I ducked through the rain and knocked on the thin door.

"*¡Bueno!*" I heard shuffling inside. This is the time of year Border Patrol agents pick through the camps. "*Pase,*" the voice then assured me to enter.

Inside, there were only two men among the four bare bunks. Arnulfo stood by a simple gas burner, blue flame under a boiling pot of macaroni. He was cleaning his one pair of black cowboy boots, or drying them over the heat, after a season in the muddy fields. "*Aja, Cristóbal,*" he said rapidly and smiled with a goateed chin-lift. He didn't chew gum, but he was that kind of jittery, fast-talking man, like some gum-chewing cabbie. Over on a bottom bunk sat the second man, Magdaleno, who smiled at me with a shy nod, his hands in his lap as usual. His forehead was high and smooth and round, and he was easily a decade younger than his cabinmate. *"No habla mucho,"* Arnulfo said of his roomie the first night we met here. *He doesn't talk much.*

Unlike most of the other cabins here provided by valley farmers for the seasonal workers, this cabin had no children inside. No pink blankets or little shoes strewn about. This was the single dudes' cabin. They were outliers in a culture where entire villages from Oaxaca cross borders and go into debt just to survive together, moving like flocks up and down the West Coast season after season. Arnulfo and Magdaleno came north alone, separated from their families and separate from each other. Arnulfo left his wife and kids in Michoacan; Magdaleno left Puebla as a silent and solitary bachelor. The two met in the asparagus fields outside Stockton earlier in the year and decided to stick together, as different as they were. No one in the camps really talked to them. Arnulfo spoke only Spanish. Magdaleno was the only one in all the camps who spoke high-tonal Zapoteco. They belonged to no one. All season they had only each other.

I met them halfway through that summer. Arnulfo stood in the distance many afternoons while I visited his neighbors, leaning into their minivans to greet the returning families from the last year, praying for bruised hands, or translating phone bills from Verizon English. Arnulfo finally approached me one afternoon among the laundry lines billowing with faded sheets. He presented no legal problem that needed assistance, no municipal court date coming up. He just wanted to make small talk, adjusting his Mexican soccer league baseball cap and poking at the dirt with the toe of his black cowboy boot, speaking faster than an announcer for a soccer match on Radio Latino. He seemed lonely.

Then the cold came, the rains, and it was time to get moving again. With no vehicle come November, and no clan to follow south to California's San Joaquin Valley, Arnulfo and Magdaleno wanted to fly. They wanted to venture in a new direction, breaking away from the West Coast's migratory loop. And they wanted me to fly with them.

A week earlier, Arnulfo had told me they wanted to get to New Jersey where some old friends of his had carpentry work waiting for both him and his new, soft-spoken pal. Traveling cross-country by bus was too risky, he'd explained, with ICE agents at dozens of Greyhound stations along the way. With a direct one-way flight, however, only two airports would need to be cleared. And maybe—this was the pitch—the two of them would look less suspicious if traveling with a *güero* (pronounced *WEH-doh*)—a tall white U.S. citizen—like me. They would not be staring at concourse screens of departure gates, looking down terminals like foreigners. They could casually stick by me as I knew where to turn, where to wait, where to get coffee, and how to look more bored than afraid of getting caught while waiting for a flight. Arnulfo now lifted his top-bunk mattress and counted out a thick wad of cash, then folded it, and put it into my hand. They wanted to buy me a round-trip flight as well, so we could move through airports and clouds side by side.

The night Arnulfo told me the plan, sitting on the edge of that lower bunk, it took me fifteen minutes to understand. He spoke too fast. I was used to the indigenous Oaxacan families who speak with slow, simple sentences, Spanish being their second, awkward language just as it is mine. Arnulfo's speech from Michoacan was a rare urban rap-speed flurry of sounds and slang with a lilt I enjoyed more than comprehended. He agreed to repeat himself, three times, each time without slowing, each time with Magdaleno nodding, until I understood. I summarized what I'd caught: *I'll turn this lump of bills into three flight reservations and we're off to New York together?* Arnulfo closed his eyes and exhaled with patient relief. Magdaleno's smile broadened, his hands still in his lap.

If I'd known how to say *Hell yes* in Spanish, I would have. Our mission, we often said at Tierra Nueva, was to "accompany" these families and folks on the margins. But that usually meant accompanying them to court, to collections' offices to pay fines, to the hospital to pray, or just across the muddy grooves of the bare camp lot to resolve a dispute with a pissed-off cousin or the underpaying supervisor with a suspicious-looking gold tooth. This was different. Here was a rare invitation to accompany two men out of this valley, across the country, into their lives, into the air. And it sounded simple enough. They didn't want any money, just my presence alongside, to stay near them.

I don't remember making the decision. Just that I couldn't wait.

A week later, the rainy night before our flight, I took a seat beside Magdaleno on the bare mattress and pulled out the boarding passes from my coat pocket. I handed the exact change in bills and quarters and pennies back to him with another printout of the electronic receipt (more for my sake than theirs) to make clear that I was not doing this for a single cent. I was a young pastor, after all—not a coyote, or paid smuggler over the U.S. border. I was becoming a regular chaplain at the local jail, but I was still not officially ordained. So in this sense, all three of us did our work in the valley without formal documentation.

We shook on it. Both of their hands were dark with deep black cracks still stained from June's ripe strawberries, which they harvest on their knees in the dirt for weeks. My hands were pale and dry, my fingernails bitten down pretty far and the names of inmates to visit scrawled in blue ink just below my wrist. We were not, as they say, birds of a feather. But for the next few days, moving with the season's change across the land, we would fly together.

Driving home that night, hours before departure, it finally dawned on me that I could get in serious trouble for this. Visiting the camps as a harmless chaplain was one thing, but now I would be aiding and abetting the movement of undocumented immigrants across the U.S. interior. And it wasn't just me. I'd persuaded my fiancée Rachel to come with us. She was reading on my bed the night I was buying the flights online and asked what I was doing, then said she wanted to go to New York with me sometime. I turned to her in my chair. Brilliant. Not only would she make us three traveling males look less suspicious, more family-like (Rachel is half Panamanian), but we could also make the most of my free ticket to the Big Apple. This is how I could take my lady to the big city. She knew from

years of getting to know my roommates—smiling gang youth,
a painter, a burned-out missionary from the slums of Caracas,
a half-toothless Honduran campesino named Lolito—that dat-
ing me was not an entirely conventional experience. Going to
New York with two undocumented fellows I met in the berry
camps, she probably shrugged, was my best idea of a date. So
Rachel and I made plans to stay with her cousin on the Upper
West Side of Manhattan and spend a dark-season week together
among the bright city nightlife with college friends. But—I now
bit my fingernails on the drive home—what if we got caught
somewhere in between? I was dragging someone who trusted
me into a potential mess of federal charges.

———————

Early the next morning we sped along the one diagonal road
that cuts through these acres of emptied fields. Outside the de-
frosting windshield, the white shoulders of the Cascade range
rose above morning plumes of vapor in the bright sun. On the
flat land ahead I saw an entire field littered with white. I knew
they were snow geese, thousands of them, newly arrived for the
winter to glean what was left on the cold earth; but at such a
distance, they looked like a great assembly of people sitting in
the mud, like at Woodstock, or the feeding of the five thousand.
Then, by the hundreds, the edge of the crowd was caught by the
wind and curled up into the air, as if the masses in their white
robes were waiting for this very rapture, and—so slowly—they
were lifted into the sky. They rose and spiraled, an enormous
pillar of wings churning across the land.

By the time our car caught up to this storm of snow geese, we were moving in parallel, at the same speed, on opposite sides of the dipping phone wires. I saw their wings open, all of them. The tips of those snowy feathers were stained black just where their fingers might have been, as if they'd had their hands in the inky mud all night.

When Rachel and I pulled up to the door with number 53 stenciled above it in primer white, the two men were waiting outside for us. Magdaleno sat on the crude bench, only a child-sized backpack on his lap. His black hair was a round bowl-cut, neatly combed, wet, and parted down the middle. Arnulfo leaned against the cabin with a shiny boot up on the bench. His only luggage was one of those clear plastic zip-cases that come with new comforters. As I lifted it into my trunk, I could see all his possessions he took with him into the future: a large plaid blanket, a toothbrush, a razor, worn-thin flip-flops, and a large, hardback *Santa Biblia* that weighed more than an extra pair of pants and shirt would have. Magdaleno's small backpack felt empty. I set the two parcels on top of Rachel's and my two rolling travel suitcases. Such baggage assumes the terrain will be smooth. And we packed them heavy enough to betray that we did not expect to run.

I told Arnulfo he'd probably have to leave the razor behind because of airport security. He removed it and set it back on the wooden bench like a parting offering in the empty camp.

We drove south through the exposed landscape. Skinny blue herons stood motionless in the winter-flattened grasses along the slough's edges and they watched us as we passed. Only a few crossed from one side of the road to the other before us, flying as they do with their heads tucked down and alone, as if not wanting to stick their necks out for anything. Brown harriers peered down from the branches of naked maples, waiting for their next catch. I looked to the tops of the tallest skeletal trees for the bald eagles at their posts, but saw none. Traveling with our two undocumented companions, I felt newly sensitized to the natural order of my valley.

I scanned the road ahead for any police. Their sharp white car doors and silhouetted light rack on top are both traits easy to identify at a distance—Audubon-style. Twice, a large white Suburban pulled up alongside us on the driver side, and my heart gripped within me. But neither had the bright green band across their doors, distinct markings of Border Patrol units, not unlike the diagonal colors across the wings of female mallards. I often see these white and green troopers parked along fields full of stooped laborers. They've been known to descend in threes or fours, out of nowhere, with buckets full of plastic zip-cinch handcuffs.

We crossed over one near-flooding salmon river after another—Samish, Skagit, Stillaguamish, Snohomish—where the last coho and chum steadily migrated under the surface, pushing from the sea up into the mountains, crossing estuarial and county lines alike, from brine into snowmelt, from Samish into Whatcom and back, winding around fields, towns, old dams, and anglers' lines and hooks, rising, rising to their birth waters. There, after beating potholes in the gravel with their weary bodies, they would lay tiny red eggs in the wet stones, the rain-dimpled shallows broken only by their exposed dorsal fins, wavering side by side.

Arnulfo and Magdaleno sat quietly in the backseat, Rachel and I up front. *What will happen,* I kept worrying, *if we get caught?* This long drive south felt just like the trips I'd taken with other friends of mine to their immigration court dates in a Tacoma detention center or downtown Seattle high-rise. I turned down the radio station playing too-early holiday music and told Arnulfo and Magdaleno how, while approaching such court dates in the past, my undocumented friends and I had experimented in praying for the judges and prosecutors, blessing our potential enemies. I suggested we might try that now, approaching airport security at seventy miles an hour. We would pass under their watchful gaze without shoes or belts and arms outstretched. In my rearview mirror I saw both men nod. So I awkwardly prayed aloud in Spanish. *"Te bendecimos, oficiales. Ayúdanos, Espíritu Santo. Mis amigos no más quieren pasar al otro lado pa' seguir trabajando con sus amigos."* *We bless you, officials. Help us, Holy Spirit. My friends just want to get to the other side of the country, where they can keep working with their friends.*

Just before we left the open valleys behind us and dropped into the urban corridor that begins in the stinking lumber mills of Everett, full of seagulls, tugboats, and abandoned warehouses, I saw a red-tailed hawk. It dove straight down, open-winged, off a telephone pole into the grass alongside the freeway. Wings flapping, it rose with a squirming mouse or small rabbit in its talons and then came down again, slamming the furry creature into the earth with three savage hops as we sped by, Christmas carols on the radio.

Inside the high-ceilinged airport, the same music continued. Just overhead hung decorations, golden silhouettes of winged beings blowing long, thin trumpets. They appear around this time every year, touting the long-ago arrival of a child to migrant and homeless parents, an incognito God who'd crossed a vast cosmic border, defying religious customs and evading Roman guard, to be with his people.

All around us families bustled on their way to their gates while Arnulfo, Magdaleno, Rachel, and I stuck close and tried to blend in with our environment—to look like we belonged to each other.

The lines for security clearance were backed up. Ahead I finally saw a bald eagle: wings spread on the red, white, and blue crest of the official TSA podium. We stepped closer, slowly. The official, a gray mustachioed man, was bent forward, both his bifocaled eyes and a third blue light passing over each boarding document and plastic ID. Rachel and I were cleared with a quick scrawl of initials on our papers. We stood in our winter coats, turned and waiting, while our two friends handed theirs over. The man looked up and around from his podium, and spoke to me.

"These men here with you?"

"Yes," I said, and swallowed.

The officer turned and called to others standing by the x-ray conveyors. Another man and young woman with badges around their necks descended around the first officer's side, and the three of them picked at the two IDs on the podium. The second officer's golden nameplate said "Ramirez," and he spoke in Spanish to Arnulfo and Magdaleno. I saw a spray of those plastic zip-cinch ties sticking out of his back pocket.

"These IDs have no expiration date," he then repeated to me in English.

"I called the airport ahead of time," I squeaked, "and they said Mexican national *células* would be no problem."

"Every ID," he snapped, "must have an expiration date."

I knew those national identity cards were legit, not forged. Apparently Mexican citizenship does not expire.

"I'm going to have to ask you four to step into this line over here." It was partitioned off from the other lanes with thin cubicle-style boards. We were trapped. Sent down a trouble chute with no escape. We'd been caught.

I wanted to say something reassuring to Arnulfo and Magdaleno as we stood and waited in the government-gray corral, maybe explain that this was normal and that we had nothing to fear. Maybe make some small talk as Arnulfo and I had done among the aisles of billowing laundry that summer in the camps. But we remained as still as Magdaleno. And even he was not smiling now.

The two men then looked up at me and barely nodded.

Yes, I thought to myself. Yes I am a failure. A bad coyote. A bad pastor. Mission failed.

Rachel looked at me with large eyes of fear, maybe with some blame. Would I lose her, too, over this stunt? I took her hand, releasing my vision of ice-skating together at Rockefeller Center among all the nations' flags and twinkling lights, swooping in circles alongside that luxuriant golden angel's welcoming gaze.

Arnulfo and Magdaleno would not go home tonight with friends waiting for them on the other side of the country. They would not be working this winter in carpentry in New Jersey nor be sending money home to their families. Instead, they would be pressing their thumbs and fingers into ink pads and reviewing stacks of legal paperwork in large rooms full of Somalis and Guatemalans and Ukrainians and others from around the world, signing for voluntary departure and skipping a bond hearing, waiting weeks at stainless steel tables just to be flown south and left with their small carry-ons in a border town. We would not be taking off together into the clouds, sipping complimentary beverages at cruising altitude. We would spend the afternoon being questioned separately and waiting in small offices to the sound of CB radios on officials' shoulders and heavy staplers on cheap desks.

I wanted to apologize to Arnulfo and Magdaleno. I wanted to quietly scribble down their families' contact information and promise to notify anyone they wanted, visit them in the Tacoma detention center as soon as possible, immediately contact our organization's best pro bono attorneys if I wasn't taken into custody as well. I wanted to tell Rachel to go ahead without me if they even let us two through, to enjoy New York with her real family.

Officer Ramirez marched over to us and handed the two IDs back to Arnulfo and Magdaleno over the partition. "When you get to the other side," he said and pointed to the bins disappearing into the x-ray machine, "we'll be waiting for you. And you'll come with us for questioning." That meant immigration had been called. They wait for any mistake that causes immigrants to stick out from the rest of the flock—a broken headlight or late turn signal on the road, an ID without an expiration date at the airport—and they snatch them up. Now I knew how it felt to move with the migrants.

My toes curled inside my shoes. My hands squeezed into fists and my jaw clenched. We were totally powerless, in their grasp like prey. I began cursing them under my breath now, the eagle-emblazoned TSA officials. It sounded like when I hear myself whispering prayers in court. And in the jail, holding hands with violent aggressors and known predators. *I love the eagles of my valley,* I reminded myself. *And I believe our nature might still be transformed.* So I took a deep breath and switched back to the idiotic mumbling of blessing toward our captors.

"Cristóbal," Arnulfo hissed to me as I bent down to slide off my shoes and put them in a gray bin. He discreetly pointed with his eyes down at his boots, whispering in his rapid diction that his blue social security card was inside his left boot, which he now had to remove and place on the conveyor. Hiding valuables in your boots is standard traveling protocol for crossing the desert, where thieves lurk who may tell you to empty your pockets with a loaded pistol pressed to your forehead.

"Forward, please, gentlemen." A TSA agent waved us toward her.

Every undocumented worker in the United States has a false social security number like this for employment purposes, but normally you leave it under your mattress at home. If you get caught with one, it is an additional federal charge.

"Um . . . put it in your pocket," was my best idea. He did just that, as casually as if it were a gum wrapper.

I went through first, opened my arms and legs as they wanded me, stripped of belt and shoes and belongings. Then the men. Then Rachel. I put my watch back on, laced up, buckled up, and was ready for a firm hand to grab my upper arm and guide me toward an "Official Personnel" door.

But no one came to get us.

All four of us stood clustered together once again, looking around on the other side of security.

There was no one.

Just the massive wall of windows here at the edge of the airport, opening out to planes taking off and seagulls flying about in a gust of wind. And we were so close to joining them, to lifting off. No officer looked in our direction. Nothing was stopping us.

"*Vamos,*" I said. It was soft. It was instinctual.

No one disagreed.

The four of us curled left out of the cage of benches and cruised down the wide-open concourse in plain sight. There was nowhere to hide. I tried not to run but, with my heart pounding in my ears, strode with my head high and my rolling suitcase in tow. I felt my neck stiffening against the temptation to look back and jinx my companions, waiting to hear "Excuse me, Sir? Sir?—*stop!*"

Our gate was amazingly just around the corner. We had only thirty yards before we'd turn and be out of sight. The flight would be boarding just as we got there. With no shouts behind us yet, no walkie-talkies fuzzing alerts from any shoulders, we hustled. Above us, more golden-winged heralds trumpeted us along noiselessly. Below us, there were bronze inlays of rivery lines running through the concourse floor, chinook salmon pushing against the current with us. They darted between our feet as Arnulfo's boots clicked on the polished terminal causeway and the little plastic wheels on our suitcases hummed.

We turned behind the wall by our boarding gate and caught our breath. Red flashing letters on the screen: *FLIGHT DELAYED. Estimated Time: One Hour.*

We were sitting ducks.

We gathered on a padded square bench. I pretended that I had a plan, but as I explained it like a coach in a Spanish-language huddle, I realized I had nothing. *So . . . we wait here . . . for an hour.*

Rachel had a better idea. She pulled out of her suitcase a zip-locked sandwich she'd made and broke it into four. Magdaleno zipped his small backpack open and took out a thin plaid blanket, folded neatly to fit. Then the only other thing he'd brought, besides the toothbrush: a still-glossy paperback *Santa Biblia*. Magdaleno nodded and held it out to me. *"Cristóbal,"* Arnulfo translated his companion's suggestion, *"él dice quizás hacemos una lectura." He says maybe we can have a reading of the scriptures.* He then respectfully removed his Team Morelia soccer hat and smoothed down his thinning hair.

I flipped through the fat stack of recycled pages and wondered what on earth to read in our anxious waiting, sitting here out in the open, unable to keep my eyes off the spot where someone in uniform would come around the corner and take us away. Magdaleno, though, unfolded the thin blanket and quietly prepared a table before us, setting the sandwich quarters back down upon it.

I decided on the same story I'd read with circles of men in the jail two nights before, from the Acts of the Apostles: when Peter, himself jailed, escapes the authorities. Though he is chained, both hands and feet, and guards stand on his right and his left, angels wake Peter in the night and guide him past four levels of security. For a moment the New Testament struck me as a kind of outlaw literature.

I pointed to the passage on the open page and invited Magdaleno to read. He stared down at it, and it occurred to me he might not know how to read. Then he began, slowly. The story of Peter, in Magdaleno's soft voice describing the chains and the soldiers, filled much of our remaining time there in the terminal. It covered us with a thin, warm sense that we might belong within this narrative, with the disciples whom Jesus instructed to carry no extra belongings through occupied territory, who would be cared for even more than the birds of the air.

"¡Levántate enseguida!" Magdaleno read the angel's words to Peter while the guards slept close by: *Get up, quick!* Peter was instructed to flee just as we had done minutes earlier. *"Ponte el cinturón y las sandalias,"* he continued the angel's hushed escape command to put on his belt and sandals. *"Ponte el manto y sígueme."* Put on your coat and follow me.

Magdaleno smiled and looked up at us with his still-parted hair. Any sense of penitent guilt about this little impromptu service we were having melted then. Gone the sense that these two men were illegal, keeping their heads down before bosses and cameras. And for me, as well: gone were my double-thoughts of Manhattan late nights, of glasses of wine, of stiff cocktails with Rachel and friends in loud Williamsburg bars. Though still afraid, I felt I belonged right here, suspended in trust with my fellow travelers.

This same prison-escapee—Peter, Jesus's friend—later wrote a letter to a network of communities scattered across Asia Minor, now Turkey, calling them all "aliens and strangers" in their land. It was a common politic for early Christians: "We are citizens of heaven," the author of Philippians wrote. Another New Testament letter says the heroes of the faith "admitted they were immigrants and foreigners on this earth." My undocumented companions helped me feel this shift in citizenship, in allegiance, within me.

By the end of the story—when Peter has flown the coop and is restored to his friends and community waiting for him—the attendant's voice came over the PA system. It was time to begin boarding. We all got our passes out, and then I noticed something missing: Arnulfo's and Magdaleno's boarding documents had never been initialed by the TSA agent like Rachel's and mine had been. They were never cleared. I looked over at the attendant by the open gate; sure enough, she examined every boarding pass handed to her.

I got out a pen. I studied the initials on mine. I'd forged signatures before, like my mom's on checks for pizza and my dad's for field trip permissions as a kid. This was even easier now, only two capital letters. But they were a government employee's initials, not my legal guardians'. What if, I thought, I used my *own* two initials? I imagined myself sitting in an interrogation office, or on the stand in court, trying to explain what right *I* had to approve these travelers. What authority did I have? I'd heard preachers yell "He has given us authority!" and "Claim it in faith!" and "In the name of Jesus!" much of my life. I'd never really known what that meant, or where that authority became tangible. Now, however, I had an idea. Or at least a place to try it out, on real documents.

So with a lift of nonresident faith, I quickly rehearsed signing my friends' papers with two very famous initials—*JC*—like a personal signature. It would feel good to exercise a foreign authority, one that would allow my friends to step through that gate with us into the sky. I wasn't sure—and I'm still not—what the right thing to do would have been. I was sinking in this dilemma while the plane engine fired up. What's important is this: Arnulfo and Magdaleno approached the gate ahead of me, treading lightly toward takeoff in their black boots, white long-sleeved shirts, and earth-stained fingers. I watched the attendant carefully examine their boarding passes. We held our breath. Then, one at a time, she tore them in half and placed a piece into each man's open hand—then Rachel's, then mine— with a liturgical smile. "Enjoy your flight."

This may be the closest I've come to stepping out of the muck and into the air with the migratory swans I've watched cycle through my valley.

That night the cabin was dark, and it hummed while most passengers slept. I couldn't read. I just sat in the stillness. I couldn't believe it. Several times I got up from my seat beside Rachel, her hand resting on mine as she slept, and walked back down the aisle to check on Arnulfo and Magdaleno. Arnulfo snored peacefully with his arms crossed, his cap removed and rising and falling on his chest. In the seat next to him, Magdaleno was happily absorbed in season five of *America's Next Top Model*. All the while, state lines passed thousands of feet below us.

———

Each winter now, when our windows are sealed up, I can expect their calls. Arnulfo's voice, six Christmases running, has reached me across miles of cold earth, from New Jersey apartments, then shared laborer homes with bachelors in Pennsylvania, and finally his home village in Michoacan, Mexico, just this year. He sends me Magdaleno's greetings, as usual. In all-caps text messages, he asks about Rachel, congratulates me on our recent marriage. I tell him the two of us are hanging ornaments on the bright-bulbed tree, two turtle doves. He tells me he, himself, is finally with his wife and children, together in a home he finally saved for, and built for them, in a land I've never seen.

NO CONTACT

MOST OF THE CRIMES I HEAR ABOUT FROM THE men I meet in the jail don't alarm me. Even murders. To threaten, steal, destroy, cheat, evade, rage, attack, smother, and self-medicate are all impulses I recognize in myself. Most men who come to our bible studies I can welcome as tragic extensions of my own hypothetical selves. And these men in rubber slippers are frankly more honest about their sins than I am about the distortion hidden within me. So to embrace these men is to see and embrace my own darkness. I've often considered the jail a kind of warped existential mirror.

People on the outside, though, people I meet at loud bars or backyard barbecues, when they learn I spend my time as a volunteer chaplain among locked-up criminals, often say something like "That must be scary," and they say it in an honoring way, as if I had the virtue of courage. I usually can't help but smile when someone projects such fearlessness onto me, because

I am full of fears. I panic like a little kid, for instance, when I feel lost or alone, in a forest at dusk or a big city without a friend or in my study at home alone with my head in my hands. This, I tell them, is possibly why I go to the jail so often: I find myself less alone among the anxious men there.

Growing up in many churches, I never found them to be raw or extremely honest places—not places where you could show the worst side of yourself. But I found the jail to be a place where inmates didn't have the option to hide their problems. Hard as one may try with weak laughter or macho fronts before guards, you can't pretend your life is working out just fine when you're locked in the county jail. Here, people are left staring—innocent or guilty of the specific charges—at the wreck of their lives. And in this place, in these rooms of unadorned life, I found something that clergy call sacrament, mysteries I could feel.

More than the bible studies, the one-on-one visits with the men were the sites of holy encounters for me. The holding cells up near the front desk, closet-sized, small, had walls of white-washed cinder sblocks. Many of the men who invited me to visit them didn't have family show up on Saturday's normal visiting hours. When the officer would bring one of the men up front whom I'd asked for—from the growing list inside my journal—many of them would wait until the door was shut, sure that the officer had turned away, before collapsing out of a hard posture into a surprisingly vulnerable embrace that often caught me off guard. Others, though, didn't care what the officers saw and shouted affectionate greetings at me—"Hell yeah! Wassup, Chris! You came!"—as they strutted down the hall, held between two armed escorts. Maybe they'd expected a lawyer. Most of the time we hardly knew each other—maybe we'd had one visit before this.

We'd sit down at the little lawyer's table. Between us, though, it functioned more like an altar. Young tattooed men would lay their ink-storied heads on it. They'd often weep. Everything they held to themselves—burdens of pain and stashes of truth—could be emptied. They would open their hands on the narrow table, vulnerably asking for something invisible, yet waiting for my hands at the same time. I was always surprised at how reticent they were to let go of them, even to wipe their own noses. As they ventured simple prayers, crying, holding my hands, many times I saw a long, clear ointment slowly extend from their eyes, nose, and chin to their laps or the table between us. On more than one occasion, I remember young Chicano gangsters' tattooed fists not letting go of my own after an initial prayer, keeping an intense, unashamed, sweaty grip as we spoke face-to-face for the next thirty minutes or more. I never felt a need to slide out of that grip.

Some nights we would simply sit together in the stillness like this. We'd try to listen the way monks and mystics listen in prayer—it was easier when we were together in this quiet cell. My eyes often wandered across the wall behind the other's bowed head; my mind can quickly wander when I close my eyes. I became familiar with the lines of grout between the white cinder blocks. Some nights these lines that trace the standard pattern of stacked bricks looked to me like infinite stairs ascending and descending upon the inmates' heads. Some nights the grid of lines looked more like a mechanical web in which the person speaking to me was caught in the middle. Other nights all I saw was a maze with no way out—all paths terminated inside these four walls, low ceiling, and hard floor.

One night, as I sat still with an older man on trial for murder, trying to "listen" with all my senses, I noticed something new on the wall behind him: tiny lettering scrawled between some of the bricks. It was too small to decipher. I'd read how pilgrims stuff their written prayers into the cracks of Jerusalem's "wailing wall," tiny pieces of paper filled with silent cries and hopes in the form of similarly small script. People roll them like cigarettes and jam them between the stones, as if such fragile messages could eventually seep through the walls of this world. I wondered in this silence whether the insides of every prison and jail cell might be a wailing wall. These pencil hieroglyphs in the grout cracks of this holding cell were only the visible stains of some wails. The narrow window in the door beside me, when I looked closely, had gang signs, declarations of devotion and raw curses all scratched faintly into the bulletproof glass. I considered how the narrow columns of psalms in the Bible are composed of the same things.

These men were giving me the riches of their lives in this small space, and they didn't know it. What they had been trying to trash, or avoid—their feelings, their pasts, their stories, their tears and confessions and secret fragile dreams—were to me the precious material of psalms, prayers, and poems. It was also the stuff of friendship. And they offered more of that, connecting me to their friends. They'd say, "If it's alright with you, I wanna cut this visit short so you can do a visit with my celly.

He never comes to the bible studies, but he'd be down with this right here." Or, "When I get out, can I call you? There's someone I want you to meet."

The fellowship grew. Communion expanded. Contact increased.

Even in group settings, our gatherings became more than bible study. Many of the most fiercely postured men would begin to whimper as Bob slowly circled around the inmates laying his hands gently on their shoulders, one by one, whispering blessings as I played soft music on the beat-up old classical guitar I'd found at the Tierra Nueva building. Sometimes they would weep uncontrollably, these men starved of kindness and care.

I felt like I was falling deeper in love as all this happened. It wasn't just with these broken lives at the table with me. It was love for the One through whose eyes I was possibly learning to see. I began to suspect I was sensing the desire of Another—God's desire for the locked-up. It was for this direct spiritual contact that I came so many nights a week, excusing myself early from dinners with friends, missing movies and participation in evening soccer leagues. I came to the jail to keep the connection.

Guys would ask me about my own life in our one-on-one visits. I could confess my own private issues, and they wouldn't judge me. I could smile and whisper my latest good news—like when I met Rachel and first took her out, or when I recorded a new song I'd written and loved—and share my most unrefined questions about God, uncensored. It was safe. Going to the jail most nights didn't feel like altruism, charity, volunteer work, organizing, obedience, or any of those labels I'd been told motivated acts of service to others in hard places. It was more like a seed finding soil and light.

But one evening a few years in, the guards at the front desk informed us chaplains that a new policy was in place. A no-touch policy. This policy was shared by most correctional facilities in the nation, and our little jail, I was told, was finally catching up. No longer could we have any physical contact with the inmates. This included the thousands of hugs men came to expect in our gatherings. Some confessed they came to our bible studies for that embrace alone. When the door opened to our multipurpose room, they'd be lined up, several guys opening their arms for one hug after another. Men I'd never met would say, "Do I get a hug, too?" These were hardened dudes. Grisly old men with beards, biker types, gangster types. They all wanted hugs. Some would say, "Just came to get my fix, man."

But with the new policy, all this was now off-limits.

This included the regular huddle with the men, when they'd come in close together at the end of our group and put their arms around each other. It always struck me as something rare, a chain linking every race and age and offense. Sometimes each guy would lay a hand, or both, on someone sitting in the middle who was in pain, all these men reaching in with one hand, like petals of a ragged flower. In the center of it was one vulnerable man, sobbing or silent, in the one safe place inside this world of emotional lockdown, a spiritual shelter where he could receive such healthy contact and grace from everyone else. Now, that was all taken away. Everything except a professional handshake upon greeting.

That day the facility became a darker place.

It seemed like men slowly were becoming more violent. We heard of more fights breaking out, the men swinging fiercely for some kind of contact. More clampdown measures were installed. Bob and I were even instructed, as chaplains, to bluntly turn down any advance from any inmate for any kind of embrace. The guards, after all, would be watching us through the mirrored windows, and we could lose all visiting access if we were found in violation. So when men threw their arms open to us upon coming out of their cells and into the room where we met for bible studies—men we missed, whom we hadn't seen in months—we had to pinch off our theology and our affection, twisting our torsos away from these men. It was awkward, seizing back like that, our bodies communicating that they were untouchable before words could clarify. There was nothing I could say that could take this new, sad, confused look out of their eyes.

The one-on-one visits were even worse. No longer could we meet in those private cells across a table. Security concerns, they told us. Too many things could be passed between the chaplain and the inmate. Contraband. Now we had to meet in the long row of public visiting stalls. We'd sit with a pane of thick glass between us. Instead of hugging we'd wave, smile, nod, point, mouth exaggerated words. They'd pick up a phone and dial in their inmate identification code. I'd pick up a phone on my side. "Hey." Much of the time, we still couldn't hear each other.

Phone's not working, we'd mime. But even when they did work, everything we said was now taped, digitally available to prosecutors. Their crimes, their pasts, their emotions, even the tones of their voices—anything they wanted to talk about—it could all be used against them. The confessional booth was tapped.

There were no more tears during these visits. With the glass, all was sealed up. Now the men would always have to insist on their innocence, even when looking me in the eye. When hearts don't have a place to break, they become harder.

I watched them become harder.

Good-byes came sooner. The shorter visits no longer ended with laughter, no catharsis where something deep inside the men emerged and blossomed between us, no wiping their eyes on the sleeves of their red scrubs. The visits now ended with a limp, unfelt knuckle-bump against the bulletproof glass. "Later." Doors would pop open automatically, and they would go back to passing in and out of their confined spaces, passing each other, on schedule, keeping their composure. The pane of glass was everywhere.

That is the point, after all, the purpose of a "no-contact order" (formerly known as a court-enforced restraining order): that more walls of protection might extend throughout the community, invisible panes, protecting us from specific people. For better or for worse, these walls are multiplying.

———

One of the guys, Neaners, kept in touch with me over the next few years—even after he was shipped off to prison and ended up in solitary confinement. I drove long hours over the Cascade Mountains, across the high Washington desert plateau, and waited on my side of the glass while guards uncuffed him on the other side. I was worried, because what he began to tell me in his letters confirmed what I'd been learning in documentaries I'd been watching on solitary confinement. *Guys lose their minds in here,* he wrote. There is truly no contact. It wasn't just prayer or hugs taken away as in the county jail. He was alone in a roughly nine-by-six room. He'd have panic attacks, trouble breathing.

Visits in solitary confinement happened in a small booth, with extra thick Plexiglas between us and a dated and crackling intercom system through which to speak. Years of lettering and designs had been scratched into the glass on both sides, adding a hazy film to the distance between us.

One of the things he asked of me in our letters was, "Can you help me build a relationship with my daughters? They don't know me. One of them, she's five. Can you go build trust with her mom, and bring our daughter to come visit me? She's never seen me."

So I did that. I found her, drafted and signed and notarized paperwork between her mother and the prison system giving me permission to carry Neaners's daughter Adelita across this chasm between them. She and I got in the car, drove six hours across the state, and I thought, *He's in for a treat to meet his amazing little daughter.* She was chatting me up the whole time from the backseat, singing songs before she'd fall asleep against the seatbelt. I would practice with her, slowly teaching songs she'd never heard like "You Are My Sunshine." She loved this one, but could never remember the words. So we sang it over and over, through the rearview mirror.

We pulled into the prison. I carried her though the metal detector. The next automatic door opened. This little girl in pigtails, red stockings, and patent leather shoes was clipping along the tile floor with me deeper into the cold solitary confinement wing of the prison. We opened the door to the visiting cell, and there on the other side of the glass Adelita saw her dad, for the first time: a paling man in a white jumpsuit, Velcro up the middle, tattoos of letters and numbers and tears down his cheeks, the name of his gang straight across his forehead. He opened his arms wide to her, smiling, an embrace only in gesture. That's all he could offer on the other side of the glass. And she just smiled back. She beamed at him. I saw him beaming back at her. She was shy at first, but as our visit progressed, as Neaners and I talked, Adelita would crawl up onto the small counter and take the black phone from me. She'd say, "Daddy!" He'd say, "What's up, mamas?" She'd say, "I love you!" She hadn't even met him before. And she didn't judge him. She was not afraid of him.

His nose started to turn red, his eyes glassy.

She was into Justin Bieber at the time, so she held the phone like a tiny pop star and sang to her dad, pretending to be Selena Gomez. Her voice echoed through the intercom, pouring into the tight space on his side of the glass, soaking him in his daughter's song. "What's that other song, again?" she turned and whispered to me. She'd forgotten the words again. So I whispered the words in her ear, and she sang to him: *You are my sunshine, my . . . my only sun-shine. You make me hap-py . . .*

when skies are gray. I always forget this part . . . Oh yeah—*You'll never know, dear . . . how much I love you . . .*"

Neaners's eyes were now wet, the tattoos blurred under his tears. The pane of glass was gone.

"*. . . please don't take my sunshine away . . .*"

WANTED III

DURING RICHARD MEJIA'S FATEFUL WEEK ON THE run, before he was caught, when he was still dodging authorities, crashing cars, and stealing new ones, he had crawled out of a cornfield and up to the front door of a small house on a county road. He knocked and rang the doorbell. A frail elderly woman, Mavis Browne, opened the stained-glass door to this frantic stranger and invited him in. He was being chased, he explained, out of breath. He wouldn't hide there and endanger her, but, he panted, he needed the keys to her car. Alarmed by this troubled young man in her living room, her instinct was to help him, but in the same way he'd been helped by the nurse the day he was born: she picked up her coil-cord telephone to call the police. This time Richard would stop the call.

This is one of many places where court testimonies hotly dispute. According to one version of the story, when he lunged to put the phone back on the receiver, Mavis startled backward, tripped over the coffee table, and cracked her hip against the side of the couch. The press and the prosecution, however, both allege Richard pushed her down. And guys who were locked up with "Baby Jokes," who find ways to get police reports on each other, tell a different story entirely: that Richard came into Mavis Browne's house through the garage to steal a getaway car, and when she saw him in the pantry entrance to the garage, she startled and grabbed not a phone but, in terror, a pair of kitchen scissors and tried to stab the stranger in her house. In this version, Richard dodged Mavis's scissor swings, she crashed past him into the floor, and Richard yelled something like, *The hell you do that for? I'm not trying to hurt you!* At this point, some reports say Richard picked her up, apologizing, and helped her onto the couch before fleeing through the kitchen's back door, sirens blaring in the distance. But those reports leave out that "helping her onto the couch" included binding Mavis's frail hands and feet with that phone cord. And how he maybe tarried a while and cooked himself some food in her kitchen before fleeing. Maybe it wasn't food, but just a fresh hit of crack he sparked with the coils from her electric stove and some foil he had found in her drawers, being on the run without proper equipment for nearly two days and all. That part of Mavis's testimony was never confirmed. She would die in the coming weeks.

Her eighty-five-year-old hip would not mend quickly in the hospital. The authorities arresting Richard and charging him with eight felonies had done nothing to help heal the damage to her bones. Both victim and perpetrator, both innocent and guilty, sat waiting in small beds with bleached sheets under unnatural lights in large facilities—the hospital and the county jail—less than a mile from one another. Their fates would be eerily similar. Only hers would come first: she eventually contracted a virus while stuck in the institution, developed pneumonia, and died of lung complications.

With Mavis's pulse suddenly flat, Richard's bail jumped to one million dollars. New charges from the prosecutor transformed Richard overnight from a strung-out addict guilty of mischief and theft and with a chance at rehabilitation to a murderer in the first degree. A savage old-lady-killer. They said Richard had robbed the elderly Mrs. Browne of what would have been her golden, peaceful, and final years. So they charged him a minimum of twenty-five of his own years to balance the ledger. But he would not have that many to give.

IN SEARCH OF SACRED SPACE

L.A. IS THE JERUSALEM OF GANGS. THE LOS ANGE-
les River is their Jordan. But it is dry. Between the chain-
link fences and sidewalks, its empty belly of concrete lining
yawns several stories into the earth, like a drained pool. Remaining trickles gather along the bottom like a Protestant dunking
tank on a Monday morning.

So when Fabian Debora wanted to renounce his life and go
under, he stepped into a much more crushing current than a river,
one that carves through the Southern California desert: I-5 South,
trade pipeline of the West Coast, running from the Canadian
border just north of the Skagit Valley through our town, roaring
by our jail at night, then twelve hundred miles south, where it
becomes a gangland boundary line splitting East L.A. from the
rest before slamming into Tijuana. Fabian's baptizers in this current were more severe than the original Baptist, or any other Bap-
tists since: despair, methamphetamines, self-hatred, and heroine

pushed him toward the ten lanes of speeding trucks and traffic lights; shouting voices of disgust and contempt past and present in his ears; years of domestic violence, loved ones eaten by the prison system, drug dealing and gang banging all now heavy on his shoulders, constantly pushing down on him. Parched and famished from days on a jag, he stood in unlaced sneakers on the freeway's barrier wall. He hesitated at the edge, hovered above the surface. No one noticed him. He expected someone to stop, call the authorities, maybe shout: *Crazy fucker, get down from there! What the hell are you doing?* But no one did. He dropped in, gave himself over fully.

He made it across one lane, two lanes, then the semi roared forward. He took a final breath over the broken yellow line, stepping in front of the charging truck. His last thought was that of a father. *My kids!*

Fabian describes something pulling him, in this headlights-and-horn-blaring instant. The next two lanes he does not remember. Only standing on the dividing median, stuck between northbound and southbound, in the middle of the eight P.M. freeway, unscathed and alive.

Home for the holidays in Southern California a few winters ago, I made a point on New Year's Day to pass through what used to be downtown Los Angeles. I stood on the corner of Fifth and Main, where Fabian told me to meet him. The sun had just set. My neck was bent back as I walked slowly, scanning the old high-rises as he told me on my cell phone that he was waving down at me from a second-tier balcony on a corner building. Its twentieth-floor roof was lit ominously by red glowing electric letters, the letter *S* missing: WIND–OR HOTEL.

"I'll be right down to let you in." Click.

I came here to visit Fabian Debora at work in his studio. He is an artist now, a painter. Only four years earlier he was strung out on the interstate wall, a lifelong Chicano gang member and a graffiti artist of East L.A.'s streets. Now, for his day job, he is the lead drug and alcohol counselor at Homeboy Industries, one of the most successful gang intervention programs—and prophetic communities, in my opinion—in the nation. But Fabian's real joy is his art. He now paints large canvases with oils, shows his work in trendy galleries, and, when I visited him, he had recently begun to create murals in communities from Kansas to northwest Washington, where he had spoken just weeks earlier at Tierra Nueva. These days, churches and neighborhood organizations fly him to their cities just to draw on their walls.

The elevator opened in the unpreserved lobby, and Fabian stepped out warily, looking around. His long black hair shined in a tight ponytail down his back, black elastic bands every few inches. And there was paint on his baggy pants, sweatshirt, and shoes, like a day laborer doing touch-ups or remodeling some space upstairs.

"Come on," he motioned to me, stealing a wary look around the lobby. No greeting. He didn't seem at ease.

On the second floor, he was quick to step out and pull his keys from deep in his pockets. There was no life, no beauty in this building. A single fluorescent bulb glared down on half of what used to be a hallway for apartments. A wooden dresser lay on its side, open, picked-over clothes strewn about. A plywood ramp led to a door with no handle where Fabian put a key into the bolt lock and pushed.

"It's through here."

Inside, the room was almost black. Streetlights from outside the dirty and broken windows revealed a gutted cocktail lounge. Tiles torn away exposed the concrete floor. Shredded AC ducts hung from the pipework above, and Fabian swatted one as he walked through this gloomy space, loosening a veil of dust and shadow between us. It looked like something from a movie, the climactic nail-biter scene of violence in some abandoned building where evil things happen and the lost hide and squat together in squalor. I told him so.

"It's funny you say that," he laughed over his shoulder as he led me around the corner into an even darker passage. I could tell by his voice and silhouette that he was more at ease here, at home. "Just last week when I came back from doing that show in Kansas City, there was a movie crew here filming. I said, 'Excuse me, I have to get all these pieces to my studio in the back.' 'There's no studio here,' the guy tells me. 'Yes there is,' I said. 'I'm an artist and I need to get back there so please let me through.' Man, they had to radio in to cut the filming, and I carried my heavy pieces through a totally redone, like, mafia-ritzy hotel room. They'd brought in fake walls, furniture, rugs, the whole bit. There was a guy all bloody on the ground, you know, some actor being dead. He winked at me when I had to step right over him—right here, actually."

All was desolate now, an empty shell left by Hollywood.

There was light at the end of another plywood plank passage, and I heard hip-hop music pulsing toward us. I followed both

Fabian and the music, watching my feet for nails or holes, and we stepped into a high-ceilinged warehouse-like space. In one corner was a rug where a massive blue canvas, depicting a sad Chicana young woman, leaned against some plastic milk crates. She seemed to hold her breath and look past me, into the shadows of this concrete construction zone. I turned, and the pool of light from this painter's corner barely reached the far wall where his growing opus waited. In the half-darkness, I could barely see more enormous canvases against the walls, full of more colors, many with faces, human forms, muscles, bright maroon hearts in the style of anatomy textbooks. I felt something similar to when I first faced that Rothko canvas across the MOMA's open loft. I thought of Rothko's explanation of why he painted. Here, in the shadows, I saw live organs, tendons spreading over grim backgrounds of hypodermic syringes, gang lettering, street gutters, skulls, and general chaos. Who would have thought such beauty was being made here?

This was the world of Fabian Debora.

He smiled, finally. "Welcome to my sanctuary." His voice echoed through the unadorned space as he saw me squinting into the shadows. It was a bare-bones sepulchre.

I turned around and he was already at work again, deepening with a thin brush the edges around gilded hieroglyphs behind the blue woman's face. They looked like Sanskrit characters, but I found out later that they were old gang graffiti letters from his adolescent days tagging buildings with spray paint for his hood. Hidden in this urban calligraphy was a poem he had written. It looked like what Orthodox icon painters would do with the space around their portraits of the saints—words from the Psalms filling the space around their haloed and penetrating gazes. Here, the saint was a woman Fabian knows, a survivor of the violence of gang hatred. He preserved the scar on her cheek. He did not call her a saint, nor did he inscribe her name.

"I come here to get away. I don't really bring many people here. Guys at work say, 'Hey Fabian, take me to where you get down on those paintings, man.' I tell 'em no most of the time. If you're not clean, still hooked on that shit, sorry. I'm there for you, but I won't bring you here. It's my . . . how do you say? *Sacred space.* You know?"

He looked at me, and stepped back from the six-foot canvas.

"I mean, when I come here and pour out the images of my past, and work through it all, it's like hours and hours of therapy. The hurt, the shit I've been through, the damage I've caused. Like here"—he nodded at the blue woman, wiped his nose on his sleeve—"this series I'm doing with women. I used to disrespect women. My mom, girlfriends. I used them. I talked shit to them like they were nothing. But now . . ." A pause. There was a reverence here that made me want my own *But now . . . ,* a bend in my own story that could bring me to my knees, or my craft, or both. "Now I'm showing them honor. Their suffering. What I didn't see before.

"And when I step back," he shifted his weight to the other hip, as if he were a French *en plein air* landscape painter squinting at his distant subject, head thrust even farther back behind his shoulders, "and look at what I've done—*Whooooosssshhh.*" He gestured like he was being washed from head to foot with a force from above. "I get this incredible feeling, dawg." He pressed his fists together as if holding a baseball bat or a piece of rebar, and slowly pulled one up and the other down: "Connection. With my higher power. With God."

Just then my cell phone buzzed in my pocket, a collect call from prison in Washington State. I was surprised the signal connected through these tomb-like walls. It was Neaners, one of my closer friends by now, halfway through his seven years in prison. He'd remembered I would be with Fabian around this time. So I put him on speaker, and for fifteen expensive minutes Fabian listened to the heart of a man just like him, a voice transported from a solitary cell a thousand miles away. He counseled Neaners as he painted.

I turned an empty milk crate upside down, sat on it, and looked around as they talked. As a privileged youth, I traveled to European cities and stepped into every hushed museum and grand cathedral I could find. But I always felt disappointed, a gnawing sense of depression I couldn't shake. I was unmoved, trying to muster some profound feeling. What I remembered from three semesters of art history did what it could to connect me analytically to the glorified oil works and architecture encasing me. I was always surrounded by people of various nations and tongues, everyone stepping politely past each other, avoiding eye or any other kind of contact, and I was lonely. I'd gather my coat or backpack at the lobby desk and step outside feeling more lost than ever, disconnected from my own story or anything higher, let alone power. No whoosh.

Minutes after saying a speakerphone prayer for the three of us and good-bye, my phone vibrated again. I recognized the number from the Skagit Valley hospital back home: it was Nate,

the guy who'd climbed my fire escape and broken into my bedroom at night more than once, who'd tried to drown himself
in the Skagit River twice, ravaged by the dual demons of meth
addiction and schizophrenia. He was a tormented young man,
sensitive, a true North American orphan. Understandably, he
wanted to die. I was so happy to hear his voice, though, that I
cut short his opening lament to tell him I was here with this
guy I'd told him about once before, a guy who'd been down the
same road Nate had. Nate was quiet on the other end, there in
the crisis wing of the hospital, and Fabian and I both leaned in.

"That *vato* who tried to take his life but then had a connection with God, like, in the middle of the freeway?"

"Yep."

Silence. I passed the phone.

"Hey . . ." Nate timidly began the conversation, not seeing
any face or direction to turn, as in prayer. "It's good to meet
you, dawg."

As happens to sought-after priests seeking solitude in a monastery, those in need had somehow found Fabian here in his
refuge. He struck me as a Mexican-American Father Zosima, the
wise Russian monk glowing through the pages of *The Brothers
Karamazov*. Now, with modern communication, from prison
cells and hospital wards, the saints could commune in this hidden
place.

There was no sacramental wine, nor any alcohol for that
matter, since Fabian had been more than four years sober. But
he tossed his empty black can of Monster energy drink onto a
pile of nearly a hundred just like it in the corner. He stepped out

onto the balcony from which he had first waved to me on the streets below. This monk smoked Marlboro Lights. He leaned against the crumbling, Art Deco–era cement balcony rim. Traffic honked below. Clouds and smog formed a low ceiling of orange haze just above us.

As he put his lighter in his pocket and took a drag, we both looked down on the meager flow of late-night cars.

"You know what?" he said. "Sometimes, I feel like a little hummingbird flying through this big city. One place to another." He opened his arms wide. I pictured a hummingbird's wings ablur, its heart held high and forward in its steady chest.

"I'm small, I know. Easy to overlook—just one person. But I'm like"—he lifted his chin in supplication, arms of flight still wide—*"let me show you what I got."*

Most weeknights, he told me, after drug testing new homies, traveling, eating with his wife and daughters, Fabian wipes his mouth and excuses himself from their apartment's small dinner table to get back to his work.

"Daddy's trying to make the history books, I tell my little girls. You know Diego Rivera, Siqueiros? I've seen their stuff, read their stories." He wiped his forehead on his rolled-up cotton sleeves, fingers still wet with pigment. "Why can't I?"

I was still struck that both Neaners and Nate had called from different institutions of half-life, and within my first hour at Fabian's studio. I wasn't sure to whom Fabian wanted to show what he's got, the princes of industry or what. But two captives, the nearly dead in their graves, had found us here, hidden, in a dark building in an endless city. They received a glimpse of who

Fabian is, what he's got—and only by hearing, not yet seeing. They got to hear a man who has crawled through their same hells and found a way out. Who kisses his kids goodnight. Who now flies.

———————

I sat down at the solitary folding table while Fabian corrected the blue woman's nose. An old boombox stereo from the eighties, covered in dust, emitted a warm and scratchy signal from one of L.A.'s major hip-hop radio stations. In this place, I felt I remembered what I wanted with my life. Earlier that day, walking the afternoon beach of San Clemente where I woke up that New Year's Day, feet in the pristine surf, the tide pools, I had felt anxious once again, lost. But in this downtown den I, like Fabian, had regained a connection. I saw in the life across the room most of what I believe in: a walking dead man at work; visceral mysticism; a heart under reconstruction; street-savvy wisdom and the rare strength of friendship it shares with the outcast; a fine art as well as a story rooted in the pain of a forgotten generation, the orphans, the oppressed. Simply, a thumbnail of the narrative of the Bible.

"I could write full books here," I shouted awkwardly over the radio commercials. With this, I had confessed a dream that I'd hardly shared with anyone else.

"Stay as long as you want," Fabian shrugged.

I wandered back along the dark walls and unhung works leaning in the shadows.

Whooooosssshhh.

What do we mean when we speak of sacred spaces? There must be a difference between the religious and the sacred, between the merely ornate and the nakedly spiritual. Moses grew up in the magnificent temples of Egypt, amid the wonders of Ramses II and the gods whom historians and archaeologists still flock to study. But only later, as a murderer in hiding, working a nothing job tending flocks in a desolate nowhere later in life, at the base of a dry mountain, did Moses stumble upon the sacred. It found him. A holy presence, a peculiar fire aglow on an ordinary bush. A connection happened there, a new movement Moses couldn't anticipate nor understand. But he knew enough to take off his sandals. He felt it. That desert was holy ground for a moment, sacred. Such wasteland was where the God of the Bible began his new work.

Getting my nose within feet of the unfinished canvases in the far corners of this bare loft, I studied the theme of sinews and tendons erupting from the centers of Fabian's dry canvases, shapes of hearts and arteries. In the shadows it looked surreal, new life pumping over and across the dead images of the past. Through the hip-hop music I shouted to Fabian that it all reminded me of the vision God shows Ezekiel, the valley of dry bones suddenly covered by the flesh and blood of a new generation: *Mortal one,* the Lord asked the prophet, *can these bones live?*

Fabian shrugged with his brush, paused, and shouted back over his shoulder. "Never heard that one. Sounds cool, though."

I hear there is a new monastic movement out there, a generation of would-be monks, men and women, young families and small communities, fleeing the excesses of society once again. They don't run to the forests, nor to the arid wastelands like the early Desert Fathers and Mothers with their bare-bones communes. Instead, one of the core values for such "new monastics" is relocating to, and inhabiting, abandoned places within the empire. Like this nearly abandoned building.

Two days before my evening with Fabian, I'd visited Mission San Juan Capistrano on my way up the Southern California coast. Thousands of brown-hooded swallows perched among and looped through the ruins. They made the rubble buzz with ecstatic life. Theirs was an unfixed beauty far greater than the now-decaying Spanish façade of polished religion and genocide, long-gutted of sacred relics. Today, people flock to see the swallows in their untrained adornment of the wreckage, pulsing with their unclean wings like a rapturous host of seraphim. New life in forsaken spaces—that seems to be God's style. Ever since the very beginning, when God first began to create, his spirit brooded, like an artist, above the desolation and deadness. The opening lines of Genesis say it hovered. Maybe like a cloud of swallows swooping over the surface of the deep at twilight. Or like one small hummingbird through the bad part of town—small, invasive, magical.

THE ANGLE OF DESCENT

I WAS JUST GETTING OFF MY SHIFT AT THE FARM, still early in my years in the valley, my hands and knees still caked with dry mud, when I got the call from the jail. An attempted suicide wanted to meet with me.

I finished washing the small red potatoes my coworker and I had just unearthed. Under the hot water, they turned from dull stony lumps to the color of rubies, live organs. I wiped my hands and drove straight to the facility in the early winter dark of the Pacific Northwest. I didn't recognize the name the sergeant gave me on the phone. So I imagined sitting silently in the visitation booth, facing through thick glass a man I didn't know, feeling clueless as to what I could say, watching him hardening before my eyes in the anticipated shame: *I'm such a fuckup I can't even kill myself right.*

When I arrived, the sergeant at his desk told me they couldn't remove the attempted suicide from his emergency isolation room for at least twenty-four hours. So I'd have to sit in that bare, chairless room on the floor with him. This was just after the no-touch policy had begun. But tonight, the sergeant nodded, they would make an exception.

The officers shut the loud metal door behind me. The skinny man who was curled up in the corner stood up and came to me, still a bit wobbly, like a newborn horse, wet and angular, fragile and very much alive. His cheekbones were high and round, his skin smooth. The sides of his head were shaved, but a sprout of thick black hair shot up from the top of his head, the way it looks in cartoons when a character is falling.

"Duuuude! Hey!" he cooed in eager, poor English. He seemed to know me, but I didn't recognize him.

He said he wanted to thank me. Didn't I remember? He was the downcast man in one of our thirty-minute bible study groups who, only five days earlier, had complained of ongoing back pain. The circle of men had extended our hands toward his crumpled body and crushed spirit, and we had prayed for him, careful to leave a couple inches of no-contact space. Nothing had changed in the moment. And he certainly had not, at the time, expressed his other desire: to die. Within days, he would hang himself. And live. Not only that: his back pain was now gone as well.

"Yeah, no shit, dude. I'm serious." He swayed and twisted his back, there on his bare legs and feet, and laughed, looking around us. "Like my cell here?" He laughed again, and invited me to sit down with him on the one thin pad they'd given him. I took off my coat and made myself comfortable there by Edgar's side.

"Why am I here?" I asked.

He told me the story.

His cellmate probably hadn't noticed what was happening. Ripping the bleach-white bedsheets is common among inmates at the county jail. Men pass the long hours using the threads they gather to braid crosses and jewelry to sell, or to make knuckle wraps for weight lifting and push-ups. Edgar had knotted two wide strips of the sheet he'd slept under that afternoon and the eight nights before into a single crude rope, like those lumpy cotton cords in the cartoons that prisoners or captive princesses toss out of windows to scale safely down castle walls. But Edgar had a different escape in mind. He sat on his lower bunk with one end wrapped and knotted around his neck, the other in his trembling hands. He waited with heavy breaths for the cell door to pop open on schedule for the evening's single hour of free time. When the automated bolts clanged open in the row of doors, Edgar rushed out onto the second-tier balcony outside his cell, kicked off his standard-issue rubber slippers, knotted his sheet to the railing, and threw himself over.

At this point in the story's telling, Edgar shrugged with embarrassment.

I tried—and still try—to imagine the arc of his fall. He had to have lifted one leg over the railing first. But did he lay his belly onto the handrail and slip over the edge, clumsily dropping until caught by that linen knot secured around his neck? Or did he leap over the edge with one foot and push off with the other, as an escapee hops a fence?

I envisioned him arcing gracefully out into the open space above the steel dining tables below like a Chinese acrobat, the sheet-rope extending and unfurling behind him. After the fall, his upright form must have swung in the wide pendulum of a trapeze artist, out from the far reaches of the recreation space, under the railing and clear back under his cell. There he would maybe bump against the newly opened first-tier cell doors and the groggy, unshaven men just stepping through them for dinner.

To me, the angle of descent was important, because when he hit the end of his rope, the moment of lights-out he was leaping for, Edgar did not find death. Nor pain, he told me. Instead of trauma, he described the moment the rope yanked tight as a moment of sudden *gusto,* or pleasure—a relief. Somehow his spine rippled from head to tailbone, yanked into sudden alignment. In his telling, he made no attempt to re-create the snap, crackle, or pop, leaving me listening for a more profound alignment.

Edgar sat with his skinny legs crossed, his back upright in the blue Velcro no-harm suit mandatory for suicidal inmates. He laughed as he told me this story.

He had them call me that evening, he summarized, not for counsel in the wake of trauma, not to keep him from harming himself again, but because he wanted to sing. "Dude, I wanted to show you this song." In this holding cell with his sudden new life, he didn't want to sing alone. He said he remembered I brought my guitar to sing in our gatherings with the men. "They don't let you bring your guitar in *here,* though, huh?"

Sure, we can sing, I said. But I was still trying to get my mind around what had happened, how he went from suicide to song in one night.

So, not at all shy, he loudly performed for me the only song that had kept him company so far in the starkly uneventful hours following his pseudo-resurrection. He smiled as he sang. During what I assumed to be the refrain, the part he kept repeating, he pressed one fist atop the other in front of his chin as if holding a microphone and rocked back and forth with eyes closed. It sounded like a radio love song he had only partially remembered. He improvised the lyrics—*I need you baby . . . I love only you, only you*—with simple and ecstatic melodies.

"You know that one?" he asked and laughed. "Come on, sing with me."

I just watched and listened, speechless, while Edgar swayed and sang to me. I was still trying to come up with any natural explanations for this odd spinal fix.

I saw that Edgar, however, was not primarily thrilled about his healed lower back pain. Watching him sing, it was clear: I was sitting inches away from a man who'd passed through death and was now alive. In my imagination I replayed his descent from the jail's upper tier, in slow motion:

Edgar Lopez, suspended in space, deliberately crossing a spiritual line from his unwanted life into death, from suffocating panic and despair into the waiting black nirvana of nothingness and total nonattachment. Blue skies above Mexican fields; the smell of burning trash; nights locked in a closet alone; hiding in dry bushes across the Arizona border at night, following behind uncles he never knew; gunshots in the projects; running down the stairwell high as a third girlfriend screams his name with hate from the bedroom above—all this behind him now, washed away in a blaze of white adrenaline. He is gone. Only the sound of blood pumping through the ears remains as he falls. Maybe another man with one expectant foot out of his cell sees the absurd: Edgar in the air, a white rainbow stretched over their prison sky, a holy vision of the patron saint of inmates—a man suspended somewhere between life and death.

At the end of his rope, Edgar undergoes the most existential and orthopedic of surprises. He is jerked back into unsolicited new life by the very rope he'd fashioned like a tourniquet to cut off the flow of pain. Something clicks in the spine, the ear, the heart.

End of slow motion. Press play.

Below and all around this unwitting protagonist, the rest of B Pod is jolting into unexpected life as well. The sound comes back on. Men's hollering ricocheting along the hard walls, alarms sounding, more heavy doors clanging open as the swing-shift guards rush in to grab Edgar's legs and torso, taking the weight off his merely sore neck. Hanging there in his white socks, held tight by the guards, aligned and alive, he breathes again. He's never been so happy.

All this happened in no more than nine or ten seconds.

Why did his neck not break, as it should have? Or his spinal nerves, why did they not pop from their delicate connections at the base of his skull? So many possible angles at which the twenty-two-year-old body could have yanked that head—all uniquely fatal, or at least crippling. Of all the ways the sheet could have been wrapped, twisted, or knotted around the young man's throat. Had it been tied in just the right way?

———

I'm a child of modernity's twilight, somewhere in between rationalism and the outer dark beyond rationalism's collapse.

So I am deeply conflicted about miracles. I listen to National Public Radio's science programs with one ear and the claims of the early church—as well as those who practice Jesus's ministry of healing even today—with the other. I'm skeptical, and yet I believe it happens, believe I've seen it and participated myself in healing within these jail walls, over telephone calls crossing state and national borders. I have friends who today will tell you the hour their knee or wrist pain stopped hurting, and never came back. That said, I couldn't easily, or immediately, give credit to our laying-on-of-hands, or God's hand, for Edgar's relieved lower back. At least not with a quick certainty. Accidents, autosuggestion, and shock adrenaline could—maybe—account for that.

But there's another issue beneath all this: I do not believe God is in control of everything that happens. It's not a question of whether God is able; it's that God never *wanted* that. Control is the desire of prison wardens and emperors, pharaohs, and caesars. The story we receive in the Bible tells of a God who creates, who created out of chaos, and whose fragile creation was quickly hijacked by other powers. The trust, the intimate contact, between this God and creation was broken. This is a God who later returned to challenge the pharaoh's control over his people, a God who liberates. God appeared on the scene as a rogue, unrecognized presence in the desert, showing himself in fire and mystery to Moses in a desolate place, to a murderer in hiding, working a shit job, probably on the night shift, tending flocks. The fire said, *We're gonna crash that mighty place like a prison break and bring the captives out who are languishing in chains. I am inviting them to a feast in the wilderness. I want them. Badly. And you're gonna help. I have no face, so your stuttering criminal face will be the face of God to them, and they will laugh. Your voice will be my voice. Tell the powerful and the mighty that there is Another out there, even now approaching his gates.*

Out there is different from *everywhere,* omnipresence. The story we receive is of a much more elusive God, who is afoot, who *could* be anywhere, who *can* go anywhere, whom walls cannot keep in nor out. I've wondered whether this is what it means that God is "sovereign," like an independent nation: under no one's control, and therefore, and always, a threat to those who seek control. A threat, even, to a suicidal man—suicide being the ultimate act of taking control of one's future.

I remembered a scene from Shakespeare's *King Lear,* my favorite play from high school English class. In it, a man tries to kill himself by stepping off a cliff. With his eyes gouged out by his political enemies and his face a bloody mess, this despairing Earl of Gloucester asks a stranger he meets on the windy plains to take his hand and lead him to the cliffs of Dover, where he hopes to toss himself over. The "stranger"—Gloucester's son in disguise, a son with the name of Edgar, no less—tricks Gloucester and guides him to the edge of a small rise in the middle of a field instead of a cliff. He fancifully describes to the old man how tiny the waves are below. Gloucester takes his final step and drops a comic two feet, collapsing face first. The "stranger" changes his voice and pretends to be a rough fisherman on the beach below, claiming he saw the old man plummeting from the cliff's dizzying heights. "Thy life's a miracle!" he sings out from the suicide's side, crumpled there on the ground. "Speak yet again."

Surviving that small drop was hardly a miracle. But something significant happened within Gloucester in that fall. He'd said his farewell to the world and the gods he'd feared, and took his last step. He stepped out of the failed and lonely project of his life so far, out of his identity and social role, out of his beliefs, out of his entire story. He came to nothing. He died somewhere in that step, in the space of what turned out to be maybe thirty inches. Only then, *surprised* to find himself on his knees and alive, could he hear another's voice singing a new wonder and gratitude into his life.

———

"Okay. Your turn, man," Edgar nudged me on the shoulder. Part of the reason he requested this chaplain visit, asking for me by name, was that he'd hoped I could teach him a new song tonight. Apparently, these stammering bits of radio love songs were not enough to hold the weight of what had just happened to him. And he wanted me to join my voice to his, in this madman's cell. "What do we sing?" He smiled, patient with me in his suicide smock.

I simply couldn't think of a song. I felt a certain stage fright, being all too aware of the guards at their desks or moving about outside the door's open food-tray slot. Many nights I had passed through that same lobby and heard the miserable bellowing of drunken men or the profane threats of angry women from this very cell, echoing loudly through the facility as if played on the intercom loudspeakers. I knew how clearly the stern officers at their desks would hear my every note. Sure, the crazy people could sing, but me?

"Um . . ." I stalled.

What in my repertoire could Edgar and I sing in harmony? What would be appropriate for this occasion? No songs came to mind, but memories from my own life started to surface. Do I share with Edgar the story of when my best friend in junior high hung himself with his small belt in his closet, just across the street from me in the suburbs? Do I tell him how, when I was his age, I too wanted to step off a ledge and throw myself away?

The emotions from those miserable mornings in my early twenties now returned as I sat with Edgar on the cold floor. In fact, the isolation cell around us felt eerily similar to my college apartment's cold kitchen floor where many mornings I sat in my boxer shorts, slumped and defeated. And hearing Edgar sing here in this jail reminded me how some afternoons I sang alone in the dry shower of my cramped bathroom, taking my guitar and four-track recorder into the tub, duct-taping the mic to the shower head. My voice resounded and wrapped back around me in there, holding me.

In those lonely, panicked days, I found myself reading a lot of Wendell Berry, the farmer-poet. His essays read like a survival manual for our age, its instructions clear: rebuild human connections; get back to the land; plant yourself in local soil, in a place, in its web of relationships; most importantly, "give love to the work of your hands." I wrote a letter to him, confessed my morbid state, asked whether I could come out to his farm. He wrote back: surely I could find a farm closer than his all the way out in Kentucky, and, farm or not, I should definitely learn how to do something with my hands after finishing school. Get grounded and give back, essentially. I had an obligation to the world to do my part, he said. And to do it well.

So I did that. I moved up here. I'd found the local organic farm to learn to plant vegetables, poor as I was at it. I had fallen from the ambitious upward track of higher education and disappeared in this remote Skagit Valley, into this small jail where I'd also learned a curious craft of laying hands of prayer on men more desperate and lonely than myself. And here I was, dirt still on my knees and under my fingernails, sitting at Edgar's side. Within the same evening, I had held the fruit of the harvest at the farm and now at the jail. I had lived into Wendell's instructions, I realized, and I felt a wholeness in my story, sitting in the cell with Edgar singing. "That is happiness," reads one of my favorite passages in a Willa Cather novel, "to be dissolved into something complete and great. When it comes to one, it comes as naturally as sleep." Indeed, I'd spent the past few years lulled into a sweet reverie in this valley, not noticing the larger fulfillment of my college dreams. Until now. Edgar was forcing me to look back on the trajectory of both his and my own short, transformative falls. I too had found myself strangely and fully alive inside this jail. His eyes seemed to be singing out to *me,* here on the ground together: *Look! Thy life's a miracle!*

————

"Unless a kernel of wheat falls to the ground and dies," Christ said, "it remains alone." By this time, I'd read that Gospel passage many times with circles of inmates. I'd underlined it in the front-page epigraph to *The Brothers Karamazov*. I'd seen it engraved on Dostoevsky's tombstone the year before, rising out of a snowy Saint Petersburg cemetery. But only on the ground of this jail cell did the verse begin to open itself to me. Unless we fall, we remain alone.

In the weeks precipitating my falling visions, I had been an isolated student in an upward-bound academy. Edgar? An uprooted migrant youth in the sealed case of a second-story jail. Maybe we were just itching to drop, like grains of wheat suffocating in their isolated casings. All those mornings I woke longing to step off buildings, I never imagined slitting my wrists, sticking my head in an oven, swallowing a bottle of pills, finding a gun, or stepping into traffic. It was a distinct desire to fall, plummeting through the air and to the ground.

———

"Why are you so afraid?" Edgar laughed and brought his legs beneath him to sit up straight in his smock. The nylon casing with Velcro straps left his bare sides exposed. "Come on, dude"—Edgar's skinny arms reached across the space between us and landed on my shoulders—"*sing!*"

It was time for me to do my part.

I remember the sound of my timid first melody opening in the cell's lush reverb, like in my old college apartment shower, but better now. It was a song I'd written for our jail gatherings, after reading a poem that named "how we die daily of unexpressed affections." *Lord, release the affection in our hearts . . . for you.* I sang slowly, used my hands, so that my new friend could learn the words. Edgar joined me. Our voices came together within the painted cinder-block walls around us. *Lord, release the affection in our hearts . . .* His smile helped me forget the listening guards and continue into the second verse. I like to think, although we could not have heard it, that one of the uniformed officers at his computer, or maybe some strung-out new arrest in her red jumpsuit getting booked and fingerprinted just outside our door, softly sang along.

I never saw Edgar again. When I asked for him two weeks later at the front desk, the officers told me Mr. Lopez was no longer in their custody. Three years would pass before I learned what happened after I'd left him in that cell.

It was raining, and I had driven half an hour upriver, away from the valley and up into the Cascades. To my right, the Skagit ran high and muddy. In my small silver car I crossed a narrow suspension bridge over the churning waters below. The man I was looking for, another guy I'd met that year, was hiding somewhere on the other side.

They called him Dirty. But now that he was cleaning up his life, hiding from the streets way upriver and out of cell phone range, he wanted to go by his birth name, Alejandro. Or Alex. Alex called me that day because he wanted to record music with me. Just out from a few months of prison, he had landed in a good place and wanted to rap about it. He was happy. But he was tired of singing alone in his room with his recording equipment. In jail, he'd always take the plastic chair next to mine in the multipurpose room when I'd play guitar and sing over the men for the first few minutes of every group. The genre had grown since Edgar Lopez invited me to try such a thing years earlier. Alex would close his eyes most of the time. He'd lean in close. Only I could hear him singing softly along, behind barely parted lips.

He now opened the door to his trailer. I knew well the tattoos on his cheeks, above his eyelids, around his bottom lip. When Alex's face is hardened, the tattoos have an intimidating, postmodern-warrior look. But with his sheepish grin now, his nice teeth, and happy-to-see-you eye contact, the tattoos looked all wrong—like monster makeup still on your friend's face when he greets you backstage after the play with open arms.

In our socks, Alex walked me past his girlfriend, who greeted me from the kitchen, past their four-year-old son watching cartoons on the carpet, and into a room plastered with glossy posters of Chicano rappers, blue rags, the obligatory Al Pacino as Scarface, and an impressive collage of snapshots of all his homies taped to the wall. I knew many of the faces. Some were in prison. The two who'd died—whose funerals I'd spoken at—had "R.I.P." in formal Old English lettering emblazoned around the last hazy photos taken of them. Both were holding up either gang signs or peace signs with their fingers. It was as if they knew they'd never get a proper tombstone and each rare photo op could be their only chance at leaving an epitaph or last message above their grave.

"Did I ever tell you the story," I asked as I perused the wall, "of the guy who tried to hang himself in County, years ago? He survived the fall. And, it's amazing, his messed-up back actually snapped into place . . ."

Alex set down the coil-cord headphones he was unwrapping and looked down.

I continued telling him the story while examining the mosaic of photos on the wall. They made a kind of missing persons poster, all young men no longer with us. "His name was Edgar Lopez," I finished. "I'm pretty sure. Ever heard of him?"

"Of course, man."

I turned and faced Alex, surprised.

"He's in Mexico. They deported his ass a long time ago, probably right after you saw him." He waited for me to say something more. I was shocked. "You're asking me because you saw him in the news recently, right?"

"News?"

"Yeah, he got caught up with the cartels down there in Juárez. His cousins and shit. I mean, he killed something like fourteen people. It's all online, man."

No, I told Alex, we were probably talking about different people. The young man *I* was thinking of would hurt him*self* long before going after someone else, let alone fourteen. He was a loner type, a sensitive kid who didn't fall in with the others and adapt. Edgar Lopez is probably a pretty common name, too, I suggested. Especially in a city as vast as Ciudad Juárez.

"No, I know who you're talking about. Edgar. He's got that baby face, why they called him El Carita when he got here as a teenager." Alex pulled out his duct-taped microphone stand as he spoke, connected the black-market condenser mic to its clip, ran the wire to his crumbling laptop with a new audio file open on the screen, ready to record.

"Skagit Valley's not a big place, man. I grew up around him, used to run the same streets."

Alex said all this matter-of-factly, while leaning the microphone to my face, hand on the record button.

"So you ready to do your part?"

———

Back at home that evening, I opened the browser on my computer. I was ready for a long and difficult search, clicking and scrolling for some old postings of an arrest in some Spanish-language news source. Instead, five bold headlines came up in my first search entry.

"EL CARITA ASESINÓ A 14, DECLARÓ ERA POR PURO GUSTO." El Carita murders fourteen. Says it was for pure pleasure. I could take my pick: LaPolicia.com, ElMexicano.com .mx, Yucatan.com. Everyone knew.

I wasn't sure whether I'd recognize him if there were photos. *Click.* My screen filled with Edgar. Full-color, high-resolution images. Boyish eyes, high soft cheeks, small mouth in the exact same expression: as if not sure whether he should let himself smile, given his situation. I scrolled through one large paparazzi shot after another of Edgar standing handcuffed between two black-ski-masked officers holding large automatic rifles, each frame capturing him from a different angle. The color photos stood out among all the gray news text on my screen, like bright paintings of past saints hung against plain monastery walls. It was him. Illuminated by the flash of the press, haloed by the oval insignia of the private security corporation printed across the press conference wall behind him. He'd become a high-profile killer.

My room seemed to close in on me. This was the nightmare that haunts any chaplain who visits criminals: I pray for a guy who then gets out and slaughters more than a dozen people. What had been my part in this? Would it have been better for those fourteen people if Edgar had had no prayer in the circle of inmates at the Samish County Jail? Would it have been better if he'd had no miracle and had hung limp and harmless there on his bedsheet rope, in his socks, somewhere between the first and second tier—rather than upright before the press while fourteen lives were zipped into body bags? Would it have been better if he'd carried out his plan with the white bedsheets, conveniently self-executed?

I drove to the jail that night. I waited between the automated doors of the entry bay with my guitar. It felt cumbersome in my hands, absurd. Maybe I'd been making up the mystery in all these stories, making way too much out of a few sentimental encounters with highly unstable men caged in cells. I saw myself, for the first time, reflected in the guards' unamused gaze as I approached the front desk: *Dumb young pastor holding hands with criminals, reading fairy tales and singing songs, exploiting the First Amendment guarantee of religious expression in here, requiring the overworked staff to accommodate dumb pastors and their chatty sessions and story times during the few evening hours deputy guards have to rest from the day's rush of lawyers, of new arrivals, of snapping mug shots and distributing meds and breaking up fights into the night.*

Signing myself into the logbook, I looked at the emergency cell there next to the front desk, where I had sat with Edgar years earlier. Someone else's mumbling echoed through the food tray slot. The staff ignored it.

Back at home that night, and in the days to come, I kept going back online. The Mexican crime tabloids all described how Edgar Lopez-Escalante, twenty-five years old, had been working for a drug cartel. The cartel patrolled the streets and controlled the profits from the addictions of the continent's most desperate postal zone. Edgar's victims were other underlings caught peddling drugs on the cartel's turf—those who had not paid their rent. Some had no names, belonged to no one, their bodies still unclaimed at the morgue.

Each article noted how Edgar, when presented to the media, spit into his shackled hands secured at the chain around his waist and leaned down to comb his hair back before lifting his face to the news cameras and shouting questions. One reporter noted that as he did this, his lips were trembling.

With this picture of the microphones before Edgar, I remembered how he had gripped his imaginary one that night in the jail, how he had swayed happily in his song by my side.

Why did you kill them? the reporters pressed, several microphones outstretched—*the fourteen people in the past ten months?* Each news outlet quoted his flat answer: *"Las mataba así no más por gusto."* I killed them, just like that, for the pleasure of it. The *gusto*.

Gusto. It was the same word he had used in the cell with me years earlier, to describe the first time he'd reached the end of his rope.

Now he had fallen much further. I imagined the arc of this second, much larger drop. It would have gone something like this: An officer from the Department of Homeland Security would have removed Edgar's padded suicide smock and wrapped him in an orange jumpsuit and chains, transferring him from our county jail's "close supervision" where I saw him, to immigration detention in a waste management district in Tacoma. There he would have awaited removal. Deportation flights soar southward over the deserts to an El Paso tarmac. From there, the plane's contents, including Edgar, would have been effectively swept back over the Mexican border into the Wild West concrete of Juárez. Cartels scoop him up, threaten him, train him. If he were a seed that needed to fall, he was redirected once again. And down there, he did not land on good soil.

Dumped in a border town, Edgar's distant relatives got him back on his feet by teaching him how to extort money, move kilos of cocaine, and put a gun to people's heads. In Wendell Berry's terms, the drug cartel had surely planted him in a local web of economic relationships and put his hands to use in the world.

They had probably taught him a new song as well. Cities like Juárez are famous for their *narco-corridos,* folk ballads on the radio commissioned by the cartels themselves. Crooning voices and accordions fill the airwaves with multiverse ballads celebrating the *valientes,* the brave drug runners and their heroic adventures for the cartels.

So, there before the media flash, trembling, were Edgar's lips trying to find another radio song? One, this time, that could make him hard and valiant? Or, while the reporters asked about his minimum prison sentence, was he already ripping the bedsheets in his mind?

Ever since that night, facing Edgar on the screen, I have continued scrolling over the story.

————

Many miles from Edgar, in a solitary confinement cube within a maximum-security prison in the state of Washington, Neaners is peeling the bleach-white sheet off his concrete bed shelf and thin sleeping pad. He is not ripping or knotting it. Instead, every morning he spreads it over the smaller concrete shelf of his "desk," like a tablecloth, and sets his only plate upon it, a notebook of lined paper. And he writes to me.

When he gets so alone in that bathroom-sized room that he wants to snap a guard's neck, or his own, he now lets himself fall onto the page. Into memory. Heartbreak. Sometimes tears. He writes raps, new songs, angry and tender lyrics. He calls me collect to sing them across the miles between us. He is feeling his worth, coming alive. When he is not writing letters, he is working through his life story, one lined page of paper at a time, all loopy cursive, tracing the arc of his fall so far.

In one early memory he mailed to me recently, he told me about when he was twelve, coming down the apartment stairs to see his stepdad, his only father figure, hanging from a rope. As a boy, he felt helpless, frozen, watching his caretaker's feet dangle and rotate slowly against the edge of the chair.

"I'm really sorry to hear about Edgar," he wrote in the same letter. "If I got deported like that or dumped in some city like that all alone on the streets, I honestly don't know if I'd turn out much different than him. And lot of guys snap here in the hole, all alone, before they even get thrown onto the streets." He told me I should write about his and Edgar's stories, side by side. "A tale of two homies."

"The difference between me and Edgar is I got *contact* going on with you, bro. In a ongoing way. It's fucken beautiful. And we got plans for when I get out. You're not gonna just leave me hanging, fallin' to the streets again, right?"

We've made a plan: when his seven years in prison are over, he will come live with our community at Tierra Nueva, maybe move in with me and Rachel for a while, raise his daughters among us, become part of our ministry organization, be sown into a new family. He knows where he is going to land, if he makes it out. I am learning to do my part.

"It's like that parable," he wrote in another letter. "The one where seeds fall on different kinds of dirt. The way I see it, each little homie who falls out of his family or out of juvie or prison or whatever is like a good seed still. They can fall on the streets, like it says, 'some fall in the road.' They can get shipped off to prison or some other place, where they'll just stay hard or get snatched up by more evil shit. Or, they can fall in a loving kinda place like what we're gonna make, where they'll open up, like I am now, and really grow. You know what I'm sayin'?"

All Neaners thinks about now is starting a small farm when he gets out. He envisions a place where the kinds of rootless migrant boys he grew up with—those in a gang he knew how to lead, control, train, knowing their panic from the inside out—can breathe fresh air and plant vegetables. He has never heard of Wendell Berry.

He has no experience of the kind of farm he imagines. Only crawling through mile-long rows as a child in the migrant camps as a boy. He planted nothing but raced to fill the buckets for pennies on the pound, trying to keep up with his bandana'd mother and her different boyfriends who would hit them in the cramped, moldy housing the night before and most likely again that night. And he rarely got to keep the fruit, or the pennies. So he hated the dirt, hated the plants, and went to the streets. Then the prisons, and back and forth. The vision of a small farm just came to him in the solitary confinement cell after lonely, visionless months where sudden panic attacks left him regularly hyperventilating, pacing in circles, hands on the bare walls. Now, when he has trouble breathing, he starts designing which crops go where, and with every day the vision grows.

He wants there to be a house on the farm where such lonely lives can all live together, and where he can teach them what he's learned in the dirt. Though he was a gang leader most of his young life, on the streets as well as inside the prison labyrinths, he wants to put his hands and leadership to good use now.

"What do you think about this name? Check it out: *Harvesting Homies.*"

In the most recent blueprint he's sketched of this garden home, which arrived only weeks ago in a hand-addressed envelope, there is a small circle in the very middle, right between the house and the crops and the flowerbeds. A small arrow points at this circle. In crooked letters: "A bonfire for singing together at nights."

Yesterday he called me collect from his weekly break in the Intensive Management Unit hallway, his two hands unshackled to clutch the phone, a guard standing near him, his voice echoing in the chamber. He wanted to tell me that he'd seen something when he was trying to pray that week, squeezing his eyes shut and pressing his fingers into his ears against the shouting of the cell block. He said he'd seen himself walking through an open field, full of a ripe crop he didn't fully recognize.

"It was all golden and light. It came up to my waist as I walked through it, like up to my hands. I'm pretty sure it's the same plant I seen on the sides of trucks. Bread trucks, you know? That's *wheat,* right?"

I was smiling on the other end.

"So anyway, I'm walking through this beautiful-ass field, and I hear this voice, through all that noise outside my cell. It says to me, *All this is yours.*"

A guard's voice in the background: "Wrap it up, Garcia."

"So I wanted to ask you—what do you think it means?"

I am not certain what his vision means, but while I listened through the collect call, this is what I saw: *All the fallen lives, lonely college students, migrant kids, criminals, all fallen to good soil, rising together as a chorus of new life, waving like grain around this felon in years to come, his hands brushing over the harvest.*

WANTED IV

I SAT ACROSS THE SMALL VISITATION TABLE FROM Richard. His hands had just gripped mine. This was before the no-touch policy. We were about to pray. He squeezed his eyes shut, trying as best he could. I remembered his story about sitting in strangers' living rooms, stealing a sense of peace that never belonged to him. So I invited him to just lay his head down, on the table, and rest.

"Siiiiiick," he smiled and made himself comfortable.

I said I just wanted to bless him, and that prayer sometimes might be just trying to sit still and let ourselves start to feel at home in a love we're not used to.

Richard released my hands and left his lying open between mine.

I looked at the top of his head, new stubble once again sprouting through the dark ink on his scalp. The rain was so heavy outside that I could hear it through the facility's chambers, in our cell's silence now. I let one hand rest lightly on Richard's head, and I barely whispered words of simple blessing.

My mind wandered.

I was back in Harold's greenhouse, four years earlier. That day the heavy rain was pounding on the foggy greenhouse panes all around me, blurry with streams of water running vertically. It created a kind of watery cage. I'd spent the morning tipping two seeds at a time, tiny and insignificant as grains of sand, into the little pods of soft soil I'd prepared for them. I had just recently begun spending time with Bob in the jail in the evenings, barely learning how to open my heart to both intimidating men and to ancient spiritual phenomena. And so, during my farm mornings, I stood vulnerably before Harold as he yelled at me in one greenhouse. And I stood with an open mind in this other greenhouse that afternoon, trying to follow Julia's quite serious instructions to make sure I took extra time to "bless the lettuce seeds"—in a New-Age-y kind of way—after tucking them into tiny cells of potting soil. I had no idea how to do this, but I was open to trying. I'd watched Bob rest his hands on the shoulders and forehead of that meth cook a week earlier. I wasn't quite ready for *that,* at the time, but I could practice with the trays of warm certified organic soil there in the greenhouse, with nobody watching.

And so I began, carefully resting my white, dirty palms over the flats of lettuce seeds, whispering improvised prayers of blessing. Many seeds would not germinate in the days ahead, and many more would not survive the shock in months to come when they were transplanted into the real world, where cold and rain and wind punish the weak. This is why, I assumed, Julia had sent me in here to pray over them.

While doing so on this particular afternoon, several things happened.

First, the sun came out. The greenhouse became a womb of warmth and pure light.

Then I heard what was hushing from my own lips as I passed my hands from one bed of quiet seeds to another. *God, bless my boy,* I was saying, *give him a good night's sleep.* This is what my dad said every night he tucked me in as a boy, his hands heavy on the comforter pulled up to my chin. Without thinking, I had been passing on the same blessing I'd received long ago. Apparently, it was the only one I knew. The words had taken root in me. I stood there among the long rows of assorted green seedlings, suddenly crying, transported to my childhood bedside beneath my father's voice and hands, my own hands and tears now pressing into the dirt before me, blessing the hidden life to come, buried just beneath my fingertips.

Julia clattered in as this happened, to dump some empty compost tea buckets by the giant plastic teapot. She paused and stared at what I was doing before stepping back out. "*Gee,* Chris," she said. "Now don't you think you're over*doing* it?"

I snapped out of the memory. The same words, though, were right there in my mind, in the quiet, as my hand lay lightly on Richard's resting head: *God bless my boy, give him a good night's sleep.* His eyes were still closed, and relaxed.

I removed my hand and sat back.

"How do you feel?"

"Weird." He barely smiled, eyes still closed. "Light."

He sat up, rubbed his eyes, looked at the same white cinder-block walls around us, focused on me.

"All the color . . . it's lighter. Brighter. I mean, maybe it's cuz I had my eyes closed so long! But I feel kinda giddy." He stretched his arms back, thought for a second. "Hella weird. I feel happy. Like I said, *lighter* . . ." He looked down, taking this inventory of his self, his feelings. "I got this pain in my ribs, actually." He wasn't used to paying attention to his feelings. "I'm not sure what it's from. Can we pray for that, too?"

We both rested a hand on where he said it hurt. We said a small prayer, words I don't remember. And when he stretched, twisted his torso back and forth in the creaky chair, he laughed. "It's fuckin' gone, bro."

I tried not to let my excitement show too obviously on my face, always afraid of encouraging guys to tell me what they think I want to hear. Because that's not why I come to the jail, to hear right answers. So I just raised my eyebrows receptively.

"I'm serious, dawg, I'm feelin' like the afterburn of heavy meds, or drugs. Like, off-the-charts *good*. My hands are all tingly an' prickly, like . . . like, you know when your leg that's asleep starts wakin' up?" He said he wanted to go tell the guys in the pod about this.

I told him something I'd heard from some Pentecostal types, who describe a similar warm pressure in their hands at times. "They say it's a sign that God's Spirit is welling up in you, and you're supposed to give it away, quickly. Like, actually lay your hands in prayer on someone nearby who really needs it. Like it wants to be shared."

Richard slapped a fist into his other palm at this idea. He imagined aloud how to "handle fools that 'need' it," and laughed. "I'd be like, 'Man, you should get your ass kicked for that, cuz you disrespected me. But I tell you what, homie. I'm gonna lay hands of love on your sorry ass instead. Because that's what God did to me: I done all sorts of shit deserving to get beat, but God *touched* me with *love* instead.'"

For a moment, as he said this, I was aware that this was possibly the most hated man in our valley, his face in the newspapers regularly, and how nobody would get to hear him talking like this. I thought of the charges, how Richard was headed off to prison. It was just a matter of time.

Then he got silent again.

"What happens when the feeling goes away, huh? I'm not gonna feel like this tomorrow."

I went with the first thing that came to my mind: "It's like a paintbrush that runs out. Maybe you just have to keep dipping your hands into God's heart, you have to keep going back, again and again." I imagined his restless hands splashing into an invisible substance and painting this uncommon art across the lockdown boneyards of America to which he'd soon be sent.

"How do I do that?"

"I dunno."

We smiled across the table at the absurdity and obvious improvisation in all this.

"Maybe it doesn't have to be that hard," I said. "Maybe, before bed each night, just say *Here are my hands, God*"— and I held mine out in a gesture of *use them, fill them, they're yours*—"and then . . ." I mocked letting my head drop suddenly, snoring loudly.

"That's *tiiiiiiiiiight*! Gangster. I'm gonna do that every night now. Watch."

Maybe he was moved by how he didn't have to hustle to get what he wanted. This was just asking and receiving.

"That's tight," Richard said again as we said good-bye for the night, and again as the guard escorted him down the hall. "I'ma give my hands to God like that every night!"

I looked for a trace of sarcasm. But I saw only sincere pleasure. His hands were wanted for good work.

The sound of the heavy rain outside still weighed over the facility with an ominous drone.

FLY FISHING WITH
THE DAMMED

M Y FLIGHT WAS DELAYED AN ENTIRE DAY. MY bags were packed for a two-week stay in Guatemala City where I would accompany an underground cadre of ex-gang members who were now volunteer chaplains entering Central America's infamous gang prisons. This would be my third trip. Such young radicals in Guatemala had become my heroes. These were extreme fishers of men.

Since I'd already said good-bye to my roommates and co-workers, I decided to spend the extra day hiding at Rachel's house until my flight the following morning. I'd give myself a mini-vacation, read. The book was *My Story As Told by Water*, by David James Duncan. I started the lengthy centerpiece essay, "A Prayer for the Salmon's Second Coming," in the passenger seat on the ride home from the airport that misty morning and did not stop reading until I was two beers deep at Rachel's place around noon (the vacation part started early), looking out her back window and over the bend in the Skagit River shimmering far below.

An unashamed, over-the-top devotion spilled from every page of Duncan's plea on behalf of wild Northwest salmon. I knew little about these fish, yet somehow I deeply resonated with it all. Why did his informed political fury to defend—and his tender personal anecdotes to describe—anadromous fish move me so? His obsession with salmon carried an unmistakable sense of spiritual wonder, his words caught up in the labor and joy of something close to worship. Then it hit me: this fly fisherman was confessing something akin to my own haunted relationship of brotherhood and advocacy among young tattooed gangsters.

Half-buzzed and fully inspired, I started a long letter to the man right there at the kitchen table, comparing our callings to adore and defend beings so different from ourselves. That is, I'm not a displaced minority youth in a street gang; Duncan's not a salmon. So what explains our compulsion? I tried to compare wild salmon and Chicano *pandilleros*. Both emerge from generations of migration up and down the Pacific coast. Both bear permanent identifying markings and scars from their respective journeys and groupings. Both move in surprisingly large numbers quietly beneath the surface of Washington State's picturesque Skagit Valley, I wrote.

Then the differences. While Duncan's salmon were disappearing at an alarming rate, gangs were multiplying at the same clip. And yet, both those trends coincide with industrial agriculture and urban sprawl. I went on. Salmon are timid; gang youth are aggressive. (In later correspondence, though, Duncan busted that distinction: "Hmm. Salmon can be damned aggressive at sea and on the spawn—and gang youth are shy of many things. The paradox is interesting.") I continued to find meaningful differences: salmon are appreciated for their beauty and historically revered as divine in the regional totem. Gang youth, on the other hand, with tattoos and oversized clothing, inspire fear in schools and neighborhoods.

In my letter I went on to give the lifelong fisherman some good news: I'd recently started fishing. But—and this was the real news—for all the power of his renowned fishing prose I'd enjoyed for years, it took a shaved-head kid known on the streets as Pipe (*PEE-pay*) to actually get me to a river's edge with a pole (not yet a rod) in hand.

As the youngest member of the local gang I was working with, Pipe had adopted me over the prior year. Now that he was trying to live clean from drugs and crime, he had been pestering me to take him fishing. To put it mildly, I was not thrilled at the idea of gathering dusty poles and rusty hooks and talking to neighbors to find some "fishing hole"—even if it was to aid my new recruit in reliving what might have been his single positive childhood memory.

Yet I knew how often the men I meet in the jail lose touch with me once they are "on the outs." Fishing might be a simple way to stay in relationship, I thought. So we bought some shiny fifteen-dollar spinning poles for trout and a foam cup of chilled soil filled with sleepy night crawlers. After an hour looking for a decent spot and trying to figure out how to knot our new line onto the spool, we rolled up our pants and flung the lead-and-dead-worm combo into the massive Skagit River before us, from the same bend of river below Rachel's house I'd looked out on so many times, but now on the other side, in another city. When that line arced in the sunlight and broke the surface of the water eighty feet out, I tasted something that had addicted generations of men before me. I looked over at Pipe, and his toothy grin said the same: *Fishing!*

We were on to something. Soon the homies were lined up in threes and fours at the river's edge, teaching each other how to cast: snapping the safety off their reels and flinging wads of up to four lead weights and two squirming worms at a time, as far as they could, out into the formidable green current of the lower Skagit.

Molonko (Spanish for "Baby Corn") and his girl Daisy came. Playboy and Danny were crawling into my backseat without beckoning and telling me where to pick up other homeboys. We knocked on the housing project doors covered in graffiti. Guys who rarely came to events at our church were now regularly calling my cell phone: "We going fishing today or what?" I even talked Diablito out of leading his followers on a vengeful drive-by shooting, after an enemy gang had assaulted him, when I simply suggested we could just go fishing instead. He shut off his cell phone, set down the crowbar in the garage, and emerged from the old rental house with his girlfriend, baby boy, and some sandwiches for the riverside.

Duncan wrote back promptly. He told me about a fly-fishing and river science class he helped start just north of us, in Bellingham, a few years before. It was a response to death and disaster. In 1999, a major gas pipeline burst over a tributary of Whatcom Creek, which cuts the city of Bellingham in two. Two ten-year-olds at play near the invisible fumes lit a bottle rocket—and 330,000 gallons of fuel exploded. We are told that the cloud of smoke rose 28,000 feet into the air, and the heat burned down into the underwater substrata. It looked nuclear from above, and it wiped the river below of every form of life. The two kids at play were killed. So was a solo fly fisher on the creek that day named Liam Wood—a young man about the same age as the young gang members I worked with. In his name, a seasonal school, the Liam Wood Fly Fishers and River Guardians, began. This was its restorative premise: make someone a fly fisher, and there's a good chance you've created a lifelong lover and defender of local rivers.

If these gangsters were fishing as I described, Duncan reasoned, he wanted to give two of them, plus me, a place in the class the following summer, all expenses paid.

Cool as it sounded, I had my doubts. I wasn't sure whether these bait-hucking juvenile offenders would appreciate sitting in a university classroom during hot summer afternoons when it would be easier to cruise their native streets with windows down, seeing as how local trouble is easier to find than local trout. Learning about bugs and stream ecology? Would they have the patience for the subtle art of casting with a fly rod? And wasn't that a bourgeois kind of hobby?

I was, however, struck by the similarity between Duncan's proposed "River Guardians" and the gang ethic of defending one's turf. Gangsters know what kind of trouble is brewing in their territory, and they place a high social value on taking action. In conversations by the river I repeatedly heard whispering about rival graffiti seen in their neighborhood. "So what are we going to *do* about this?" What better river guardians for the Pacific Northwest? Maybe, I began to think, it is just a matter of *deepening* their already-loyal sense of place—so obvious from the towns and area codes tattooed on their hands and necks. From streets to streams.

Months passed, and I chose my two classmates only days before the Liam School began that June. There was Juan, fresh out on bail and looking to stay out of trouble in the afternoons after picking strawberries for pennies in the morning fields. And there was Teddy, a teenager as tall as me and more than a hundred pounds my weight, who'd tried to beat me up the first two times we met, before his homies told him to kick back; both times I was the suspicious white guy showing up at late-night gang meetings. It wasn't until Pipe called me one night—"Ey Chris, I got the homie Teddy here, and he needs some prayer, know what I mean?"—and brokered a new relationship that I saw a different side of the only homie who ever posed a direct threat to me. Teddy was laying low up north on the reservation with his girlfriend and her family, trying to start a new life away from the streets of his hometown. Both

Juan and Teddy were painfully in need of something new—bourgeois or not.

And maybe they weren't the only ones in need. The Apostle Paul, once a violent man, had a different view on the natural world than our imagination of it today. He sent a letter to his comrades in Rome, likely written from prison, in which he wrote "all creation groans," waiting to be set free—as if the earth and rivers and mountains and life teeming through it all were a restless prison population held captive, not yet its true self, caught in chains of predation since the beginning of time. The whole letter never lets up on the haunt that grace can save what is dead, what is captive to a tangle of laws, human and natural, all the way down through the whole sad system. All of creation groans, waiting for the children of God, Paul wrote. Juan and Teddy and the homeboys needed the river. And maybe the river—Paul, as well as the class title, suggested—needed them.

I'd been looking for a craft to teach the guys, something to do with their hands as part of my work as a pastor. What Wendell Berry had urged me to do myself. I'd also been reading articles by the theologian Stanley Hauerwas, as well as other scholars teaching at the divinity schools I'd been looking into, and they said all spiritual training is learned through actions, like apprentices. Not through ideas. Hauerwas said cabinetmakers and T-ball leagues both knew more about making disciples than churches did. Here, with fly fishing, fly tying, stalking and reading rivers, casting and mending a line into the current, I wondered whether I'd found a sort of craft, something to which these young men out of jail could put their idle hands. I would soon find out.

———

The first day of class we were late. I had to drive to the outer limits of two different counties to pick up these unlikely students. I first arrived at a gravel parking lot in front of some low-income migrant houses in south Mount Vernon where Juan emerged from an array of cars in disrepair—with two casual roosters pecking among the tires—to hop in my front seat. Then we sped north, over the Chuckanut pass through the evergreen foothills, past Bellingham and the university, to the distant reservation exit, right around the casino, right on Smokehouse Road, left on the street with no posted name to scoop up Teddy. Each evening he would clutch his oversized (fifty-eight-inch-waist) Dickies below his hips with one hand, holding his class-loaned books and fly rod in the other, and run to our car before the jaw-snapping, seething dogs Jasmine and Precious could bite a hole in my tire again (which had stranded us and cost me fifty bucks the week before, no lie). We spanned the width of two watersheds—to the outer margins of the Skagit and Nooksack river basins—before arriving at the campus. Then back again, late into the golden Northwest twilight.

As we found the last remaining seats at the front of the classroom that first day, these burly young men in baggy black-and-blue attire were timid amid the lean, all-white undergrads surrounding them with hipster haircuts, stylish eyeglass frames, and REI water bottles. The professors had asked each student to state his or her name, declared major, and reason for taking the class. Most announced majors like biology, environmental studies, economic development, journalism. Many said they needed an extra elective and were around for the summer. I mentioned I was a jail chaplain and hoped it wasn't too obvious where I had met the two characters accompanying me. Teddy, with his zircon earring, sideways ball cap, and fresh neck tattoo, was last to share. He kept it simple: "I like to fish because . . . you know . . . it calms me down."

The room was still. Students waited to hear more.

"You know?" Teddy summarized.

———————

I came across an article that week in an outdoor magazine. It was about a growing organization called Healing Waters that takes young men home from combat zones in Iraq on fly-fishing trips to aid their traumatized nerves. I've often considered the similarities between the armed forces and gangs in the United States: kids who join gangs on the streets are drafted more often than they volunteer, and their boot camp can start as early as age eight or nine, in the home, or in an alley after school. Most guys I work with, either on the streets or in prison—and those trying to leave both—could relate to one of the Iraq veterans interviewed in the article who had been wounded when caught in multiple firefights in his Humvee. He described perfectly what the gang members I know live through, especially those who've spent a three- to four-year tour in prison: "combat . . . where you have this negative bombardment of your sight, smell, and hearing, and all your senses are on high alert because your life is on the line."

The fly-fishing program, according to the magazine, "uses the sport's serenity and grace to smooth civilian reentry."

What Teddy said.

————

As the weeks progressed, I kept waiting for one of the guys to not appear when I honked in their driveways. Instead, the front doors always opened, their class-issued fly rod tubes, book, and notebooks under their arms. They began to love the course. Juan, a high school football star in line for quarterback position before he dropped out his sophomore year for the gang, was a natural at fly casting. On the first day, he had the arm, the touch. After the first week his fish recognition quiz score improved from one out of twenty to seventeen out of twenty. While learning how to tie woolly buggers on fly-tying day, he asked the wrinkly old river veterans who were teaching that segment how he could purchase a cheap fly-tying vise and kit. They adjusted their nose-balancing spectacles while naming stores to visit, then leaned over his shoulder and praised his rather original modifications of the standard marabou streamer patterns.

"That'll catch fish for sure."

Juan beamed.

Teddy, on the other hand, appeared frustrated with the casting, the quizzes, the intricate insect-doll art. When it was time to pick books for our book report, I suggested the three of us read together Norman Maclean's *A River Runs Through It*. It was the shortest book on the list. By the next class, Juan told me he was enjoying it but had to sit in one of the gutted cars outside his house to find a quiet place to read. Teddy, likewise, sought refuge in his flat-tire car out front or locked in the bathroom his first evening with the text. Then his girlfriend read a page, and they finished the entire book reading aloud to each other in two nights. Juan said he took to the first chapter because he, too, learned how to defend himself by getting the first punch in as a small boy, just like the Maclean brothers did as Scottish immigrants in wild western Montana. How had I missed all those tough details in Maclean's first ten pages?

It became clear that this classic novella—though beloved by L.L. Bean–clad, fly-fishing buffs—had more to do with Juan's and Teddy's lives than with many of the university students' worlds, including my own. These rough young men had personal experience in getting bailed out of jail by an ashamed family member, as happens to Paul Maclean, the narrator's kid brother. Teddy and Juan both grew up around such alcoholism and compulsive gambling. They too had lost friends and brothers to early, violent deaths.

When it came time to give our verbal book reports, I encouraged Teddy to refine the rap verses he was always making up in my backseat on the way home from class. He had no memory of finishing a written homework assignment in his young life.

"Aw, *hell* naw, Chris," he protested, and I felt his knees press in the back of my driver's seat. "Why you always gotta put me on blast like that?"

The car hummed along the freeway.

"So, like, you really think they'd let me do that?"

This is what he rapped to the class the following week, with chopping hand gestures and steady hip-hop cadence, incorporating the previous day's lesson on stream entomology— which was, incidentally, the same page of notes on which he'd also composed the lyrics:

See sometimes I feel like a cockroach,
An incomplete metamorphosis
Instead of a butterfly that's pretty and gorgeous
The other day I learned how to tie flies using hair from
*   elk and horses*
In the beginning I was confused but with practice it
*   started making more sense*
To me fly fishing is like learning a language but not
*   being fluent*
See I rather cast a rod than sit in the street and
*   shoot bullets*
But beside that, I read a book called A River Runs
*   Through It*
In the book Paul reminded me of myself
'Cuz I am also a bad boy with an Indian girl
But even Paul had a peaceful and beautiful world
That was fly fishing in the river that splashed and
*   swirled*
That's a book I read by Norman Maclean
He still found peace fly fishing through all his stress
*   and his pain*

Some of the female undergrads approached Teddy to tell him how much they loved his rap. He seemed to take the rest of his homework assignments more seriously after that.

———

Halfway through the course, the apex of summer's long days, violence returned to our streets. After being up late with the girlfriend of a gang member who was murdered in a drive-by shooting from the rival gang, I almost didn't bother to get out of bed for the next class. I expected the fishing fantasy to be over. I expected to have to try to talk Juan, Teddy, and others out of rash revenge actions.

To my surprise, though, both were waiting for me to pick them up as usual. They had their phones off, reading, the night before. They used our long drive that afternoon to process their shock and grief. They were glad for an excuse to tell the other homeboys why they couldn't "put in work" that week: they had to be at their "college class."

One Friday evening Teddy's girlfriend Trina came to pick him up from the Liam School's field trip site: Whatcom Creek. After ten years of restoration work since the explosion, it was now running clear with eager summer trout. It was a new creation. Seeing her man fly casting, and surrounded by stately trees and proud instructors, had an effect. A week later, I got a call from Trina: "Now he yells at me, not 'cause he's drinking or anything, but because I walk in on his *reading* time! It's so weird. He's always asking me to take him looking for places he can fish. So every evening we take my mom's car and find places in the rivers all around the rez. And ... oh my *gosh*! ... we never really knew they were here! Normally we just drive past them or over the bridges by the casino. ... It's so *nice*. I take the dog for a walk like I've always *wanted* while Randy [his birth name] fishes. ... Oh, Chris, we're getting along better than we ever have. Randy seems so happy. I just hope this change lasts."

When several other homies caught the enthusiasm from Juan on non-class-days, they asked whether we could all take a fishing trip. So five extra homeboys with their girlfriends squeezed into two cars, and we headed up the legendary North Fork of the Stillaguamish River, one gentler watershed winding into Puget Sound just south of the Skagit. A man at the gas station in town told us how to get to the exact place he'd fished for years.

Not ten minutes into rigging up the fly rods and normal poles by the river's edge, Juan's girlfriend Gaby gave a sharp whistle from the top of the hill. She had been standing lookout, purely out of habit.

"*¡La jura!*" Police.

I thought she was joking. Maybe it was just a game warden with a name tag that looked like a badge. Each guest had a fishing license, but I still clambered up the steep grass to see a uniformed police officer with bulletproof vest and firearm coming right at us. As it turned out, Teddy's girlfriend Trina (who hadn't come along that day) wasn't the only one noticing the novelty of a Chicano in gang attire hanging out in such an unlikely environment.

"What's going on here?" he asked, looking around. Most everyone had lines in the water. I explained that we were fishing. He seemed content to tell us to move our cars from where they were parked by the roadside ten minutes' walk away to a spot twenty minutes farther down the road. Several of us moved the cars.

Then an hour later, while helping a newcomer improve his cast in the still water below, I heard a man's voice boom on the bridge above: "Freeze! Young men!—come back here!"

Teddy hollered, "Ey Chris, you better get up here! There's two more cops!"

When I got up to the bridge, one of the young officers was ordering Juan to show not a fishing license, but legal identification. I interrupted and asked why that was necessary. He told us we had trespassed on government land—the abandoned train bridge several local fishers had told us to use—and were fishing on private property. Though I knew this was a favorite fishing hole documented in local catalogs, such as the photo guide I'd checked out from the library, the officer explained that he and his partner had received several calls from local residents reporting the trespassers. I could see *two* black-and-white squad cars parked under the trees in the distance behind them.

"If everyone in my group looked like me, though," I said, "you two officers wouldn't be here."

"And who are *you?*" he peeled off his sunglasses and stepped toward me.

"I'm these men's pastor, and I'm taking them fishing."

"Sir, I'm going to have to ask you to step over here," he directed me to the edge of the bridge and pulled out his citation pad and pen. "Do you have some form of legal identification?" Meanwhile, the other officer asked several of my friends to empty their pockets.

After a lengthy riverside interrogation, the officers and I negotiated the property lines and where we could resume fishing. As they marched away toward their vehicles, I apologized to Juan and all the young guys and girls for such an experience. They had come all the way out here to get away from such hassles.

"It's okay, Chris," Juan shrugged. "We're used to it."

"When I'm out fishing," the U.S. military veteran in the article had added, "it's a chance for my senses to say that nothing but positive can happen to me out here."

In class that Monday, the professors asked how many students had explored any rivers over the weekend. When Juan, Teddy, and I told our story, the professors were perplexed.

"Trespassing? By the trestle bridge on the Stilly?" Professor Leo's white eyebrows wrinkled. He didn't scold us but laughed in surprise: "In my three or four decades of fishing the Northwest's rivers, I've never once encountered police. I've never even been asked to show my fishing license."

There was an awkward halt to the classroom rhythm. The syllabus did not take into account run-ins with armed law enforcement officials. My two friends and I were in the class, along with the rest of the college students, to learn about local freshwater aquatic life in our region. We studied the difficulties such subsurface lives endured daily and the imposed boundaries that confine them. The four-week course now turned out to be making sympathetic advocates for both Duncan's beloved recovering Northwest salmon and my beloved recovering Northwest gangsters.

The greatest hands-on lesson in this unexpected education came on our highly anticipated final three-day fishing trip to the Skagit River's headwaters high in the North Cascades. Salmon and steelhead traveling up the Skagit River eventually bump up against Ross Dam and can proceed no farther. They never see the dreamy mountain streams high above Ross Lake that feed into their churning highway of the Skagit in our valley below. Fly fishers in their privilege, however, need only drive across the Canadian border into the pristine wilderness of British Columbia to play in the crystal headwaters.

Juan and Teddy were thrilled about the trip. Neither had slept in a tent or camped outside recreationally. We were prepared with letters from both Juan's attorney and the professors explaining the educational nature of the field trip, just in case we ran into any trouble. The van full of students ahead of us was waved through the border checkpoint. But a scanning official spotted at a distance my friends' different skin colors and tattoo markings in the stream of cars. He whispered to our upcoming agent in the booth, and the man in blue seated inside flagged our passports and asked us to pull over, then come inside the customs and immigration office.

For the next six and a half hours, Juan and Teddy were separately interrogated and studied, with pictures taken of each one of their tattoos, like specimens, for future government training in gang identification. And so with that, the cold, geopolitical dam had stopped their pilgrimage upriver. They were released back onto the streets of Sumas, Washington, and told that they would be permanently detained as criminals if they ever tried to cross into Canadian territory again.

Much later that night I pulled up to the glowing cluster of cars, tents, and beers around a campfire high in the British Columbia mountains. My classmates, now quite fond of their Chicano comrades, asked where Juan and Teddy were. Duncan was there too, hoping to meet these unlikely fishermen he'd sponsored in the Liam Wood School. I alone stepped out of the car. There in the darkness, with personal experience in defeat against dams, he simply met me with a hug.

———————

Teddy had been inconsolable at the border. As we waited on the curb for my roommate Ryan to pick him and Juan up, he announced dismissively, in stoic anger, his plans to relapse on his drugs of choice as soon as he got home. My heart was heavy. But when I returned days later, Ryan told me how the three of them had made their own small field trip on the way home. Juan suggested they might as well use their fly gear at a pond where he had caught his first fish weeks earlier: behind a Kmart in Bellingham a healthy stream and ecosystem had been restored in recent years alongside the strip mall. There, the two class members taught Ryan how to fly-cast and catch his own first fish. The three of them each pulled in a small bluegill with elk hair caddis patterns Juan had tied.

And so, Teddy and Juan helped spawn another fly fisher that night in restored waters, despite the Canadian dam's unbending position.

————————

Juan saved the money he would have used on a gun for his own fly rod instead, just in time for the fall's record return of pink salmon, hundreds of thousands of them gathering like pilgrims at the salty mouth of the Skagit at summer's end, then charging up the river as the air cooled, through our valley's crisp chill and apple season, into the mountains. It was as if Duncan's prayer for their second coming had been answered. The professors generously loaned us as many pairs of waders, wading boots, and extra rods as we needed from the Liam Wood class supply to take more of Juan and Teddy's friends up the Skagit when the leaves turned.

Stepping out of the yellowing birch forests an hour's drive upriver, we could smell the Pacific Ocean among the pebbly shallows. We tromped through a cemetery of pale, spawned-out pink salmon along the rocks. We stepped in felt-soled boots around shallow eddies where dozens of oversized dorsal fins slashed in procreating frenzy.

"Daahaaammmn, that looks like a shark tank, dawg!"

Soon I was comfortably waist deep in the frigid currents alongside four other tattooed homeboys, fly casting into the abundant return. We could see the fish cruising in clusters that looked like long stains or shadows along the river's sparkling seams. I paused and looked around: several fly lines laced through the open air, the enormous Cascade mountain range dusted in early snow loomed in the background, with endless space all around us.

In that moment, I saw my gangster friends simply as boys, and their gang identities—Juan's was *Lobo,* Spanish for "wolf," *Teddy* for his big bearlike nature—mere masks allowing them to roam the streets at night together and roar against a cramped migrant childhood full of barriers and alienation. Now, cloaked in different colors, algae green waders worn over the usual colored gang clothes, I watched these boys at peace in a greater wildness. The splashes of leaping fish continued round the clock, especially at dusk. We'd see the red or chrome or green creature's glory, manifest in full arc—more often, just the wake and splash of its disappearance. Then the peace. Quiet. Current. Then another shimmering leap and splash in the distance. Over and over again. And so the homies and I continued to cast into such waters, well into the twilight, the salmon rejoicing around us. Unlike many territories, this space seemed to welcome them.

WANTED V

RICHARD GAINED WEIGHT IN JAIL AS THE MONTHS went on. He became thick with unhealthy food and the extra rations he bullied with a smile off other inmates whom he knew to be pickier about what they ate. He became pale and pasty as the seasons changed without the sun touching his skin. Over time guys' skin can become almost translucent, revealing the lines along which their blood runs.

His trial was neither simple nor short. During the nearly two years he spent in county jail, switching lawyers, turning down plea bargains from the prosecutor's office that offered more than thirty years in prison for murder, Richard became a regular in our B-Pod Sunday afternoon bible studies. As a loud and charismatic leader, Richard easily became the de facto shot caller of the entire pod. He had a sense for what needed to be done, who needed to be put in check, and how to keep everyone getting along in a small space filled with men facing years in prison, drug withdrawal, losing their wives, girlfriends, children, all the while doing everything in their power not to show any weakness.

Richard knew how to handle the variety of cultures, as well. He was, after all—at least he said—a biological and cultural mix of many: white people saw him as white, Mexicans as Mexican, gangsters as gangster, Native Americans as part Native, and so on. He contained multitudes. He was all things to all people. There were short, indigenous Oaxacan gentlemen with darker skin, awkward crew cuts, and such limited Spanish-language skills they often could not understand their legal situations nor cellmates' demands. There were grisly Caucasian men with beards, tempers, addictions, and histories in the area. There were a few black men, usually from Seattle, who'd gotten caught up in a very non-black Skagit County, many displaced by Hurricane Katrina in Louisiana. There were Natives from the Swinomish Rez over on the other side of the sailboat channel, who stuck together. In custody, they were usually just waiting out a thirty-day hold for disorderly conduct. And there were always the skinny, volatile Chicano gangster kids with everything to prove and nothing to lose. All these guys lived together, twenty-four hours a day. And guys like Richard naturally became the recognized governors over these involuntary villages.

One Sunday afternoon the door to the multipurpose room clanged open and more than twenty men filed in from the pod and greeted me one by one, shaking my hand, and taking a seat in the small circle. Some needed to sit against the wall, on the table, or on the stack of extra nylon bedding mats stored in this space. (Extra arrests jam the cells with more bodies in the summer months when the days are long and the streets are hot.) Richard stood by the door with his arms crossed, pleased, as the last straggler hurried in.

"I brought the whole upper tier for ya, Chris. Except one motherfucker who wouldn't come out of his cell. I did my best, really. I went to his bunk and got in his face. I said, *I'm not gonna tell you again, old man—get your ass in there!* But he wouldn't listen.

"Don't worry, though," Richard wanted to assure me, as he took the last seat left open beside me. "I'll kick his ass later."

I told him it was all right, that wasn't necessary.

How do you show instructive disapproval when someone is giving you a gift? Gang leaders have a gift for recruitment. They excel at gathering the unwanted and unreachable. Reaching out to others in need has been a mark of spiritual maturity in most traditions, and into which most of us, believers or not, seem reluctant to grow. So when the entire upper tier—minus the old guy who refused—now emptied into our Sunday circle, with eager interest, at Richard's jailhouse means of persuasion, I saw more than bullying, more than even his expression of gratitude toward me. I saw a raw dynamic of apostolic growth. Like the Samaritan woman Jesus met at the well, Richard was becoming an unexpected herald. He was telling even the guys he hated in his lockdown village to come and hear this shit for themselves.

Only a few minutes into our study, he piped up. "It's like this . . ."

Richard was becoming my unsolicited assistant in making sure everyone in the now-growing bible study understood exactly what Jesus was trying to say.

"Danny, Oscar, you two, get your asses up. Stand over here."

I hadn't planned on having the guys act out the parable we were reading from Matthew's Gospel, but Richard decided in the moment that it was necessary. It was, after all, a story to which he could relate: Jesus was comparing the kingdom of heaven to a wedding banquet, or a party, wanting everyone to come and celebrate with him. In the parable that an inmate had volunteered to read aloud, the ones invited to the banquet either make excuses and are too busy to come—*"they paid no attention and went off, one to his farm, another to his business"*—or they apprehend the king's heralds—*"the rest seized his servants, treated them shamefully, and killed them."*

"So, like, they tazered 'em and cuffed 'em?" Richard had asked, but looking to the group to see whether they were getting this too. "I mean, more or less?"

We kept reading.

A dark-skinned and bony man from northern Mexico named Lorenzo was reading aloud for us in passable English, slowly, verse by verse. *"The king was angry . . . he said to his servants, 'The wedding feast is ready, but . . . but those invited were not worthy. Go therefore to the main roads and invite to the wedding feast . . . as many as you find.'"*

This is when Richard really sprang into action.

"So the king sends out more of his messengers to the streets. He's lookin' for more people, right?" Richard was now out of his chair with a New Testament open like a script in one hand, ready to block out this scene with the jail roster company of players before him. In this way, the pages slowly came alive before us, words becoming flesh. "Those other motherfuckers missed their fucking chance, see, so the king is like, Go out into the streets, tell all the fuckups and bad people like *us,* to come to the party!" His inked fingers swept over the whole room at this.

The other guys were not as excited as Richard yet. But he was intent on sharing his enthusiasm, not keeping it all for himself.

"I'm not making this up. Look here, it says: *And those servants went out into the roads and gathered all whom they found, both bad and good.* The *roads*? That's the *streets,* dawg. And who do you find in the streets?"

This is when Richard dragged Danny and Oscar across the room from the circle and left them there. Then he came back to continue his instruction.

"So Jesus, I mean the king or whatever, is throwing this *gangster*-ass party, but he's all rejected an' shit by the people with money, who I guess have better things to do. But he doesn't wanna have a party and nobody come—cuz that fucking sucks—so he invites street people." He said this as he walked with exaggerated street strut over to the confused homies he'd left in the corner, grabbing them by the arms, acting it out. "Ey, check this out," he explained to the outsiders. "We're gonna roll to this party. It's a classy kinda thing, but motherfuckers like us can come." The two sheepish inmates played along, followed Richard to our circle around the table, and took a seat among us. Richard remained standing. "See, people like me, we know where all the bad people are at! So we gotta be the ones to go and invite 'em, right? I'm your messenger, right here!" he said, tapping his chest. It was as though Richard were suddenly sensing an alignment between the desire of heaven and his own frustrated story so far.

"*Both bad and good,* it says it right there." He repeated the words with his finger pointing back into the recycled paper pages, like someone standing at the entrance to a ball, holding up their personal invitation to the security staff at the door.

Maybe he imagined me as such a bouncer.

"Motherfuckers like us are bad. Thieves, drug addicts, crack heads, crack babies, gangsters, lawbreakers, bad people. There's hella of us out there. I mean if the king really wants his house to be full—shit, I'll help him find 'em. I mean it makes sense, doesn't it? If we're here at the party, having a good time with the king, there'd be less of us jackin' car stereos an' shit on the streets, right?"

He turned back to Danny and knocked a knuckle against his chest. "It'd be like, 'Ey Danny, now you call all your homies and bitches, and tell 'em to tell their homies—family, *everyone*—good and bad, don't make no difference."

The old white guys, the tattooed homies, the Natives, even the Oaxacan guys who'd gotten no translation through any of it, all smiled at each other. Richard was leading the best bible study I'd seen in this jail.

"And just like it says here," their new preacher concluded, "*The wedding hall was filled with guests!*"

Richard finally sat down next to me with a loud, exhausted sigh and smile, as if he'd just finished his job interview, been chosen, finished his appointed role, delegated others, and could now enjoy the party. Sure enough, it felt as if the party had already begun. *What would it be like,* I wondered, *to work with Richard out on the streets with me, recruiting for such a kingdom's banquet through the alleys and projects of our valley?*

Just then the narrow vertical window in the multipurpose room door squeaked open and an unhappy set of eyes scanned over our loud gathering. They'd be coming to take everyone back to their cells in just a minute.

But the parable wasn't over yet. And the guard had given us the two-minute-warning look.

So I thought our reading of the wedding banquet parable could end right there, where Richard had brought us, with the hall happily filled with guests. We didn't have time to take on the rather difficult verses that followed.

But Lorenzo had humbly plodded on in his reading of verse eleven while I was distracted with the guard's signals. We were always getting cold stares from the officers when they'd loudly pop the doors open and have to wait in the open doorframe in their stiff uniforms because we had not heeded their "Do your prayer and wrap things up" warning. It is an uncomfortable experience to pray aloud when an unhappy correctional officer is staring at you only feet away, an experience I was trying to get better at avoiding by better complying in moments like these.

"No, it's okay, Lorenzo, you can stop there," I interrupted our soft-spoken reader. "We'll read the rest next week."

That's when Richard, just like the first time I met him, cut me off.

"Naw, hold up, Chris! Fuck that, we're not done. Keep reading . . ."

He didn't like the worry he saw in the eyes of Lorenzo, who had already begun to read ahead in the parable. Richard smelled foul play, that I was covering something up. We don't have time, I explained with a forced smile to avoid the ominous verses that followed. But Richard's elation at the story was now already turning to pain, like he'd been lied to.

"Keep reading," he ordered Lorenzo, and he crossed his arms while leaning forward to listen to the rest of the story.

"But when the king came in to look at the guests, he saw there a man who had no wedding g-garment. And . . . and he said to him, 'Friend, how did you get in here without a wedding garment?' And he was speechless. Then the king said to the attendants, 'Bind him hand and foot and cast him . . . into the outer darkness. In that place there will be weeping and gnashing of teeth.' For many are called, but few are chosen." Lorenzo looked up at me from the reading.

"Just what I fucking thought!" Richard stood up and his chair screeched loudly across the floor behind him, a needle across a record. The party was over. "What the fuck, Chris? What do you expect from people like us? We don't *have* all the right clothes. We never look right! You should *know* that!" Though these were Jesus's words, and ancient, Richard nevertheless held me responsible. As a gang member, he knew what it meant to represent something bigger than yourself with full responsibility. "Why you even invite us to any of this if you're just gonna fucking humiliate us and throw us out anyway? It'd be better not to come than have you break our fucking hearts!"

The guards were going to open the doors any second. This is what I was trying to avoid and handle with proper time—and exegetical nuance—the following week.

"You get our hopes up!" he pointed at me. "And it's fucking beautiful what you tell us—that God is different, that he wants everyone. Even the bad people like me. And I'm like fucking *excited* and wanting to tell everyone—"

"Okay, hang on," I interrupted him now, looking at my watch. I hoped this would be one of the weeks when the guards have to handle a medical emergency and so leave us in here a while longer. I explained quickly that in first-century Palestine, some scholars say it was the custom for the host of the wedding feast—and especially a king—to provide these over-garments for the guests, right at the door, before they got into the banqueting hall. "Like those little birthday hats parents give to each kid who comes to the party." It was the first comparison that came to mind. "It's not about who comes dressed up nice or not; everyone is given the celebration attire. So if this guy's not wearing it, it's not about poverty. There's some other reason he's choosing not to wear it. It's an insult, a direct disrespect to the host, in front of everyone in his own home." I thought this would register with a guy who lives by the streets' code of respect, familiar with the pain of having his fragile joy mocked in front of others. "It's like this garmentless guy's refusing to celebrate for some reason."

The guys around the table sat silent, their heads moving back and forth between Richard and me, sensing something very important was at stake here.

Richard then countered with the kind of insight no seminary could teach me.

"Even if they are given little birthday hats like you say, sorry—if you're gonna invite motherfuckers like us from the streets to your party or church or house or heaven or whatever, you should know we might not wanna wear that shit on our heads. We're not gonna right away play by all the little games and rules how you do! So you didn't really want us at all! Or if you did, is it just so you can throw us back out into the darkness? What's it say?—'Chains and gnashing teeth'? Hell fucking yes, I'd be gnashing my teeth. Cuz that hurts so deep, Chris." His eyes confirmed this. "Better to stay in the streets with the bad people than be told you're wanted and then find out you're really not!"

I didn't know whether I wanted to stand with Richard or with the text. I loved both. And, like watching my parents fight as a boy, I desperately wanted them to love each other. I wanted to clear up the misunderstanding.

The unresolved question underneath all of this remained, and time was running out: Why would such a lavish host throw this guest out in the darkness?

"What if it's the other way around, Jokes?" I challenged. I had no scholar's text to back me up now. Just my own hope, a pathos pounding inside me. I had no disapproving pastor or professor to convince, only an unsavory man about to leave the table, a man I wanted as much as any other I'd met, maybe in my whole life so far, to stay.

He tilted his head to the side, willing—and waiting—to be told his worst fears weren't true.

"You're just assuming," I went on, "the one not wearing the garment is one of the 'bad' people who were invited off the streets. But it doesn't say that. What if it's one of the 'good' people who feels suddenly uncomfortable around all these 'bad' folks pouring in from the streets and sitting next to him, or her? Someone who's too good to look just like the trash seated around the table? Someone who needs to set himself apart, not putting on the same robe—putting himself on the same level—as all the undeserving fuckups?"

Richard's shoulders relaxed, but I was just getting started.

"How do you think the host would feel, watching his new flood of guests that he invited from the streets to share his joy, now all feeling judged by this one guy, who's totally killing the party?" I had never thought of this before, but I was suddenly choked with fury at this faceless character in the story who was making the mixed wedding guests in my mind as suddenly unsure of themselves as the guys around the jail table before me now.

"He'd throw that guy outside and tie him up," I almost shouted at Richard, as if it were a declaration of how I personally would defend him and his place at the table if I could, "let him get it out of his system, grumble all he wants, until he was ready to come back in and share the joy of the king who wants *everyone*. Even people like you!"

The doors clanged open with the same violent noise as ever. Richard was afraid to trust what I'd said now. It seemed too good—to be true, at least.

"Back your shit up, Chris," he said on his way out the door with a finger pointed at me. "Send me a copy of whatever *scholar* you're talking about. I wanna see that in print!"

FUCK THE WORLD

MY FIRST YEAR AT THE JAIL, I SAW A TATTOO I would never forget on an inmate's neck. It was a Thursday night, in our regular circle of chairs in the cold multipurpose room. We opened with a prayer as usual, but after Bob said *Amen,* it was silent. We all looked at him to begin with some story or greeting or question for the group. Instead, Bob's brow was furrowed as he lingered for a moment, looking at the neck of the young man seated beside him. There was no judgment in his gaze. Rather, it was a look I'd seen on his face before, when intently listening to someone tell his or her life story. He tilted his head and I could hear a soft *Hmm.*

I knew the inked man beside him, Michael Jenkins. On the streets people called him Trixter. I had visited Michael one-on-one the last time he was in here, when he had asked for a private visit and for prayer. He was one of the only Caucasians from the

Mexican gang I had been getting to know lately, behind bars and out on the streets of our town.

Michael was the last to lift his head from the postprayer silence and so was the last to see Bob looking at him. Michael stared back down at his lap, then peered out again from the corner of his eye. Bob was still fixed on him.

"What . . . ?" Michael asked, repressing a nervous smile.

All eyes were on him.

I knew exactly what had caught Bob's attention. I too had seen it as soon as Michael had come in. On the side of his neck facing Bob was a glossy new tattoo. *Fuck the World,* it read. It was not partially hidden under his collar but writ high on his neck in large, clear calligraphy. I thought of the banners hung in church sanctuaries I'd seen growing up, similar letters announcing slogans like "God Is Love" or "Shout For Joy All Ye Peoples."

"I'm just looking at your tattoo," Bob answered. Michael was clearly uncomfortable, and he lifted his hand to cover his neck, but stopped halfway.

"Yeah?" he mumbled.

Maybe Michael was thinking, *I knew I shouldn't have come to church since I got this shit on my neck.*

"Yeah," Bob finally answered. "I'm just looking at your tattoo here and thinking, That's something Jesus's disciples might have said."

Silence.

Michael's eyes weakly strained to smile.

I knew that Bob was not playing.

"Let's open to . . . ," Bob began as he flipped the onionskin pages in his Bible, "where is it . . . ?"

While everyone grabbed a thin New Testament from the ragged stack and waited, I watched Michael. His eyes darted around as he began to suspect that this was no joke, but rather that we were about to open to a page where the writing in the Bible agreed with the writing on his neck.

"Here. First John, chapter . . ."

Most men are lost when they pick up a Bible, and so we usually take a minute or so to help each person find the passage. It'd be easier to paraphrase it, or just bring photocopies of the selected passage, but Bob likes to empower those who feel unqualified to crack the book open and find their way around. Ultimately, to read it for themselves. During this moment of shuffling pages, Bob smiled at Michael and asked his name. Michael still shyly answered. Bob then quietly asked whether he would read the text for us, and Michael's face went red.

"But first," Bob started, speaking loudly so the group could hear. "Michael, what do you mean by *the world*?"

"I dunno," he shrugged. Then his eyes shot up with certainty. "The system."

When he saw that the pastor made no move to defend the system, but nodded in response, Michael elaborated.

"The *system*, you know—the courts, the laws, prisons, cops, so*ciety*," his head swayed back and forth in frustration. "Just . . . just the way the world works, you know? The *system*," he repeated and looked down.

Then he read, slowly. Michael had been expelled before high school (so he had once shared with me during our visits) and rarely made it to school thereafter. So, he now struggled with the words.

*"Do not l-love . . . the world . . . or the things in the w-world. If,
if anyone . . . l-loves the world, the love of the Father,"* he paused,
"is not in him."

———

Later that month, I was invited to lead a jail-style bible study
among homeless youth from Seattle's University District. It was
the same kind of "gutter punk" culture I'd known on the streets
in Berkeley—on dark Monday nights at the free clinic, I had
washed their toes in soapy bins, served up overcooked vegan
fare, learned how to roll cigarettes with them out on the fire
escape, but had always wanted to read the Bible with them, see
what they thought, learn about their lives. So when I got the invite from the Seattle U-District group a few years later, I was in.

But what to read together? I had been thinking about
Michael's tattoo and our conversation earlier that month, so I
decided to tell the group of twenty teenagers and young adults
strewn across the church lobby that morning about the tattoo
on my mind. Just to see what they thought. That would be our
study.

Most had not slept the night before. They slouched into each
other on the couches and on the floor, their faces hidden in the
shadows of hats and hoods. I introduced myself by saying I spent
a lot of time in a jail. Then I dragged my finger over my neck and
described Michael's tattoo.

The chatter fell silent.

It wasn't clear whether they were shocked at hearing a supposed minister say the words "Fuck the world" or whether this

declaration was a sermon in itself that they instantly recognized as true.

A young Chinese woman on the old couch across from me, her eyes sullen with heavy black mascara, pulled back her rain-soaked hood and sat up to listen. Three guys with large backpacks and straggly hair to my right opened their eyes and leaned forward. They had been pretending to be asleep after getting their share of free coffee and donuts. I then opened one of the beat-up Bibles on the center table to the same verse we'd read in the jail, as well as a new verse.

"If the world hates you," Jesus says to his disciples, *"it hated me first."*

I said I wanted to know what they thought "the world" was referring to in these passages. "Do you think it's the same *world* as in *For God so loved the world that he gave his only son*?"

"Naw," one of the young men to my right shook his hand in the air, "that's different. That's what God *created*. That's what we love, too." Everyone agreed that the verse wasn't talking about all the wild expanses of ocean, desert, and forest. Not nature. Not the earth, creation. Those things didn't hate Jesus. "Not the redwoods and salmon an' shit," as one increasingly loud young man with spikes around his choke collar clarified. "Not that."

"What's an example of *the world,* then?" I asked. "Where do you see *the world*?"

"Shit, just last night," one short teenager yelled from the coffee dispensers in the back corner. "I got locked in a dumpster. It's the only dry place to sleep during the rains like this, and I found one full of clean cardboard—collapsed boxes, you know—in one of these alleys behind an office building. But I guess they don't want people like us touching their perfectly good cardboard, even if they're just throwing it away. So they put a padlock on it at night. But I didn't know that then, I'd only heard of that kinda shit—until I woke up in the middle of the night . . . *trapped.* They locked me in! I was banging for hours under the lid, yelling."

Others around the room began to snicker.

"I don't think it's fuckin' funny," he silenced the group and looked back at me. "We're nothing to the world. We're just trash, anyway, is how we're seen."

"I got an example," another young woman actually raised her hand before continuing. "I mean, that first verse said not to love 'the world' because it's like the opposite of," she looked over and checked her neighbor's open text, "opposite of *the love of the Father,* right?" She pushed her hair behind her ear and sat forward. She saw I was listening.

"Well, check this out. So many of us street kids are trying to get a job, and I finally got one at the Starbucks here on the corner. The same Starbucks that never allows us street kids to use their bathroom. So when I started working and would sometimes let my friends here use the bathroom—because it's just about illegal to take a piss anywhere else—I was told I had to turn my friends away. Or get fired. So I left. I had to quit my job and now I'm back on the streets. I could have a studio apartment by now, a clean place to sleep. But I'd have to turn my back on people just like me. I'm not going to do that to the people I love. Where's *the love of the Father* in that?"

More voices chimed in. After a few, I was struck by how their examples were not stories of being wronged by individuals, necessarily. They didn't seem to be complaining about the anonymous employee who locked the dumpster, for instance, or the manager at the coffee shop. They all gave examples of general procedures, policies put in place to deal with unwanted people.

"Yeah, when we say *the world,* or when this verse says it, not to *love* it," the Chinese teen summarized, "it's not talking about *people,* saying we shouldn't love people. *We're* people. I don't think Jesus is saying he was hated by a few specific people. It's something else. Something bigger. Like *society.*"

I shared Michael's definition: "the system." Nearly everyone in the room nodded.

————

Michael Jenkins's tattoo took on a life of its own. Bob and I repeated the "Fuck the World" bible study in as many different kinds of groups as we could. It became a standard in our repertoire. In Guatemalan prison grottoes, the local juvenile hall, Union Gospel Missions in Seattle and Bellingham, seminary classes Bob led in England and France, we kept considering these words written by early Christians.

Most respectable people we read this with were quick to say that Jesus and his disciples were hated and arrested for *different* reasons than street criminals would be today. That is, the disciples brought life and healing, a different religious message merely, while many criminals are hunted and hated for bringing danger and dysfunction to the community: burglarizing houses, moving drugs into a town, vandalizing property with graffiti, firing guns in neighborhoods, assaulting their peers.

Yet these differences weren't always clear to Jesus's contemporaries. His words and actions were seen as profane to the faithful, his style of fellowship openly subversive to public order. He was, after all, executed as a criminal between ordinary thieves. According to Gospel narrative, Pontius Pilate agreed to release Barabbas—a convicted political assassin—in exchange for Jesus that day in court. Common thieves, violent revolutionaries, and the message Jesus embodied were apparently all threats to the system.

———————

Months later Bob got a call on our way to the jail. It was a woman in our Tierra Nueva community, Amy, who said she had received a message while praying: she had the specific sense that God wanted us to bless the hands of an inmate that night named Mike. I sat through the first three half-hour groups with various combinations of inmates, and each time Bob asked whether someone in the circle was named Mike. No one was. Then, in the last group, when Bob asked again, Michael Jenkins raised his hand.

"No one's called me that since I was a little kid."

Bob slid his chair over to Michael's and asked whether he could bless his hands. This was still before the no-contact policy. Michael nodded his head quietly, slowly offering over his thick hands, like a dead animal shot down for the safety of local children. Bob later told me that Michael's hands were cold and clammy. But, he said, they began to warm as he held them. He told Michael—the way a pastor can—that God wanted to redeem his hands, that they were not designed for pulling triggers or pushing syringes, but for transmitting love to others.

Michael said he was being transferred to prison the next day, as if that negated Bob's suggestion. But the rest of the men still came around Michael and together touched his back and shoulders, praying that his hands might be made "instruments of blessing" in that prison world, "not instruments of violence." The door clanged open and the men filed out, back to their cells, several—including Michael—to be shipped off to prison within days. And so Michael disappeared to a place where so many others had before him: large societal dumpsters with no shortage of padlocks.

Prison was a place I had only read about—first in college texts, from Michel Foucault's early treatise on prison "discipline," to the modern mess of mass incarceration in the United States. Then I read the letters from inmates. Usually they said at some point in their letters that they just couldn't tell me about certain realities inside those walls. So as more and more men we shared such evenings with in the local jail kept getting bussed off to prison over the next four years, I bought more books on the prison system.

I learned about how "the punitive large-scale imprisonment as a social practice" today ends up not preventing, but "maintaining and even promoting criminality." And how this is good news for some: dried-up rural communities across the United States, whose small family farms went belly-up with the advent of big corporate agriculture, are now bidding for and begging private prison contractors to build the next facility in their backyards. More inmates, more jobs. Then Walmart, Best Buy, and Applebee's will follow, springing up from—after first paving over—the abandoned fields and shuttered downtowns.

Everything I could find confirmed that prisons, on the inside, are a carefully maintained racial war zone, which journalists have referred to as the "Balkans in a box."

Then I read about the rape. I knew it happened, but not "how commonly guards and supervisors manage the practice and threat of rape between inmates to divide and subdue the prison population." Some sociologists called it "a thriving 'sex chattel' system." I thought about Michael. And twenty other young men I knew in prison, men with whom I've laughed and held hands and together prayed "Deliver us from evil." Sitting in my low-ceilinged room at Tierra Nueva, in my comfortable Goodwill reading chair many late nights, under a small lamp by the open window in my tiny loft, I made bold underlines with my pencil, sentence after sentence, in current studies that maintain that "the terror of prison rape . . . can be seen as the creation and manufacture of ever more brutal men" who are released into society perpetuating what they learned inside the walls.

As I read, I wondered whether there was a connection between these documented human rights violations and the anger some inmates eventually ink into their bodies and faces. Is it their most permanent and visible form of protest? I thought of Michael Jenkins's tattoo, the profane declaration, scrawled in fine cursive over the soft of his neck where the pulse is felt. While probably a dumb impulse when he got it, a brick thrown through the window of polite society, was it also his picket sign lifted against this prison world?

But his neck did not say "Fuck the prison system" or "Fuck the police and guards and officers." It said "Fuck *the world.*" I read about how each prison and prison employee was just a small player in a growing carceral industry connected to most every other system in our society. The human warehousing was woven into the fabric of the much larger economic system, a thriving "corrections industry" with financial roots pushing into every local county in our land. I learned that "a single pay phone inside a prison could earn its owner $12,000 a year" and "that a warden, if he played his cards right, could make himself a millionaire."

This is how the system works: it pays to lock more people up. Pays a lot, actually.

But *who* gets paid? I discovered that major and recognizable brands relied on the "American Gulag" of millions of pennies-an-hour captive laborers to manufacture their goods. Companies like Procter & Gamble, Honda, AT&T, Microsoft, and Victoria's Secret. When I realized that I was daily brushing my teeth with the prison, driving to the jail bible studies with the prison, talking on my cell phone with my ear pressed to the prison, typing my emails with the prison, and folding my fiancée's intimates with the prison, the reality of the prison industry hit disturbingly close to home. I began to understand the despair and magnitude of Michael Jenkins's tattoo: it seemed the whole *world* was accomplice in the suffering he knew.

"You will find prison life," I read, "to be quite reminiscent, for all its differences, of experiences in the wider society . . . the

punishments, the regimentation, the excessive brutalities oper-
ative in the prison are often only more intense versions of the
regimens and practices that characterize the population."

Each man we prayed with in the local county jail was being
shipped off not to a place outside our society, but rather to a
kind of accelerated form of it, a microcosm of the world and
its machinations, a caricature of how it all worked. I began to
wonder whether those who had been to prison and back knew
"the world"—which Jesus and his disciples denounced in the
Gospels and New Testament letters—better than anyone. Better than people like me, at least, who more often *benefit* from
the world as it is, who have never been locked inside a dumpster.

I wanted to write to Michael Jenkins. Tell him about what I'd
been reading. Ask him, *Is this what you meant by "the world"?
Is this why you got that tattoo after your first stint in prison? Tell
me more, Michael.*

But I will never know his thoughts, because I never wrote
that letter. I never wrote him at all—even though he wrote me
once. Unfortunately, Michael Jenkins wasn't as charismatic or
personable as the other men with whom I had written and developed deeper pastoral relationships. He was not as articulate
as these others, either in person or on paper. He was not as immediately lovable, the single letter he sent me probably not as
interesting as the others. Maybe that's why I never wrote back
to him, why his letter got buried under a stack of other folded,
wide-ruled papers full of inmates' handwritten greetings from
unhappy cells across the state. I forgot about him.

That's how the world works.

———

Years passed.

After seven of them as a full-time gang pastor, I moved away. Rachel and I got married weeks after she finished grad school to be a mental health therapist, and both of us planned our escape. Together we went on sabbatical in Montana—after reading *A River Runs Through It* with two sets of homies, two summers spent with the Liam Wood class, I'd spent many sunny days dreaming of Maclean's boyhood trout rivers in sunny Missoula. So that's where we moved. During those Montana months trying to learn how to be a married man and a morning person, making breakfast early for Rachel as she went to work at a Montessori school for toddlers, I took a lot of calls from guys back in Washington.

I got a call from Chavo, a large gang member I had been working with, one of the homies who toasted us at our wedding, his broad and shaved head swathed in inkwork occupying much of our wedding photos: arm in arm with aunts from Michigan, freak-dancing against my mother and high school English teacher, taking a smoke break from badminton with Pipe, the racquet over his shoulder, arm in arm with my childhood friends.

"Ey Chris," he greeted me on the phone, across two mountain ranges. "Did you hear? Trixter got out." I'd forgotten that was Michael's street name. "He's not good, man," Chavo told me in worried tones. "He don't talk much now. He used to be hella funny 'n shit. Now he just smokes that crystal meth all day. I saw him when I was picking up my cousin from my *tía*'s apartment yesterday. He looks bad, bro."

I never went to see him. I was two states away, on sabbatical, after all, reading and fly fishing. But from afar, at my desk reading about the mystics' use of fire imagery, and while standing in the Montana rivers with chilled knuckles, I found myself remembering Michael's hands, how they were cold and clammy. I was sad to think that none of us—not Bob on his one-year assignment in France, not me out here, not Ryan our new chaplain in training or anyone in our chaplain crew—was around to go visit Michael, now that he was out. There was no one to go hold those hands, warm them. He would most likely have to get arrested in order to see us pastors again.

———————

When rereading *A River Runs Through It* now, in Norman Maclean's hometown, away from my own, I realized why the book had resonated with me so deeply those past few years. The story is not really about fly fishing. Maclean wrote the novella as an old man, still haunted by the loss of his kid brother, Paul, who was "beautiful," especially with a fly rod over a trout-laden current. Only after reading the book several times—knowing how in the end Norman would get a phone call early one morning to learn that his risk-prone brother with a drinking and gambling problem had been found beaten to death by the butt of a revolver—did I understand the entire work as an older brother's retracing of his steps through prose, reviewing those last two sparkling summers with his brother before he was killed, reliving those afternoons they went fishing together, trying to find the moment in his memory where he could have said something, helped his troubled brother in some way. A darkness looms over each page, feeling in each lyrical unfurling of the fly line, each comic exchange of shouting over the sunny river, how the narrator cannot make contact with his elusive brother. He is just out of reach. Just days before pulling this book off my small shelf to re-read it, I had begun to write through my memories of guys like Lil' Jokes back in Washington, hunched over my desk in Missoula. "We are probably those referred to as 'our brothers' keepers,'" Maclean writes, "possessed of one of the oldest and possibly one of the most futile and certainly one of the most haunting of instincts. It will not let us go."

Three weeks after Chavo's first call, I got another.

"They shot Trixter."

———

U.S. marshals were chasing Michael as he fled on a bicycle. A warrant was out for his arrest, for not checking in with his parole officer and failing to attend drug and alcohol treatment, the terms of his early prison release. Michael allegedly shot a gun over his shoulder at the pursuing vehicles looking to take him back into custody.

"And that's when they opened fire on him," Chavo said. "Dropped him on the first shot. My nieces all saw it in front of their house and were texting me soon as it happened."

What really hurt Chavo, he told me, was "this fucked-up article they just ran in the paper about him." It was an extra article listing "every piece of dirt they could find on him in the court records. Basically, like, saying he was a evil motherfucker and we're all better off that they killed his ass. I mean, Jenkins was no saint, but. . . . It just feels ugly, man. Not right."

That night I researched what the Skagit paper had written. "The man shot and killed by U.S. marshals Thursday afternoon had been out of prison since October," it began, "and was considered by Mount Vernon Police to pose a 'high risk' to the community." I had to scroll over an enlarged copy of Jenkins's most recent mug shot: he looked sickly under the neon jail light, his head tilted and expressionless before the camera in the red inmate uniform. "TRIXTER," was emblazoned in dark, fresh letters across his bald forehead. He looked the part: bad guy caught and killed.

Just as Chavo had said, what followed was a public listing of every infraction and negative episode the county records had of the slain Jenkins. It read like a retroactive death sentence, the inevitable justice for a lifetime of moral failure. It was a prosecution before us readers, the public jury, though the sentence had already been carried out. There was no defense witness or counsel.

Nor was there any lament, no quote from a friend or family member, someone who maybe would mention how Michael grew up taking care of his mother and sister through various sufferings, including medical issues, that his father had already been in prison for a decade. And there was no quote from the officer who pulled the trigger. No investigation into the history of the armed marshal who aimed and fired at the back of a young man as he rode away on a bicycle. What anger I had felt for Jenkins, for firing at a police officer, melted as I scrolled down the article, reading as each small paragraph reduced him to a thing of no worth, some thing whose open-fire disposal no reader would question.

I kept reading. I learned that when he "injured a sheriff's deputy in the past," he was a juvenile being held down "during a physical struggle with two officers in his cell." With two fully grown adults in boots and uniform muscling him into submission, the unarmed boy had kicked a sock-and-slippered foot out in resistance. And so "one officer came away with torn ligaments and an injury to his lateral meniscus in his knee." The juvenile served eighty-four months in adult prison for that. The record did not mention any injuries the boy might have sustained. And when Jenkins "threatened to kill police," it turns out he was still a teenager then as well, crouching in the top of a tree as several officers and squad cars surrounded the base of the trunk. He had scrambled up there after stealing from a small local tavern. "From the tree," the news reporter stated, young Jenkins "threatened to kill police officers and was heard making calls to people, telling them to bring guns to his location and 'smoke' all of the officers, according to the affidavit." No friends ever showed up with guns.

The more closely I read the public report, the more I saw not a picture of a monster rightly put down, but something much less threatening: a vulnerable youth cornered in a cell by two armed men; a boy climbing a tree and hissing empty threats from its branches; an addict fleeing the world on a bicycle and firing loose shots over his shoulder.

———

The next night I was looking for holes in my fly-fishing waders. I was tempted to throw them away upon returning from another Montana riverbank with more river in my pants than I wanted. So I filled them with my breath and pressed them down into shallow bathwater. The legs struggled and kicked out of the water while I looked for the invisible wound, searching the water for the smallest of bubbles, little whispers of breath to tell me what was wrong.

While kneeling at the tub's edge, my cell phone buzzed. It was my old roommate, Ramón, whom I'd left in charge of our shared apartment with the guys at Tierra Nueva.

"*¿Qué honda,* bro?"

I'd met Ramón in the jail six years earlier. It was a night when I had invited the gathering of inmates to take a shot at Jesus's command to bless and pray for our enemies.

"How many of you have enemies?" I had asked the circle of men. Many men closed their eyes and snorted while raising scarred hands and arms. Men told stories of family members who had abused them, of gang rivals who had shot their friends and put them in hospitals, of old friends who had slept with their wives and stolen everything they'd had. Some said they were their own worst enemies.

"But no one forgives," said a brawny biker-type with tattooed barrels for forearms as he threw his chin up. "That's not how the world works." He was right, I said. I knew, for a formal example, that forgiveness was never a legal option in a court of law; it is unauthorized and unrecognized as a course of action. I said true forgiveness was a way, then, to defy the world, to go against its rules entirely.

Ramón stared at the concrete floor and said he wanted to forgive the man who'd killed his brother months earlier back home in Juárez. He also wanted to pray for the young woman whose false accusations of abduction and rape had landed him in there, where he currently faced thirty years in prison. Ramón, the short twenty-something with curly hair from a violent border town, was the only man who wept that night in the circle of condemned men as he forgave.

The following week he tore into the large room where we meet, before all the other inmates, to tell me "it worked!" I was confused; I hadn't expected any functional results to follow the act of forgiveness. But this was the first of many forgiveness miracles I witnessed in the jail. Ramón told me how the morning after forgiving and blessing his accuser, he received a call in the jail block from his lawyer: a handwritten letter from the young woman had appeared inside their office drop slot that morning, a full confession of her involvement at the party, her shame, and the reasons for her false testimony against several men who had seen her that night. The experience changed the direction of Ramón's life. He was free within weeks. He'd evaded the social dumpster.

Over the next two years I saw him only intermittently. Then, one day, a maroon convertible Mustang roared up next to me at a stoplight, and I recognized the laughing young man with an outstretched arm hung over the wheel, three young women in the car with him, their hair flying around him in the summer air. He wore a bright gold chain around his neck.

I called his name from my old Volvo sedan, but they could not hear me over the music. The next time I saw Ramón he was knocking on the back door of our ministry apartment late at night. I poured him coffee, but it sat cold next to him as he rubbed his brow and confessed many things. He disappeared for another year. When he returned, it was to move in for good.

This was his short speech, like an aspiring monk at the monastery gate: "I've got a house. I've got a job. I'm not homeless or a junkie or anything. I'm just tired of being an asshole and wasting my money on stupid shit. I want to move in here and learn, with you all, a new way to live."

Never in all my years growing up in American churches had I heard such a perfect summary repentance.

But back to the bathtub in Missoula.

"Your voice is all echoey, man," Ramón said over the speakerphone I'd set up on the sink. "Where are you? Sounds like you're in a jail cell or something."

I explained that I was in the bathroom, that my sleeves were rolled up at the moment and that I was trying to drown a large green version of myself in the bath, "trying to get some information out of him, but he won't peep."

"Careful, man," he laughed, "that'd look pretty bad if the neighbors saw you through the window!"

Sure enough, there was a large window as low as the tub's rim directly in front of me, and only a translucent shower curtain hung before me, upon which the bathroom light probably projected a crude silhouette of my struggle with the form in the tub, its legs kicking up occasionally. Framing is everything.

I asked Ramón whether he'd heard about the shooting. He had.

I confessed I was furious. At first, I told him, I was just sad that Michael chose to pull a gun on U.S. marshals. "But I didn't realize how angry at the cops I was"—I said over my shoulder to the phone on the sink—"until I was suddenly raising my voice at Rachel last night, almost yelling. 'Cops just open fire on a drug addict on a bike and drop him dead in the street? And all the local news does is nod and reassure us, *Hey there's nothing to worry about, look at this guy's record, he was just a piece of shit, anyway. Don't worry, the police were just cleaning up the neighborhood for us.*'"

My voice was raised again, I realized, even there in the bathroom. Neighbors outside the bathroom could definitely add this to the evidence.

I looked down and focused. Still no bubbles.

"You remember," Ramón's voice echoed around me, "Jenkins was my codefendant when you met me."

I had forgotten.

"So those rape charges the paper mentioned, some of those were probably the same charges I faced, the same young woman who falsely accused me, the one I forgave, remember?" He told me he'd rolled with those same homeboys back in those days. That he jacked car stereos, had drugs in his car, too. "Most things they said about Jenkins in that article they could say about *me*. Gangs, burglary, all that. Even the allegations, if they wanted to."

This only made me angrier. "Yeah—so if *you* got shot down, they could make *you* out to look disposable too."

I was clearly more worked up than Ramón. The thought of losing him enraged me. I'd shared daily life with Ramón since he moved into our apartment two years earlier. He'd raised his two children among us. He even named his baby boy after me, had me sign *Christopher* on the blue name card displayed on the end of the infant's clear bin. In time, Ramón was helping lead our gang ministry. He had visions of detailing a large van with lowrider paint, and he would drive it around town, to the projects. "We'll scoop up the homies hanging around on the corners, and take 'em to the forest, to the river and mountains where we fish," he'd explained. "We'll love 'em and eat with 'em. No one else may want 'em, but God wants 'em, fool." It had thrilled me that Ramón felt the call to be a recruiter with me, as Richard Mejia had acted out in our study of the banquet parable. During my sabbatical, Ramón was even preparing to leave his full-time job on a dairy farm to work with the many young felons he knew. He wanted to start an auto-detailing business where he could teach his old friends still in the gangs how to restore "piece-of-crap cars to something *beautiful*." Something had happened in this former criminal, Ramón. He now valued and sought to repair what the world had thrown away.

"Bro . . ." his voice was soothing through the speakerphone. He said he'd mentioned his codefendant status with Jenkins only as a way to get at something else: he was trying to tell me he went to visit some of the guys who were with Michael Jenkins most every day before he died. "They told me he was all meth'd out since the day he got released. He wasn't himself, they all said." Jenkins knew the Department of Corrections had put a warrant out for him for missed parole meetings. "I guess Jenkins was telling all of 'em, in the days before he got shot, *I'd rather die than go back to prison. I'll never go back.* He said, *I'd rather they fucking kill me.*"

I was silent. A thread-thin stream of bubbles rose through the still water, from the center of the waders. Everything became clear. Jenkins knew exactly what he was doing when he took some wild shots at the U.S. marshals. He wasn't trying to kill but to *be* killed, before they could send him back to the place that had changed him, that had taken away his laughter, and, with unspeakable things, had made him unspeaking, unrecognizable to friends. I took note of where the green figure beneath my hands had been pierced, then released my grip and let the breath out and the water pour into the torso as it sank to the bottom.

I reminded Ramón of how he and I together had told his story several times to church and street audiences—how he'd forgiven the young woman who accused him, how the charges were dropped, and so on. "But you've never told me much about that night," I said now, "when you were with Jenkins at the party."

"Oh," he said, "it wasn't much of a party. It was over at the Stanford Drive apartments, where all us wetbacks or poor kids with moms on drugs used to live. It was never really a party." He said they had nothing to do, stuck there most nights. They didn't have money to go anywhere else, "or parents to put them on a baseball team or something. I mean, cops'd end up pulling us over if we left the projects most nights, so we'd just stay there, bored as hell." Ramón was the only one with a car, with his prize money from ultimate fighting and working with the cows on the dairy farm. Most everyone else, he said, jacked a car if they wanted one, just to get out for an evening.

I sat on the toilet lid, holding the phone, just listening now.

"But anyway, that night, I think I remember seeing that girl pass in and out of this one apartment with a couple other guys, and maybe Jenkins got with her at some point, I don't know. But all I remember"—Ramón's voice warmed suddenly, laughing—"was *pinche* Jenkins just doing these running jumps and throwing his body against the walls." Ramón's laughter filled the bathroom. "He'd jump on the bed and do these flying kicks, just straight into the walls."

I imagined this young man's acrobatic assaults on a plain wall inside the cramped projects. It struck me as a sad portrait of the only approach Michael Jenkins knew for defying the world's shape. Like salmon leaping against the current, unseen and futile protests flying against the concrete dams. My old association between flight and faith.

"It was like—like he was trying to kick *through* them, you know?" Ramón continued. "And I think he eventually did. His shoe punched right through and left this big ol' hole. I think he even hurt his leg, tore a ligament or something."

I thought of Ramón's latest tattoo. He'd gotten it a couple years ago across his upper chest, letters curving beneath his collar line from shoulder to shoulder, gangster-style. It read *Greater is He who is in me than He who is in the world*—a passage taken from another one of John's letters in the New Testament—but I think one of the words was misspelled. I now asked Ramón what it meant to him.

"All the evil shit I used to do, I don't desire it anymore. Sure, I'm tempted and fuck up still, but it's different now. There's no pleasure in it, I don't enjoy using people how I used to. I *hate* the fucking things of the world."

I asked him what he meant by *the world*. His immediate answer impressed me.

"The world? You know . . . looking down on people. Cheating on women. Lusting." It was both a systemic and personal definition. In Ramón's mind, in his fluid answer, it seemed that the lust of the individual's eyes and the larger, dehumanizing "system"—society's spiritual condition of looking down on others—were intimately connected. The world makes humans into something less than they are.

"And I don't wanna look down on anyone like that anymore," he added. "I hate it."

I told him about Jenkins's definition of *the world*.

"Yeah. The system." Ramón said it like these were the same ideas: "How they look at us. They don't see what's happening out here. And I'm talkin' about the church, too, not just the courts and prisons and business owners. I don't wanna be too hard on the church, but so much of the help or love they give comes with *conditions*. Like pastors who are supporting the auto-detailing shop are asking me: If guys are gonna work with me, they're gonna have to come to *church* with us, too, right?" Ramón sounded impatient. "For me, it's not about who comes to church. It's who's being—what's the word?—*transformed*. And who's there to see it."

I now saw in Ramón a parallel to Michael Jenkins: a codefendant from the same neighborhood, but one who had narrowly escaped the padlocked dumpster of prison, who found a way out of the jail walls with forgiveness, out of the whole system, *the world,* with repentance. He was the model I was looking for since meeting Michael Jenkins, a modern tattooed life that said "Fuck the World" the way a disciple might have said in the early Christian movement. A man who goes against what society says about the throwaways, scooping them up like brothers in a ridiculous family van he's detailing. A man who leaves his good job on a dairy farm to pursue criminals, without any financial security, trusting that another order—an order foreign to this world—will sustain his love for those lost in the endless streets and systems.

Ramón does not look down on Michael Jenkins. In fact, he does not even remember Michael's sins that dark night, what may have transpired on the other side of that wall. Instead, he sees Jenkins with new eyes, eulogizing him now, giving *me* new eyes to see a felon's frantic yearning for deliverance, raging through our cramped walls for eternity: "Honestly, that's all I really remember from that night," Ramón said. "Michael just flying at those walls."

HEARTS LIKE RADIOS

FOR SOME TIME I'VE IMAGINED ALL OF US HAVING a fragile nerve inside of us, like a spiritual antenna deep within our core. Some people, I've thought, simply have an abnormally large antenna inside—poets, prophets, psychopaths, your slightly crazy aunt who's drawn to the paranormal, who some days is more compassionate than anyone you know and other days is aggressive and convinced everyone including the government is conspiring against her. In my work both behind jail bars and the years I continued with homeless youth on the streets of downtown Seattle, I've met a number of young people with schizophrenia. I've wondered, when talking with them about some of the abuse and trauma they've survived, whether the internal antenna-nerves of some people are damaged. Maybe they could be exposed, jutting out like a bone from a broken arm, picking up way too much of the otherwise faint spiritual frequencies coursing through this world—from "beyond," as well as from the person across the room. I've wondered whether some of these people slam heroin or meth or any street medicine they can find as a way of jamming cotton into their spiritual ears.

It's not a real theory; just how I've pictured that part inside us all.

But there are days I see this radio-antenna metaphor as somewhat compatible with the psychological definition of schizophrenia. Rachel was in grad school studying to be a therapist the same years I was encountering people with these symptoms, and every so often I still pick up her *Diagnostic and Statistical Manual of Mental Disorders IV* and textbooks that sit open around the house: due to trauma or defect, part of a person's psyche or mind is *split* (the root *schizo-*) off from the rest of the mind, and its thoughts are then "heard" as an externalized set of messages, or hallucinations. But I wonder, if all our "minds" are not purely cognitive organs, the gray matter of brains, but also internal spiritual mysteries (as all religious traditions have maintained, and even contemporary science is rediscovering), then this "splitting off" of the mind—and *psyche* is translated from the Greek often as soul—is for me a fine description of the broken and exposed spiritual antenna that I've imagined.

This is what drew me even closer to the men and women with schizophrenic symptoms: what they reported the voices to be saying never sounded very strange to me. These troubled folks usually seemed surprised that I even ask about the content of their "auditory hallucinations"; they are used to people leaning back, politely, when they mention the voices. Either their friends (what few they have kept) are weirded out by the whole phenomenon, or the mental health professionals have as little interest in *what* the voices say as a TV technician would with the "content" of the fuzzy static blaring through a busted device. But I recognize the content. Most of the time the "voices" whisper constant, taunting criticism—intelligent accusations that seem to know all their worst deeds, access to a criminal record more complete than any county's register. The mean words that fill their ears—all the contempt and ridicule and steady accusations they describe whispering through them—I recognize from my own home growing up, from political discourse, and from my own lips. But the mentally challenged were picking up the mean words right out of the air around them.

What if, sometimes, these voices are *not* just an illusion, fragmented thoughts and guilty projections bouncing back at such people off the insides of their minds? "Galileo thought comets were an optical illusion," writes Annie Dillard on a page I dog-eared recently.

What if there really is an Accuser, as Jesus named his spiritual adversary? Satan, that is, means "the one who accuses" in Hebrew. "Adversary" in Greek. The cosmic prosecutor.

There could be some good news here as well: the schizophrenic souls I talk with don't hear only negative voices. Sometimes they tell me about a voice that tells them they're okay, reminds them who they are and prompts them to notice others who are suffering and to care for them. Jesus told his friends (remember the company he kept) about such a voice, said he would send them a Defender, a Counselor—the Paraclete, or one who speaks from alongside. The street youth tell me they usually don't report this kind of voice to professionals. Because, they say, they never want to lose that voice, that presence, that visits them. Like the poet Rainer Maria Rilke's famous refusal to Freud and his chair: "If you rid me of my demons, my angels may take flight, too."

I think I've heard that wiser, kinder voice, as well. But I've always wished it were louder for me. Especially when I try to pray. So I've gotten into the habit of praying, when I can, with those who hear better than I do.

———

These questions became more serious for me one night when I sat with a sweating young gang member. He was swinging a golf club around a dark upper room of Tierra Nueva's old Victorian building. This guy, Noe Solazo, was abused growing up—repeatedly as a child, then locked in rooms by foster parents and group homes that used occasional beatings when he would rage at peers and authorities. By age twenty he had been given a diagnosis of severe paranoid schizophrenia. He called me that afternoon from the house phone of an elderly couple that lived by the Skagit River. He'd tried to drown himself in the winter current, but it spit him back out on the tangled bank. He'd crawled, scraped and wet, to the front door of the closest house and called me. I brought him to our place to shower and mend. He had lost—in the forest—the antipsychotic meds that the jail had given him upon release and was now just coming down off a meth high while in our care. This same night a class was being taught in our large meeting room downstairs about listening prayer. Quiet down, the teacher had been saying, tune in to your inner flow, focus on the face of Jesus, ask a simple question, and dare to write down whatever next shimmers through your mind.

I was taking notes when some of our volunteers tapped on my shoulder and asked me to come upstairs; our guest was getting aggressive and frightening them. I found Noe circling in the shadows of a dark room, a blue paisley bandana tied tight around his forehead, gripping a driving iron over his shoulder, threatening to strike out at tormentors that I could not see. He told me they were laughing at him, whispering from just outside the windows—we were on the second story—calling him a "faggot" and a "pussy," telling him to do the world a favor and just kill himself. As he agreed to hand over the club and sit down with me, he kept looking over his shoulder and sneering at his mockers in the shadows. I could not tell him to just ignore these voices nor persuade him they were not real.

What I did do—probably because of the class I had just stepped out of—was suggest he try a different kind of listening. I asked Noe to imagine turning his antenna toward God. Ask a question, I said, and then just listen. This seemed to him a more reasonable request than ignoring all his senses.

He began with one heaving question: "Why me?" He pressed his hands into his face, wild and unhealed cuts all over his fingers and cheeks. He started to cry. The room was silent for a moment, as when someone's on the phone listening to someone else. Then he laughed dismissively. Like he'd heard an answer that irritated him. "Fuck this," he said as he stood up.

"What did you hear?" I asked.

"Nothing—just . . . I dunno . . . what it said was: *You're the righteous one.*"

I was amazed that after days of hearing cruel contempt, he would suddenly hear such a different message. It simply seemed too good to be true, to this young man unbelievable. "This is stupid," he said. "That was probably just me."

Maybe, I said. "But is that how you see yourself? Does that sound like something *you'd* say?"

"Fuck no," he laughed. "I fucking hate myself! I mean"—he now almost whimpered—"why am I *the righteous one*? Look at me. I'm a piece of shit tweaking here on crystal. I'm filthy and homeless, a *vato* who's robbed and ripped people off in the last twenty-four hours. I tried drowning myself in the river just this morning. I'm nothing."

I didn't want to try to tell him otherwise. But I suggested he ask this same question in the form of a prayer, and listen for another answer. So Noe sat down on the floor, rolled forward on his knees, steadied his hands on the carpet, took a deep breath. "Why . . . ," he jerked his neck in an agitated tick, wiped his forehead, " . . . what do you mean I'm the righteous one?"

Silence in the room again.

Then he snorted in irritated disbelief and shook his head.

"You heard something!" I was totally absorbed now, eager to overhear again what God might sound like when speaking directly to a scraped-up criminal. That is, compared with a bunch of "normies" like me sitting downstairs, quietly penciling in our journals what the currents of heaven might say when we asked our own most vulnerable question. "What'd you hear?" I asked, there on the ground with him.

"Forget it," he said, but sat still.

"What I heard was . . . I'm 'the righteous one' . . . because I'm the only broke-down *vato* in this town on my knees tonight, on a Friday night, crying out to God with all my heart."

That night, on the floor of the upper room with a suicidal schizophrenic, I fell in love with whatever voice said that to my miserable friend.

It sounded like something Jesus would have said. That same quality of mind from the Gospels now spoke in our dark room, through Noe's unseen crowd of accusers. And it brought him sudden peace. He laughed and smiled. "Ahhhh, shit," he shook his head, exhaled. He looked at me, reached a hand out that landed on my shoulder. "Crazy, huh?" He stretched out on the floor with a blanket and pillow, disarmed and with no concern for the windows or the shadows. Within minutes, he was sleeping soundly. Noe had made contact with the voice that I seek to follow. I sat in the dark there for a long time, fully awake with the sound of his deep breathing.

———

If any of this is true, if these touched and tormented souls have sensitive calibrations being overwhelmed—the volumes in their heads turned up to eleven—then seriously listening to them has seemed to me to be the best way to eavesdrop on what spiritual frequencies are out there, still in the cosmos, in our own more subtle thoughts, all old as the earth. It might be a way to reconsider both the divine and destructive spiritual currents washing through our own minds, through history and cultures, humming all along through our soft hearts and passing through harder walls of universities, bedrooms, monasteries, prisons, governments, and asylums.

So when I got the email about a young man named Connor Harrison, I was certainly curious to learn more about the "telepathic messages" that told him to kill his father.

This quiet twenty-four-year-old son to suburban parents in the Pacific Northwest rose from his bed one night, went downstairs, selected a large knife out of the block on the kitchen counter, started an argument with his father, and then began stabbing him, pursuing him out the back door and into the wet, cold lawn. He got in only seven blows because his bleeding father tackled and held him while he himself was already dying.

Connor was not a violent kid. Nor was his father, Bill, violent. This was not a blowback from a childhood of abuse at the hands of a tyrant. Connor was not into bloody video games or guns. He did not sketch gruesome pictures in his notebooks. He did not listen to morbid metal music. But he was listening to something.

For example, two years before this incident, Connor stopped eating for a while because he said he could hear his food crying out in pain. He heard his friends' thoughts as well. He was soon diagnosed with schizophrenia. As Connor would later tell me with no recognizable emotion—through the glass in the cold jail visiting booth one of the several dark winter nights I visited him—they were not so much "voices" but more like "telepathic messages" he'd been picking up from "the world."

When I was first contacted via email about visiting Connor Harrison, I told the Harrisons' family friend that he probably wouldn't want to meet with me. The few times I'd made a jail visit that wasn't a direct request from the inmate, the visit did not go well. "No, he will," she replied. "I told him about you—'the jail chaplain who believes that the voices some people hear are real.'"

She'd heard online a talk I'd given. Both prophecy and schizophrenia, I'd said, appear to be more complicated—with more slippery overlap between the two—than either Bible readers or psychiatrists would make them seem.

I'd been studying the Hebrew prophets. They heard more than clear, verbal oracles from the Lord. Rather, they shuddered with terrors and torment, often appearing quite unstable, maybe bipolar, swinging from jubilant praises of God to rage and even suicidal despair, all right there in our Bible's thin pages. The prophet Jeremiah, for example, looked much like the homeless youth I've met: a teen making a nuisance in the city streets and locked up repeatedly by authorities. Jeremiah was put in the stocks in the public square, mocked. Ezekiel did strange things like make demonstrations with feces in the street and lie comatose for days while receiving revelations. The Jewish theologian Abraham Joshua Heschel spent much of his life studying these figures. Heschel describes the prophets not so much as official spokesmen with verbatim divine pronouncements, but as humans with a severe "sensitivity to evil." To the prophets, he writes, "even a minor injustice assumes cosmic proportions," and the prophet's "ear . . . is attuned to a cry imperceptible to others." They are so sensitive to what we overlook or have ceased to feel, they appear insane.

Heschel says the prophet is primarily burdened with the "pathos of God." An infinite vulnerability.

With *pathos* as the root of "pathology," we are not too far removed from a modern diagnosis of "mental illness." Prophets could be called divinely pathological, burdened with a suffering larger than their own. Some of the mentally ill might be suffering from a similarly severe vulnerability to evil.

And they could also be more vulnerable than others to divine presence. Paranoid schizophrenics often describe not just being accused, but being followed, pursued. Heschel wrote a book called *God in Search of Man*. The question of religion in the Bible, he says, is not so much about humans seeking God, but God seeking us. Maybe some people can actually feel that, and can't shake it.

So Connor's story clearly fascinated me on a theoretical level. But the situation's gravity set in when the young woman, a friend of the Harrisons, emailed once more: "His mother Debbie can't even legally visit Connor because she was also his stabbing victim that night." A mother had lost both her husband and son. A tormented son had lost both his father and his mother, at least for now. I rearranged my schedule and committed to visit as a chaplain.

———

Alone on the freeway where it curves through the smoky evergreen hills leading out of the valley and into the next county, I drove south on a rainy winter evening to see Connor. I pass the exit where a year earlier a guy named Isaac Zamora had obeyed local unseen voices and gunned down three neighbors, a female officer who showed up on the scene, and two other drivers on the freeway as he fled down this very stretch of shadowed highway. Weeks before those "Alger Slayings," Zamora's mother had contacted us and pleaded that someone at Tierra Nueva visit her son while he was doing a few weeks in jail. When I asked for him at the front desk, the guards came back and told me he didn't want to see anybody. Then the slaughter, when he was released weeks later. That's what happened the last time I visited an inmate who hadn't asked for the visit himself.

Tonight was my first time in this other county's jail, so I slid my ID and visiting slip under the glass to the night shift officer on duty. She gave me a bronze key that I struggled to figure out how to use once inside the elevator. I slid it into the slot by a button for the third floor, turned it, and the doors closed. Visiting Connor Harrison, I was in new territory.

I walked down the cold concrete corridor and opened a door to a closet with a cracked plastic chair inside and a wall-sized window into Connor's world. There Connor sat on the other side of the glass. He did not look like the criminals I meet with normally. I recognized him, but didn't know why at the time. He looked like me—that is, when I was his age, five years earlier. The year I was unstable, suicidal, seeing counselors, and reluctantly swallowing pills prescribed by the university's mental health professionals. Connor was pale and skinny, with straight brown hair that had grown too long during his first two months in jail, hanging and covering his blue eyes. Like me, he grew up in the suburbs. Like me, his mom was a schoolteacher, his dad an instructor. He read books and played rock music. And now something had gone terribly wrong. It was as though I were sitting down to face my younger hypothetical self—had my own antenna been tuned in to amplify quieter, darker voices.

I waved and we both picked up the black phone receivers on short metal cords, like the ones in old payphone booths. As we introduced ourselves, Connor looked down, then back at me with a shy smile and nervous laugh. I felt that the description of him in the email was right: "At the same time," the family friend had written—that is, she meant, aside from the tormenting voices and savage stabbing—"he is a very likable person, easy to talk to when he's not comatose, just really confused, really oppressed by what he senses, and really protective of his inner universe."

So on this first meeting I told Connor a bit about myself. I told him about my cautious exploration of the charismatic, or Pentecostal, Christian conference scene lately. How so many people I'd seen there, doing things like "prophetic activations," say they "struggle" with their "inability" to "hear God's voice" better. They get seriously discouraged, I told him, sometimes weeping after years of closing their eyes, relaxing their minds, and trying to be open to the faintest of impressions. "They're dying to hear a voice," I said.

Connor laughed at this.

"On the other hand," I continued, "I meet guys in jail or young women on the streets of Seattle who have the opposite problem: they're crying 'cause the voices won't stop!"

We laughed together.

I said most people, of course, see these as separate worlds. They raise their eyebrows and tell me I should be careful not to confuse contemplative listening with serious mental health issues. I confessed to Connor that not only did I suspect the two might have serious overlap, but I myself was one of those people who *wanted* to hear more, who wouldn't mind getting clearer messages.

With this, Connor nodded at me deeply. We had gotten somewhere. Or maybe Connor thought I was crazier than he was. Either way—out of fellowship, or pity, or warning—he shared his experience.

"I killed my dad," he began casually, "because of messages I was getting that . . . that I had to pass a test and prove myself. And that I had to save the universe." His free hand smoothed his hair over his forehead and he closed his eyes. "Gosh that sounds . . . weird."

Not that weird, I said. I told him a bible story.

Abraham hears a voice that tells him to take his firstborn son Isaac to the top of a mountain and sacrifice him to God. The old man—reluctantly, obediently, silently—leads his son up Mount Moriah with a knife and wood for the pyre bound to his son's young back. When he ties the boy down and lifts the knife, "an angel of the LORD" swoops in to stop him. It then directs Abraham's attention to a ram stuck in a nearby bush as a substitute. The traditional interpretation, I said, is that Abraham passed this ultimate "test of faith," willing to offer up his own son, and that the angel is essentially God's announcement of "Just kidding!," a whistle blown at the last second before he carries out the grisly order. But some scholars point out—and this interested Connor more than anything— that it was normal religious practice for the Chaldeans in that region to sacrifice their children on those same hilltops, to the god Molech. And this: in the text, the voice that tells Abraham to carry out this very common religious practice in his culture is identified in the Hebrew only as *elohim,* the more general term for "god" or "gods." The presence that *stops* the violence, however, is not called *elohim* but something entirely different: "an angel, [messenger] of the LORD," or Yahweh, a distinct and mysterious deity who would go on to liberate Abraham's many descendants from slavery in Egypt. So maybe, I told Connor, Abraham was not being tested by one God but was caught between two opposing and very real voices. One saved him from following the bloody orders of the other. Abraham could have been the patron saint for schizophrenics.

A guard tapped on the door's window behind Connor. Time was up. Connor nodded his head. He looked back at me between the locks of hair in his face and told me to come back, soon. He was ready to do the talking, it seemed, to open up his own inner universe.

———————

Before he died, Abraham Heschel went on television in the early 1970s to talk about Jewish studies and mysticism. NBC's Carl Stern interviewed him for a prime-time audience on a blue sound stage, facing the white-bearded Heschel across a small white table, both men seated in futuristic small white chairs that touched the ground beneath them like wineglass stems. Stern, with his hair parted sharply, asked the wild-bearded scholar whether the idea of prophecy or a God who cares still applied to modern humans. The grainy video shows Heschel lean forward toward his host, then look into the camera, answering, "The world in itself is so fantastically mysterious, so challengingly marvelous, that not to realize that there is more than I see—endlessly more than I could express or even conceive—is just being underdeveloped, intellectually."

————

On my second visit a couple weeks later, Connor sat in his hunter green scrubs on the other side of the glass with even longer hair and told me he'd been thinking about the Abraham of Genesis. How I'd brought up Bible stuff during the last visit. He wanted to start by telling me about his "Jesus Freak" stage three years earlier, when he believed in those things—"When I used to think everything I'd hear or see or think was God or the devil." And so began Connor's story, which I would learn over the course of several conversations that winter.

It all started on a trip to Southeast Asia. He'd gone with his mom to Cambodia to visit a child they sponsored through one of those international Christian organizations that connect kids in starving villages with suburban families of plenty in the United States. His mother had hoped it would be good for Connor after a year during which he'd stopped believing in God, started running with a drug crowd, lived in an apartment of neglect and filth, and distanced himself from his family. Connor didn't remember any of the trip to the village, really. He didn't care. That's part of the (then yet-undiagnosed) schizophrenia: being hypersensitive to select parts of the outside world while also being almost entirely disconnected from the rest of it.

Out of the whole Cambodian trip, Connor only remembered something that happened at a small motel, where they stayed by the airport their last night before leaving for the States. He was in the shower when he tapped into a current that changed the course of his life.

It was not electrocution, but his head was filled with light. His bones glowed with the fire of the sun and his chest with the power of a hundred friendships. He fell to his knees, laughing, undone, like Saint Teresa of Avila's ecstasy now in the cheap shower stall of a Cambodian motel, naked as the day he was born, there in the lukewarm water spraying over him in the squeaky tub. He tried to sing along with the heartbreakingly beautiful choir he could suddenly hear so clearly all around him. Outside the bathroom door his mother heard Connor's voice bellowing over the noise of the shower, an off-tune version of "Our God Is an Awesome God," a song he knew as a boy from Sunday school.

Connor's mother Debbie later told me her version of this story in a closed coffee shop where we met late one night, chairs upside down on the tables all around us. She was still numb and quiet in the wake of her husband's murder. Her face was hard to see in the unlit café where she wanted that night to meet me, the young chaplain visiting her son. When I asked about the Cambodian motel, she smiled. She said she remembered how Connor finally stepped out of the bathroom with a new look—a clarity—in his eyes, as if he could *see* her after months of appearing lost in an alternate universe. "Mom!" he burst out, dripping. "I know what God wants me to do with my life." *God?* she must have thought. *I thought you didn't believe in God, sweetheart.* "And . . . what's that, honey?" He said, "I think God wants me to play music. For Him."

Now, this simply could have been a biochemical blip of dopamine, the more pleasant side of a manic-depressive episode. An ecstatic blare of static in a brain's slow turn toward illness. What began to interest me, though, as the story continued, was the long-term fruit that followed this shower epiphany. It was sweet. It lasted. For weeks, then months afterward, all Connor wanted to do was share that irruption of affection with the whole world.

He started in his hometown. He'd normally kept to himself and avoided speaking with strangers. But now, he said, he felt aware of people around him on the street, at the movie theater, in the park. He heard not just the anguish and edge of all the mortal stuff like clipped grass and animals and children outside, but now he seemed to hear the things people secretly wanted. Their hearts' yearnings. It drew him to strangers. He had words for them. "People kind of came up to me, seriously, and . . . I would just *talk* to them . . . and soon they would, well, come to faith. Right there. Like, believe in *God*. It was crazy."

As Connor told me all this, his sheepishness fell away, then returned, as if he both missed this way of living and was ashamed of it as well. He said he never planned anything like this, had no agenda for evangelizing strangers, no outlined theology. He just found himself saying things—"they'd just kinda *come out* of me"—that moved people. He was transmitting the same message to others that had so moved him in the motel shower's steam.

Connor, normally the shy and awkward Harrison kid, was now asked to speak at his family's church—up front, leaning over the podium and microphone. It went well enough that he was invited to share in front of other local congregations.

He muttered what was echoing through him, and people were not troubled. They found it edifying, clear. People who had heard sermons much of their lives might have heard something as fresh as when Elvis first came through living room radios.

It wasn't just in public, or in church. At home he'd journal in his room, and often he'd slip into what he said felt like God's point of view, another heart beating, speaking *to him*. These words were almost always positive, kind, like they came from someone, he said, who truly liked him and understood him.

He tried to transmute what was moving through him into the sounds of several instruments. Acoustic guitar. Then electric guitar, plugging his cables into a loud, humming amp in the garage. He soon fell in love with the bass guitar, where he felt each note speak through his bones. But the drums were his favorite. He had an ear for the beat. In fact, even when he took piano lessons as a boy and neighbors heard how talented he was, he never understood what was written on the sheets of bars and dots. He played, as they say, by ear. By heart.

At this point Connor's voice on the other side of the glass stopped.

His lips were still, and I couldn't tell whether he was still with me. He shrugged his shoulders, apparently done with this part of his story. Through the receiver at my ear, I heard loud doors slam from the other cells and the sounds of inmates yelling back in the halls on his side of the glass. I returned his gaze in the silence. I couldn't decide whether, in his ill-fitting green jail scrubs and shaggy brown hair, he looked more like a humble prophet, a stoned twenty-something, or a serial killer.

"So what changed?" I asked. "Sounds like a good gig you had going. But now you're locked up . . . for murdering your dad."

Things changed, Connor said, at a Baptist summer camp for kids where he had gotten a job. He'd always connected well with children, but ever since the Cambodian shower epiphany, Connor had a new concern and attention for the boys and girls he'd talk with. Adults began noticing how Connor had a way with the youth, how they were drawn to him. He took them seriously. Soon he was hired at the summer camp by an alpine lake, both as kitchen staff and as an assistant counselor.

For weeks Connor heard the hiss of dozens of grilled cheese sandwiches he'd assemble on the stainless steel griddle, the splash and squeal of kids in the afternoon lake, the hushed cadence of campers reciting Bible verses from their sleeping bags in the cabin bunks, and the chorus of crickets all around him as he walked the night trail under a star-scattered sky.

Then one night around the campfire, the night each week when the young preacher hopes students are most listening, when they are encouraged to "make a decision" to give their lives to Christ, Connor was listening very closely. And he made the opposite decision.

"The preacher, he kept talking about 'the cross, the cross, the cross!' How Jesus suffered on the cross and that it was *God* punishing him, that it was a punishment *we all* deserved. I guess it freaked me out."

As Connor told this part of the story, quite animated, I could have finished his sentences. I heard that same sermon countless

times as a kid at such youth events. And in college I wrote papers
dissecting this immensely popular aberration of Christian doc-
trine that also had turned me away from the church for years.
It goes like this: as opposed to seeing in Jesus a fully human
God in the flesh, stripped bare and suffering vulnerably among
us, the cross is construed as a kind of cosmic justice where an
Almighty God is punishing His own son in lieu of killing all of
us—who, we are told, *really* deserve it—thus saving us from His
own binding and violent wrath.

The problem is, such a god looks less like the saving Yahweh
and much more like the bloodthirsty Molech. Sadly, some
Christian churches for a few hundred years have, like Abraham,
confused the voices and similarly offered their children up to
this violent message. Such "good news" has shocked generations
of children and teens into a kind of faith, only to repel almost as
many when they become adults. They trash this story, and their
faith with it, when they can no longer sustain such a hateful
image of God in their praying hearts.

But Connor, with his hypersensitivity to evil, was immediately more sensitive than most to such theology. He told me how
he withdrew from the circle of campers' faces aglow with the
flicker of the campfire and the fiery message, and he wandered
into the dark pines. *Do I believe this?* he asked himself. It caused
him to lose trust in the more direct, mysterious channel he'd
been dialed into that year that had filled him with a grace like
pure music. He decided he didn't want any part of what he was
now hearing. It turned him off. Connor left the church camp
after that week, and his heart turned the internal dial. His Jesus
Freak stage was over.

Three years would pass before Connor's very special antenna began picking up a new signal—and with equal clarity.

———————

During those three years of internal humdrum silence, Connor worked a part-time job at Guitar Center. He spent days surrounded by retail instruments riffing stale scales and thudthudding all around him. He experimented with marijuana, LSD, and mushrooms. This eased his usual hypersensitivity to pain, and yet his choice of hallucinogenics betrayed his longing for transcendence, tapping into the extrasensory currents he knew were out there. He quit the music store eventually and applied at Radio Shack. No music; pure mechanics for listening. But he was fired a year later when the manager noticed how Connor had stopped tending to customers, busy in back writing on the backs of recycled invoices—he was trying to transcribe the telepathic messages that had begun to reach him.

Connor told me about the day they'd started. He was off work, alone at the park in his hometown. He was watching the ants crawling across the dirt and saw one ant carrying another on its back. It's not like the ants were talking to him exactly, he told me. It was more like the earth or the universe was communicating just to him in this moment, through the insects. He leaned forward and paid closer attention. Passersby, hand in hand, old men walking their dogs, Connor told me, did not seem to notice any of what he was seeing. But the message was letting him—and only him—know it understood his desire: to create a world where we don't destroy each other, but instead where we live to help each other, like this ant.

Connor kept watching the coded message playing out, just for him, among the soil and sticks. He saw the ants struggling to crawl over the exposed roots, around his feet, up the tree, and more coming across the sidewalk, behind the bench where he sat. He decoded it: there were strong people and weak people in the world. Other people stepped on these insignificant lives without knowing it, all while Connor watched. Clearly, he saw, the weak would be crushed and know only torment. Was he any different from the ants? Would he be crushed? Or would he resist?

If he were to create a better world from scratch (so he slowly understood in the messages), "there would need to be obstacles, like tests," he said, "to climb or conquer. You'd have to do stuff like that to become a king or something, to set an example for others." He would need to prove himself. Unfortunately, Connor now understood, death and suffering were part of the deal. He would obey.

The messages continued. They came to him "telepathically," he said, because when they came through people—friends, coworkers at Radio Shack, customers, family—their lips weren't moving. But he picked up these signals coming through them, loud and clear: about the ordering of power, the relationships between the strong and the weak. It became urgent: *Wasn't he getting the message?*

When I met with Debbie in that dark café, she helped me understand the basics of Connor's story—starting with the order of events, since Connor's version was all over the place. She said it was sometime after Connor was fired from Radio Shack that Debbie and her husband Bill began to worry. Connor no longer took an interest in children or strangers or even the rest of the family. The disarming light about him was gone, like it'd been switched off. "A kind of darkness grew about him," she said. He withdrew into solitude, spent long days alone in his room. He said even the sound of a lawn mower across the street, when he stepped outside, was overwhelming: the motor and spinning blades were a menacing threat of pain and horror. The messages were coming through in this way. *This is how it is. You can't hide. What are you going to do about it?* They shamed him and bullied him. He became more agitated. He said things that did not make sense.

That's when Connor's parents took him to a professional and he was diagnosed with paranoid schizophrenia and prescribed a series of antipsychotics. Bill and Debbie were warned that their son might become aggressive. But they insisted they wanted Connor to come home from his apartment's squalor and live with them. They fully accepted the risks. They would take care of their son, making themselves vulnerable to his illness, for better or for worse.

The pills dampened the messages pulsing through Connor's head. I imagine they functioned like the blankets and pillows my musician friends used growing up to stuff inside their kick drums in the garage so the neighbors wouldn't complain. But the telepathic messages still throbbed through the chemical blanket lining his head. They came through smoother now, with a tone of cold logic. These new messages brought the cosmic lessons down to an immediate level, where the universe's crisis now really hit home: he, Connor, was one of the weak; his father was one of the strong. It was up to him to take a stand against the tyranny of the mighty.

Connor resisted this idea for months. But soon his dad became less of a real person, no longer the father who'd loved him, taught him guitar, taken him to picnics in the park, and stayed up late with him, cooling his forehead with a damp towel at three A.M. and helping him take his medicine to calm down. Connor moved into a more intense, more ideological realm of abstraction. The telepathic messages kept coming, telling him that he couldn't be weak and survive. He would have to fight back. There were powers at work that were observing him, waiting for him to make up his mind. He would have to prove himself.

———

In my conversations with Connor I never directly asked about what led up to his assaulting his dad with a kitchen knife. I mainly asked him about how he "hears," or what it's like to pick up telepathic messages around him. He gave me an example. It was the Christmas season, he told me, switching the visiting booth phone to his other ear. He remembered walking through the mall with his parents and older brother, trying to act normal while they shopped through holiday sales racks, each of them unaware of the much more urgent decision he would soon have to make. Christmas carols may have been lilting through the commercial air, but they were faint compared with the increasing pressure around Connor to stop wasting time and kill his father. *If you don't do this today,* the messages pushed, *then shit*

*will hit the fan, many people will get hurt because of your coward-
ice and delay.* It had the seductive power of wartime propaganda
on the radio, severing any basic concern for who might be at-
tacked. He had to act quickly. His feelings were only getting in
the way.

The manner with which Connor continued to narrate the
days leading up to his final act, it sounded like a surreal trial spiraling around him. Any sense of time and place fell away from
his story. Would he do what he had to do? Did he have what it
takes? Kill or be killed. Connor knew this was the test of his
life, and it became more complicated as he tried to interpret
the mounting messages. He began to second-guess everything.
*Was this actually the opposite kind of test than it seemed? Was
the unseen council that bullied him just trying to see whether he
would cave to these demands, proving himself a weakling after all?
What if he steeled himself to obey and end his dad's life—only to
discover that he had failed, was responsible for untold suffering
and therefore certainly deserving of eternal torment?* "I went back
and forth like that," Connor told me, rubbing his face the way
anyone would if they were up for three nights facing a decision
like this. "I had to decide."

Debbie said that in the days leading up to her husband's murder, Connor was lying in bed in a dark room upstairs, almost
catatonic, hardly responding. They grew increasingly worried
about their son. Something was very wrong.

————

Connor, with his hypersensitive antenna, seemed to have made
contact with more than divine signals. He spent time dialed

into two very different wavelengths. One frequency filled him with light, flooded him with song. The other filled him with dread and a need to prove himself.

What troubled me most is that the second wavelength seemed more powerful.

In the torn paperback New Testaments I've read with circles of inmates in jail, Jesus deals with these same two frequencies. One comes to him early, like light between the clouds, like the wings and song of common pigeons, when he stands dripping in a river baptism. *This is my son,* it says, *in whom I am well pleased.* This is the rare frequency that propels Jesus through villages, touching blind eyes and lepers, stopping funeral processions to wake the dead. He seems compelled to constantly forgive the condemned, calling strangers his friends, proclaiming a heavenly order on earth. He has compassion for the crowds. He stops for every cry he hears. He feels. He seems infinitely vulnerable.

But he's also tormented by a persistent and very different set of messages when he walks alone in the desert. *If you are the son of God,* the telepathic messages reason, *throw yourself off the top of the highest building.* The same suicidal logic. *Prove yourself.* Who hasn't heard this voice? The experience, as Connor felt, is that of being tested. In the wilderness, Jesus also hears ongoing, whispering offers to gain control of all the nations, power to rebuild the world. The logic is tempting. In John's Gospel, Jesus calls this spiritual voice not the "devil," but something much bigger: "The Ruler of this World." This is the disturbing intuition of those who have ears to hear: that death-dealing channel fixed on controlling nations and throwing lives away is the one that rules our world and its airwaves.

In the desert, Jesus doesn't dismiss it as hallucination. Rather, he turns his extraordinary antenna away from the wavelengths that rule the world and follows the steady signal of a revolution, a kind of guerrilla radio frequency still alive today that advances the resistance of a new kingdom. Unlike most of us—large or small antenna, schizophrenic or not—he knew the difference between the two messages.

And so, as I drove through a few more dark winter nights on the evergreen highway to Connor's jail, taking the elevator up to the top floor and talking through the glass with a young man still trying to reckon with his own horrific violence, my goal meeting with Connor the schizophrenic young man became the same as my conversations with any inmate, with any friend, with my wife, and with myself: What do we listen *to*? Amidst so many spiritual currents in our age—where even the charismatic Christians at those conferences I attended, who believed they could hear God's voice, also supported sending thousands of our young men and women to two different wars cased in flak jackets and trained to kill—the problem remained the same as what Abraham faced long ago. That is, hearing voices and messages is one thing, but discerning which to follow is another. What Connor needed, medicated or not, was what I needed, what I was learning in my jail fellowships: to learn to pray, and listen, together.

———

At our next visit, I told Connor the story of Noe Solazo, my friend who went from aggressive paranoia to peace within minutes, by merely listening in a new direction. Connor listened carefully. He seemed to understand. He told me about a private experiment of his—something he'd developed a few years earlier. He called it *The Method*.

Back when his sensitivity to any suffering had been most extreme, the noise of lawn mower blades and the sight of a kid standing alone waiting for a bus gave him a chronic knot in his stomach. Antipsychotic meds couldn't take the nausea away. "I tried to find," he said, "or experiment with, different techniques to make the pain go away. Make the knot loosen, you know?"

One technique worked. "It would happen when talking with someone. Like if I were talking with you, it wouldn't be so much about what we were *saying* to each other, but more about *connecting*, in another way. Does that make any sense?"

I asked how they would connect.

"Like, maybe affirming each other," he said, tilting his head and squinting his eyes at me. He said he'd try to wait until he felt, in some way, that his friend let him know he was okay. "Or that he liked me. I'd just try waiting. Watching closely, kinda." When it came, he explained, he'd try to do the same thing back. "It's hard to explain." This technique was the only thing he'd found that conquered the evil ringing in his ears. For months, he said, it was the only thing that calmed his nausea from the storm of suffering, the soundless crying-out all around him. All he had to do was find that subtle, invisible frequency between his heart and another's. Shortwave radio. Back and forth. A kind of focused, mutual vulnerability. It sounded like a fine description of love. A kind of I-Thou encounter. But not just between two people. I heard it as a pure definition for the very heart of prayer. Mother Teresa famously said that when she prayed, she listened. What does God say to you? an interviewer asked her. *Nothing,* she answered. *He just listens.*

I've since kept Connor's definition of The Method written inside the covers of some of my journals. It is not the language a yogi or mystic-saint would use. It is as precise and without sentimentality as how I imagine Thomas Edison's first raw observational notes might have read when he was discovering electricity. Waiting for the connection beneath the words. Something like being liked and wanted. Then sending that fragile affection, that naked desire, back in the same direction—either with another person, or with heaven.

I asked Connor whether he was interested in trying The Method again, but this time as a way to begin praying, after years away from such things. He looked skeptical. The courts were still trying to determine whether he was legally insane. He was still trying to determine whether he'd done the right thing, whether he'd passed the test (the telepathic messages had been only dampened by the heavy medication in his head). He feared coming torment. I said the only way Jesus could deal with his own impending torment was by practicing this kind of Method the night of his arrest. And even he—who famously advised taking your prayers into a closet and shutting the door—didn't want to do it alone on this night. Jesus wished his friends would fight sleep and join him in prayer even as his betrayers and tormenters neared through the dark garden trees. I told Connor I would join him. He could experiment with me, here where we could visit and together practice through the glass in this closet-like space, the doors shut behind both of us.

He kind of smiled, and let me know that would be okay. And that he liked me, wanted me to stay with him. It wasn't so much what he was saying—he spoke little, and even then his voice was thin and distant through the few feet of metal cord connecting the two black phones at our ears and mouths in our separate spaces. But I felt it. I tried to do the same thing back. And so we began.

That was the last time I saw Connor in the county jail. Soon after that night, he was ruled mentally incompetent, acquitted of criminal charges, and transferred to Western State Hospital two hours south in Tacoma, the largest mental asylum west of the Mississippi, for an indefinite stay.

Over the next five years, I often thought of my conversations with Connor. After Rachel and I moved back from Missoula to the Skagit Valley, I pulled out a dusty moving box in my garage filled with old jail journals. I found the page from our last visit together, when I had barely begun to pray with him. The words "REPENTANCE" and "CONTRITION" were written in all caps at the bottom, words I'd forgotten scribbling in that small room years earlier. Maybe, in those last visits, I was witnessing what repentance could look like. The word means more than feeling sorry for one's actions; *metanoia,* the Greek word usually translated as "repentance," can also be translated as *greater mind,* or *new mind.* As we'd opened ourselves to the affection of God, between ourselves, had I sensed in Connor or myself a new mind? And contrition means, literally, a crushing, a damaging—*breaking-of-heart.* The troubled, large-hearted King David sang, "My sacrifice, O God, is a broken spirit; a broken and crushed heart, God, you will not reject." This psalm, I've recently read, is the one recited by Eastern Orthodox monks almost every day: "It is the way the saints pray. They ask of God to crush their hearts." I thought of my image of a broken spiritual radio deep within some of us. Contrition might be the moment when our hearts break into the hypersensitive condition of people like Connor.

Thinking about his story, my heart had not yet broken. I had not become vulnerable to this tragedy. I was too intact.

So I called Debbie. I got her on the line when she was stuck in a snowy overpass in the Cascade Mountains but somehow had cell reception. I did not ask much about Connor's voices or telepathic messages. I asked about her marriage with Bill. She shared stories with me until her phone died two hours later. Bill came alive in my mind: the middle-aged man whose "waddle" through the big box stores had endeared him to his wife; the award-winning high school choir instructor who had published several "method books" for beginning instructors to hear and hone the music of young people into something coherent; the friend who she heard composing on the piano most evenings; the husband who lay with her some nights and bemoaned his inability to compose his symphonies from bed like Mozart.

She emailed me an eighty-five-page manuscript she'd begun four years earlier as part of her therapy—with a counselor who worked with soldiers home from war. I read the entire thing on a long shuttle ride home from the airport. She told each step of the bloody evening in their kitchen and backyard. But between each scream and slash of the knife from the kitchen block and grab at the sliding back door, Debbie's narration was punctured with elegant flashbacks of when she first bought the house with Bill; of developing those photos that hung on the wall of the crime scene at Costco with Bill, holding his hand inside his coat pocket all the way home; of sliding that back door open in the summer to hear Bill composing his own music in his office; of helping their son sell those pyramid-scheme knives. The manuscript was an unnerving descent into grief, a woman's heart breaking open fully for the man she loved most in this world and lost at the hands of her son. As I read, I began to feel something stir inside me for this man who wanted to "hear" the music no one had heard before and bring it into the world. This man had chosen to leave himself vulnerable to a sensitive son whose gifting might turn dark and betray him, even into death.

When I finished Debbie's manuscript, I stepped off the shuttle feeling oddly euphoric. Despite the terror in many of those pages, some still-present frequency of immense affection between this woman and her husband was stronger. It conquered the knot in my own stomach as I read. I stood on the curb waiting for Rachel to pick me up that night under the stars and I felt at ease, at home in the world, for the first time in months. I began to pray, I think. And I wondered what Rachel was feeling as she drove. It felt like my heart was beginning to break. My antenna was opening, vulnerable in the night air.

I visited Debbie at her home. She pulled out pictures of Connor and Bill. We sat on her couch and she showed me grainy home videos of when Connor, during his Jesus Freak phase, spoke from the platform at his church about a greater love, he said, than most of the churchgoers imagined. He stuttered and waved his hands like how Mozart did in bed.

In the manuscript, I remembered, Debbie wrote vividly about a moment during the night of the murder that Connor had never mentioned to me during our visits. She had woken to Bill's screaming for help in the backyard, ran out panicked in her pajamas and wrested her son with the knife away so Bill could release his tackle-hold on Connor and scramble in blood up the steps into the house. Connor pushed her off and she followed him back inside; he had kicked at the back door and pursued his dying father under the kitchen table (the same table upon which, just hours earlier, they had eaten their last supper together). She pulled her own serrated blade out of the pyramid-scheme knife block and swung instinctively at her husband's attacker/son. It was as if, she said, Connor couldn't even see her, a "faraway look" even in his determined eyes. When her strength and even her knife failed her, and Connor climbed a chair to finally fall upon his father with a last blow, she helplessly screamed, *"Jesus, stop him! Jesus take this evil presence away from my son!"* In that moment, the kitchen was stilled. Connor turned and looked at her, "as if," she wrote, "he finally *saw* me for the first time in weeks." He stepped down off the chair, set the knife on the ground, and sat down at her feet like a child. "It's okay, Mom," he told her as she trembled and Bill died. "I'm all done."

I was tempted to dissect the spiritual and psychological wiring in this climax. Even in her manuscript, Debbie admits that this story can make her sound like a lunatic. While grieving, talking to prosecutors and public defenders and psychiatrists and a few pastors, she has longed for answers—*"Why, when I tried everything, from pills to knives in self-defense, did these words, this prayer in this name, bring my son back?"* I underlined this passage in my printout of her manuscript. Had her cry turned Connor's inner dial more than any chemical could, albeit tragically too late? Or was he merely called away from illness-enhanced primal father-rage to an even more primal motherly attachment? My need to put all the invisible pieces together fell apart as I sat by Debbie's side there on the couch, watching home videos. I surrendered to the wavelengths of affection filling the room as she watched her son and husband playing guitars together on the screen. I set down my pen.

———

Eventually, I made the long drive down to Western State Hospital and waited for Connor at a plastic table in an open day room with thick, thick walls. When he came in, he looked different. He'd gained weight. He wore a big college football sweatshirt. His hair was clipped short and fuzzy, and his round cheeks were covered by a thick, trimmed beard. He looked like his father, Bill. And he waddled in thick running sneakers when he approached me, shyly shook my hand, and sat down.

There was no glass between us this time. He said he'd been wondering where I was. I caught him up, told him I'd often thought about our conversations in that jail several winters ago. I asked him what he remembered from those conversations. He looked at the table and scratched his neck. "I was kind of crazy back then, when you last saw me," he said. "If I were you, I wouldn't take anything I said to heart." He'd gone off his meds once last year, he added, and the same telepathic messages interrogated him about whether he had carried out his mission correctly or not. He took a deep breath. "I don't want to talk about that stuff any more, if that's okay."

So I asked him about what his mom had told me, how he had taken up the guitar and bass again. How he was writing his own songs. That original family friend had recently told me he had become fascinated with ambidexterity—playing each instrument right-handed as well as left-handed, restringing all his instruments, regluing the bridges and stretching his unfamiliar fingers into unfamiliar shapes. Ambidexterity, I'd heard, is about engaging both sides of the brain. On the drive down, I'd wondered whether Connor was laboring to let music wash through his entire brain, training all of his mind and heart and limbs to follow his original call in the Cambodian shower.

But he wasn't going to talk music, either. "I feel like you're asking me a lot of questions. It's kinda intense. I'd rather just, I don't know, talk about cars. You like cars?"

Not really, I said. Did *he* like cars?

He shrugged and looked out the window.

There was something he remembered from our past visits, he offered a minute later, and smiled. "How you put your feet up against the glass between us, like, how you crossed your ankles. You were all kicked back and relaxed in your chair. Like we weren't even in jail." I had forgotten doing this. "That was cool," he smiled. Connor was once again reflecting an earlier version of myself back to me. Now, I realized, I was more intense, trying to solve abstract puzzles, figure out all the messages. In the same span of years, Connor had been heavily medicated, interviewed repeatedly by forensic psychologists about the telepathic messages. He'd been examined by new doctors on the ward here every few months or so, had his inner world probed and analyzed, his thoughts held under the surgical light so many times he now had no interest in talking about any spiritual stuff anymore. He was still coming to terms with the reality that not only had he taken his father's life, but he'd also lost the prime of his own life to walking these sterile halls for the next decade or two amidst people he did not trust.

When I tried to lead into the conversation with my own life, as I had when we first met—this time, telling him about a monastery I'd visited lately called Gethsemani, how moved I was by the utter strangeness of a choir of adults singing to heaven together in chapel out on the winter plains of Nowhere, Kentucky—Connor's eyes wandered the ceiling in clear disinterest. He asked whether I had brought money to get snacks out of the vending machines. We drank sugar-free soda I bought for us (all the sodas were sugar-free by policy) and munched pork rinds in the institution's silence. It was the hardest single hour of all my years visiting guys in lockdown facilities. It was the opposite of what had drawn me all these years to such places: none of the sharpened hunger for God, open hands and hearts and stories coming together. No music. No fire. It felt familiar: almost a caricature of my postfaith generation in their late twenties, Connor was now cynical about things like prayer, not sure what to believe anymore.

"We don't have to use the whole three hours," I offered one hour in, looking at the plain, caged clock on the wall. "I can leave early."

"No," he cut me off. "I can do this." His eyes told me not to leave. "Let's just take it real . . ."—he finally smiled again, moved his open hand through the air as if to a slow jam—"slow."

I took it as a sober corrective to my whole inquiry among hearts like Connor's. Opening yourself directly to the spiritual sources—be they evil or holy—is dangerous business. You risk opening the front door of your heart to forces as complicated and conflicted as the streets and prisons. (As inmates have made sure to remind me, regarding such environments: "Not everyone's there to help you, Chris. You can get fucked up really quickly." Those words, I think, apply to the unmediated spiritual realm.) But there's an even greater danger. You risk making contact with a Love somewhere out there that is so pure, so good, it makes you feel more, hurt more, notice more, care more, makes you embarrassingly odd and terribly sensitive, welcoming strangers, touching the lepers like Francis in Assisi, or getting dragged to court and stuck with the death penalty between two thieves like Jesus did. Or—and this is most common—if you lose that connection that filled you like the sun, it can be a loss so disorienting that even the hope required for real prayer—someone suggesting you open up again, say, to God—can drive you mad. Any way you come at it, it's a dangerous game.

So we played cards. Children's games, like slapjack.

Time flew. We laughed. There at the table, with three sleepy chaperone guards reading magazines by the door and the vending machines humming behind me, Connor and I pulled jacks with knives, clubs, and hearts off the two stacks by our chests, not sure what would come out with each draw, every now and then his hand landing on top of mine, mine on his. In this way, Connor was still training me in the simplest mysteries of prayer: for the next two hours, it wasn't so much what we said, but how we found other ways to sit in the silence, even in a hostile environment, and rebuild a fragile connection after years apart.

STRANGER ON THE
EDGE OF TOWN

I SPENT TWO DAYS IN NEW HAVEN. YALE TOWN. I WAS
invited to speak in a small class at the divinity school there.
They were studying the history of Pentecostalism in North
America—small-town revivals, people speaking in tongues,
healings, signs and wonders. They invited me because the young
teacher was a friend of a friend, and this in-between friend said
that the div students would probably be interested in hearing a
fresh perspective about the Holy Spirit when the syllabus took
a turn toward "how this stuff is practiced today." I suppose this
is because the students were all too wary about big glossy "charismatic" conferences these days, where wealthy white suburban-
ites shake on the ground and scream jibber jabber and jangle
their jewelry and stuff velvet baskets full of money to support
Israel and big-haired GOP candidates.

I was different, our friend said, since I spent time in a jail, and with teachers like Bob. Our faith community in the Northwest was more a kind of hippie-anarchist, shoestring budget, early church–type crew. And like that early church crew two millennia ago, he added, we also had gotten pretty deep into the Holy Spirit stuff.

Here's how. Bob the liberation theologian and agrarian revolutionary had come to despair as two forces in America ravaged the flocks he tended—methamphetamines on the streets, and post-9/11 prowar anti-immigrant patriotism throughout the local churches, in which he'd been trying to cultivate compassion for the outsider. He'd grown desperate for a greater power that could save. Something that could challenge the crushing powers of the world. Jesus, after all, had authority to heal sickness, cast out tormenting spirits, and send away the "Legion" of Roman imperial occupying forces. So Bob went to one of those "renewal" conferences in Toronto. He'd heard rumors—mainly from his family—of something gentle and invisible sweeping through the room, making people laugh, making stiff bankers in ties like his father convulse in strange but sweet seizures that left them teary and kinder, making people like his troubled young relative finally quit drugs and care for his family. Bob thought maybe he could sneak in the back door, steal what was good from the flag-waving, shofar-blowing circus, and bring it back to the jail where the men languishing in there needed something more. Third day at the conference, Bob found himself falling, knees out from under him, when the pastor rested his hand on Bob's forehead softly and spoke simple words of blessing, just as Bob had done with so many inmates and migrant families. He felt a wavering heat on his brow even when he picked himself up and walked out the back door into the snow. The heat continued upon his brow still back in Washington, then Paris, then Honduras, then Mozambique as he traveled to preach. He described this tangible sense of presence to me as we sat in his car in the jail parking lot, under the ten P.M. streetlights.

This was just when I was arriving at Tierra Nueva, new to the strange valley, not far from my own despair. A sense of wonder, for me, went through the roof. I wasn't reading many of those glossy-covered charismatic manuals about how to "catch the fire"—yet. I was reading Annie Dillard and slamming the brakes in my car when huge herons lifted out of farm road sloughs. I was waking to schizophrenic men crawling through my window and watching bright green sprouts appear out of black dirt in a sealed greenhouse. In that season, for me, anything was possible. I'd begun to write about it. Both wonder and terror await, I'd argued, when you allow yourself to trust and follow the Holy Spirit. Rarely does the Spirit look like what you'd think.

I suppose this is what interested the divinity class instructor: contemporary Christians who took the mystical-magical side of the New Testament seriously, but who had their hands in the dirt, who served the poor instead of spectacle and capitalism. Plus, my hair wasn't big. I was just a prematurely balding, bearded, blue-eyed smoker in Converse sneakers.

———

It was the first night I flew in to New Haven, and Sam the instructor had picked me up from the airport in an electric car set aside for such faculty business. I was hungry. At midnight, other than Taco Bell, only the rustic local pizza joint was open late.

That's when I met the man whom this story is about. He was outside the brick oven pizza parking lot amid piles of chopped firewood—rounds of cedar and sawdust to fire the thin-crust oven within. He was sitting on a stump smoking a cigarette. And he greeted me as I entered the city.

"How are you my-*fhrend*," he said, blowing smoke with an accent I did not recognize.

I like strangers. Especially if they look strange. This guy looked like a street fighter. He was a strong man, thick and plain as the wood he chopped. His eyes were small, set within a pale face that looked like it'd been punched repeatedly and healed just as many times over the years. He had a fresh cut on his lip, like he'd just finished a good round. I asked whether the pizza here was any good. He said, "Eez delishious." An hour later, Sam and I emerged satisfied and saw this same man splitting more cylinders of wood with a heavy awl. He sat down and pulled out his smokes as we approached. I asked him whether I could bum a cigarette.

"Of course," he said wearily. There was kindness in his small blue eyes.

I thanked him and we exchanged names. His was Kadir. I recognized that name. David James Duncan, in one of my favorite essays of his, calls his invisible fly-fishing guide "Khwaja Khadir," after the Sufi version of the Koran's Holy Spirit.

"Yes, my name," he nodded, "it mean Spirit. That is good. So you like the pizza, my-fhrend?"

"Yep," I said. "You work here, then?"

"This is my restaurant. I start it eight years ago."

"Wow. So where're you from?" I asked as we lit the Marlboros and Sam declined.

"I am fhrom Turkey."

Excited, I told our new friend I'd been learning all about Turkish coffee lately. It was the first culture to turn the caffeinated cherry pit from Ethiopia into a dark-roasted, fine-ground, triple-steeped beverage, still famous among coffee geeks for the elaborate brewing ceremony performed for nomadic guests in bedouin tents with three shiny, curvy pots. I asked Kadir whether he knew where I could find and try some authentic Turkish-style coffee here in New Haven.

"Of course," he closed his eyes and almost smiled. "But why you learn about the Turkish khohffee?" I told him I'd recently gotten into the coffee-roasting scene in Seattle. "You," he asked, "are businessman?"

No, I said, I am a kind of pastor. But the organization I work with started in Honduras, I explained, and our founding partners grow coffee in the cool mountains there. Outside Seattle is where I work with undocumented folks and men out of jail. I told him about a tall, tatted-up guy named Zach who used to be a meth cook and who had been going to coffee-roasting workshops with me lately. Zach was collaborating with us to start our enterprise where ex-cons like him who can't get jobs because of long criminal records can artisan-roast—then slang—the coffee from Honduras under our new label we were developing: Underground Coffee. They could use their past, their normally unwanted drug-world experience (weighing, selling, maintaining customers, cooking up batches with an attention to quality control and without blowing up) as a set of cross-over job skills. This way they could step out of the underground economy, getting connected to cafés and churches. "And churches love coffee," I wrapped up the spiel, probably sounding exactly like a businessman.

Kadir eyed me and now truly smiled. "You come tomorrow, my-fhrend. Here. I will take you to experience real Turkish khohffee."

Sweet, I thought. An off-campus adventure.

———

The next night, around ten P.M., I hoisted myself up into Kadir's large white truck behind the pizza shop and slammed the creaky old door shut. The talk at the divinity school had gone well that afternoon—we even got the Skype connection to work for one of the homies back home, Evaristo, to join the class as a guest speaker, his face large on the flat screen, his soft voice loud through the lecture speakers. My work was done for this trip, all the cautious preparation and performance anxiety now lifted. This truck was a welcome opposite to the polished "smart classroom" with digital projectors where I'd sat much of the afternoon, as well as the well-furnished living room of a student's home prayer group I'd just left, where they'd hosted me for hushed guitar music and organic tea.

"You rheddy?" my boxer-faced host asked me.

"Let's roll, Kadir."

There was still pizza dough flour on his big hands as he put the vehicle in reverse. I was suddenly in a rather intimate space with this stranger. An unfamiliar mix of odors particular to each person's habits hung in the car, none of which I could recognize now. It smelled, well, *foreign*. And I had no idea where we were going exactly. Just a cup of coffee, some place around the corner, I thought he'd said. We rumbled down a dark street that was not turning just around any corner. My right hand felt my thigh pocket for my cell phone. I remembered that I'd left it in my bag at Sam's house. So my right hand slid inconspicuously to the cold lever that opens the door and it stayed there.

I knew nothing of my guide. He beat me to the friendly interrogation before I could find my own polite angle of inquiry.

"You say you help the immigrant, people with no paper," he turned to me from the wheel, his face lit only by passing streetlights.

"Yes." I kept it short. "Well, not me anymore, really, but my organization does. I work with guys in jail."

"The immigrants are Mexicans?"

Yes, I said again. Mostly southern Mexicans from Oaxaca. And some Central Americans. He told me he had been to Oaxaca, he knows the place. All of Central America, in fact.

"I cross—how do you say here—with wet back? The Rio Grande. The Mexicans, they help me. You know this river?"

I told him I needed to hear this story.

He adjusted in his seat and leaned back, as if we still had a long way to drive.

"I'm sorry," I interrupted. "This place we're going for coffee, it's . . . it's close by, you said?"

"Yes, yes, the khohffee. Don't worry."

He then told me about his village in Turkey, where many people had left for America over the years. He wanted to leave as a youth, but could only get a visa to Guatemala with his sister's help. Then, a late teen alone on the other side of the world, he was picked up by Guatemalan police at the Mexican border, held in a cell for two days, released, and caught again by Mexican officials on his second try. He told me how he was transferred to a Mexico City facility, detained with hundreds of Central Americans who did not understand him, and then deported to Ecuador. *Ecuador?* It was the closest nation that would accept him without a visa. He then made his way as a lone Turkish foreigner through Colombian smuggling routes to Costa Rica, then Honduras, learning enough Spanish along the way to barter his way back into Guatemala. "Bad people," he said. "Have to work with them. Have to learn." Kadir was recognized by officials in Guatemala just before attempting to cross into Belize through the Petén jungle. "They told me, *We throw you in jail.* And I thought, No way man, so I tell the police, *Baño, baño,* you know. He let me go to the bathroom but I sneak out the small window and run. I leave behind my leather jhacket. My family make it, Turkish leather, traditional style. The police he liked it, I could tell. I leave it there on my seat with the police. It was a good jacket." A week later, after being taken in by an attractive hotel clerk and shuttled north through her family networks, Kadir put what remained of his clothing in a plastic trash bag knotted with air and, at three in the morning, swam across the deep, dark river between Matamoros and Brownsville, Texas. He told me that all he could see above the waterline as the current lapped at his neck, sweeping him downstream, was a glowing Holiday Inn sign. On the other side, "very very happy," he dried off, put his clothes back on, and walked through an empty parking lot right past that Holiday Inn and into the night of America.

It looked like we were far outside the city now, in some remote industrial district. Half an hour must have passed during that story. Kadir pulled us into the massive and empty parking lot of what may have been an old strip mall.

"This it?" I tried to sound casual.

"Yes. This is it," he said with better grammar and killed the engine.

There was not a single car around us. Not a single window aglow across the street. Only a few fluorescent parking lot lights flickering above.

Oh shit, I thought. His shady-networking-through-Latin-America story might have been a superb read if I held it in a magazine in my apartment, safe with a cup of coffee at my side. Or even inside a jail, or a crowded trailer park. But at this point, alone with him in his weird truck in the middle of nowhere, that whole story made it plausible to suspect that he might pull a knife out from under his seat any moment and duct tape my mouth with those wood-chopping, dough-pounding fists. Maybe he'd make me dial my family on his cell and squeal while he flatly informed them I would be left in some Connecticut dumpster if they didn't Western Union a lot of money to some Colombian country code within the hour.

Kadir turned to me in the silent cab. He seemed to notice my fear. "You whork with the criminals, in the jhail, you say?" He smiled and almost laughed. Was he taunting me now? I thought of a man I visited in the jail once. The guy had looked normal enough, but he'd driven people out to the woods upriver and pounded a needle-nose hammer into their temples. A voice had told him to do it. *Perfect setup,* I thought now, about my driver. *And I'm the naïve out-of-towner. Completely disposable.*

I rehearsed in my mind a single body movement that could unlock and open the door while slipping out before he could seize me. I could run faster than he could, I knew, even with these tight jeans. I pictured myself racing into the night to who-knows-where while his bright truck lights roared behind me like the movie poster for *No Country for Old Men.* In fact, Kadir (*was that even his real name? damn me and my fly-fishing Spirit guide naïveté!*) looked a bit like that vaguely foreign, flat-expressioned killer in the movie, cartel connections and all.

Kadir finally opened his side of the car and stepped out. I exhaled. I stepped out as well, slammed my door, and kept a calculated distance as I followed this stranger cautiously through the empty parking lot and across the street, asking about his family but not really listening. Just a lame pastor's way of whistling in the dark.

We approached a creepy building that looked like an abandoned office tower with six stories. *Where the hell were we?* This was not like following Fabian Debora in L.A. I knew Fabian's story well beforehand. This Kadir guy, however, was an unsafe bet. The cramped foyer ahead of us was not lit. Inside, he pushed the elevator button for *Up* and smiled again at me. It did not put me at ease. The stairwell was open to my right. I heard unhappy sounds echoing down the concrete passage from above.

I've been to crack houses before. But all those times I knew who I was looking for. Often I was carrying a personal message from an inmate I'd just met with in the visitation rooms, usually

a tender message, and it felt good to climb piss-smelling stair-
wells and knock on strange doors knowing I held such a thing
of original beauty in my pocket, an unexpected gift to give to
some unhappy soul on the other side of that apartment door.
But now, here on the other side of the country in a forsaken
place on the edge of some Connecticut town, I was armed with
nothing like that to give.

A skinny couple stumbled out of the stairwell, arguing, but
grew silent when they saw Kadir and me still standing by the
elevator. I don't like elevators. Since I was a kid I have always
feared they will malfunction, leaving me trapped in a cell with
no toilet, suspended between stories, pressing all the buttons,
eventually screaming, pounding the mute walls, hyperventilating, nobody hearing me. This elevator looked well below inspec-
tion as we stepped in.

"That eez good, you help the immigrants. That eez good,"
Kadir repeated. It felt like he was just killing time with flattery
over the few things he remembered about me. His mind was
clearly elsewhere. Probably coordinating something that would
happen to me in a moment when the elevator doors opened.

I'd like to think I began to pray in that moment. I didn't. But
I remembered how, at a conference once, I heard some laugh-
ingly joyful, Holy-Spirit-addled Italian monks who worked in
the slums of Brazil tell how they offered to pray for a man who
was robbing them at gunpoint. When they rested their monkish
hands on the panicky thief's brow in blessing, the guy dropped
to the ground, right there by the ATM, like they do in big
prayer services. The laughing little bald men had lots of stories
like this. Most of them ended with how they bought groceries

for the criminal and dined with his family the next day. I looked
at Kadir out of the corner of my eye as we rumbled upward. I
wondered whether he even had a family, and whether I could
even get my fingertips to his forehead before his street-fighter
skills would block me and crush my hand.

Then the doors opened—and it was all color. Smoky red.

It could have been the set of a Guy Ritchie film, that hidden
mafia hangout where a low-ceilinged room is filled with round
tables of foreign-looking men playing cards and smoking cigarettes with stony faces just like this. I followed Kadir into the
room. Through the haze I could see ashtrays, Marlboro packs,
cell phones, and hairy knuckles on the felt-topped tables. Men
in Adidas jogging suits with curly hair and 1980s muscle tees,
many with curious facial hair patterns, looked up from their
dominoes (not cards) and greeted Kadir, then me. Like he was
the kingpin. Like he owned the joint. Their glares said I was
with the boss.

Beside each seated man I saw an eerie red cocktail in what
looked like a curvy Long Island glass, but barely bigger than a
shot glass. That was the only drink. And everyone was sipping.

Kadir and I sat at a small table for two in the back that was
apparently waiting for him. A short man with a broken nose
and wearing a white apron appeared at the table. He spoke with
Kadir in a language I had never heard.

"Do you like eggplant, my-fhrend?" Kadir then asked me.
"Mustafa wants to know." The man bowed.

Sure, I like eggplant.

Kadir and I faced each other for the first time since meeting
on the lumber rounds the night before. Soon plates of eggplant

and lamb ("Not pork. We're Muslim.") in red sauce came out and filled the space between us. Then rice. Then yogurt and spices. Then hot sesame bread. Then soup. Then water. Then shotlike glasses of sour cherry juice Kadir had imported from Turkey for his homesick guests.

"Kadir," I said, leaning in to whisper to my now-beaming host, then turning around to take in the room, "what is this place?"

"This Turkish social club," he said like it was obvious.

Of course.

"There are many men from Turkey here in New Haven. But we had no place to come togehther. No social club, like our people have for five thousand years. Our ancestors in Anatolia, they call this 'reading rooms.' Here, I fill up that place that was missing in Turkish community, you see. Like missing brick from wall."

As he spoke, I ate, and continued looking around the room. On the wide-screen TV over in the corner was a Turkish talk show. Musicians played long, twangy sitar-like instruments, but they were wearing modern suits and ties, sitting cross-legged with their shoes off on the studio's couches as guests.

"Let us drink tea, yes?"

"Cool with me."

He leaned back and called into the kitchen in Turkish. Though I did not understand the words, Kadir made sense to me with these sounds. It was as if the eerie song of our night so far had, for just a few notes, resolved into his major key. In response Mustafa emerged to take the order, a quick duet with smiles. I noticed this time a scar across the cook's face. Then he disappeared. "This man serving us," Kadir said, "he lost his family. Everything. I hire him. He eez so happy to be cooking. His specialties."

More men approached our table and Kadir kept introducing me to them as a man from the West Coast who works with undocumented immigrants. These stony characters we'd passed on our way in now nodded their heads in warm reception upon hearing this.

Mustafa brought out two of the curvy-hipped glasses on little saucers, filled with that red liquid and a tiny metal spoon in each. Two sugar cubes with mini-tongs rested on the saucer. It was not a liqueur. "We are Muslim," he shook his head. "We do not drink alcohol. But we love strong tea. Addicted, like cigarette." He pushed a single Marlboro across the red tablecloth to me. It had been a long time since I'd smoked indoors.

"You are Christian," he began. "What do you think of Muslim? Of us?"

He caught me in the middle of lighting my cigarette. I smiled with my lips still pinched around the filter and leaned forward to the cheap blue lighter he flicked aflame for me. All of my previous knee-jerk distrust and fear were gone; I was drawn to this man seated opposite me. I felt taken care of. Treated like a friend. Together we were feasting in a warm upper room on the dark outer limits of town. I liked how he spoke plainly, much like my friends in the jail back home, naming the difference between us and asking how I saw him—and everything connected to him—from my side of the table.

"Many Christians, President Bush," he continued, "they don't like the Muslims. They see us as terrorist. Migrant, too. I am both Muslim and migrant. But I like Christians. I like Jesus. We all are from Abraham, no?"

"Well, that's who I talked about today," I replied, "in the small divinity school class."

Pause here.

Part of me usually dreads these conversations. Either it's shit-talking another religion, some secondhand debate, or waving away centuries of differences with too-easy "it's all the same" kind of talk. But this conversation with Kadir already felt different from either the conservative church lobby or the liberal café. My border-crossing, pizza-tossing host from the other side of the world wanted to talk Abraham, the founder of both our faiths that are now so alien to each other. And here we were in a Turkish social club, the globe's foundation of all coffee houses. We were getting back to origins.

He tipped his ash in the glass tray. "In the Yale seminary?" His brow furrowed, head tilted. "What do you say of Abraham?"

I told him I was fascinated by the figure of Abraham—a mystic and a migrant, a guy who listened to a strange voice, totally foreign to his culture and gods, that told him to leave it all. "And he believed it," I said. Abraham risked his life on it, took his wife and goats and goods and became a wanderer, a nomad, leaning into the unknown. He trusted and followed this voice that told him he would be the beginning of something new that would one day bless the whole world, all the strange nations under the stars.

"Anyway," I caught myself from getting too far off track, "that was the connection to the class today, because they're studying Pentecostals in America." I told him how students are skeptical about "hearing God's voice" in a nation where the commander-in-chief of the most powerful empire in history says he is an evangelical believer who "talks to God every morning"—with waves of U.S. flags behind him, directing two wars.

"Yes," Kadir nodded.

"But Abraham," I continued, "the 'hero of faith' at the start of three religions, for him 'hearing God's voice' led to the opposite. It meant leaving home, like *you* sojourning through Central America as a Turk with no one to guide you."

I looked down and saw that in the middle of my excitement, someone had refilled my tea.

I told Kadir my favorite story about Abraham: when he's in his wandering tent and he sees three figures approaching on the horizon. They outnumbered him and his wife. But Abraham doesn't defend himself. He runs out to them and bows low, insisting that the strangers join him and dine in his tent. He serves them a feast of the fattest goat in his wandering flock. Turns out, these strangers are undercover angels. I told Kadir how we piped Evaristo into the class from Skagit Valley, how Evaristo's street name was Stranger, how he was a unique blessing that came to us at Tierra Nueva in the middle of the night, undocumented, covered in blood. In the same way, the stranger-angels bless Abraham in return.

"But then," I said, "the angels visit the cities—"

"Sodom and Gomorrah, yes?"

Yep. These undercover angels approach the city, I continued while sipping more tea, and they're welcomed there only by Lot, Abraham's in-law. Lot, I said, was a resident alien living on the edge of the town. He too bows to the three figures and invites them into his home. Again, the foreigner is first to welcome the stranger. "Like you," I said, tipping the last of my cigarette ash and looking back at my host. "You invited me here last night, when I barely got off the plane. You didn't know me at all."

I was speaking freely now, as I do with close friends. Kadir smiled and leaned against the wall, put his feet up on another chair, as if we had all the time in the world.

"But the citizens, of Sodom," he asked, "they are different?"

I crushed the butt in the ashtray. "Totally." I said they try to kick down Lot's door, demanding the foreigner hand over the newcomers so the mob could "know" them. That is, hold him down and rape him. "The sin of Sodom," I said, now thinking of guys I know who have come home from penitentiaries, like ghosts, never speaking about what happened to them, "is no more about homosexuality . . . than the gang rapes that happen in prison or the military." I told Kadir that the shower of famous brimstone that falls on Sodom is a judgment on a wealthy, powerful city that is cruel to the outsider. Meanwhile Abraham, way outside of town that night, sits with the angel's odd blessing aglow in his tiny home. He becomes the start of a different society, I said, his tent the new haven for the stranger.

"I want to show you something." Kadir took a frame of pictures off the wall by his special table, our table. "This eez a church I bought for my people. There was no place for the little boys and girls to study Turkish language, or the Holy Bhook."

He told me how he bought the nondescript, single-story Bible church in the dreary photograph, in upstate Connecticut, with money he raised from the Turkish migrant community in three states.

Church?

"Mosque, you can say. I show you this because it make me very proud. Eez why I keep this photo here, by my table. I go every Friday, when I can get away from the pizza to go and pray, here." His thick finger tapped the framed glass over the photos. One showed the interior: a high wood-beamed sanctuary adorned with padded floors and walls of bright green fabric. It reminded me of Japanese tea ceremony rooms, where you have to remove your shoes to walk. Or childhood sleepover forts that occupy family rooms with blankets, transforming the space into a secret, intimate realm where best friends tell stories into the late hours. "All the green, it is for paradise," he said. "Where we feast with God eternally."

"Cool," I said.

He laughed. His eyes smiled at me with surprise. "You come with me next time you visit. We go together."

I wanted it to be the next time already. I wanted to go tonight.

"Brother, Chris," Kadir said with sudden seriousness, "I almost forgoht. You still want the Turkish khohffee?"

"Hell yes I do."

———

Mustafa bowed low when he set the two china cups on more matching saucers before us, steaming with the smell of cardamom and sage. Together we bowed forward across the space between us to sip the fine-ground and triple-boiled Turkish coffee. It left dark foam on my short beard. The fine silt around the rim of the cup stuck on my tongue and teeth. I imagined the sand of the Turkish desert night lining the eyelashes and lips of nomads sipping this in the barren steppes outside Constantinople hundreds of years before. And Abraham before that.

We sipped our coffee and lit more cigarettes. "This eez how I see you and me," Kadir said, pushing aside the finished plates and arranging the unused knives into shiny paths between the many cups. He spoke of religions as freeways—"this eez the 95 freeway, and this eez the 91"—both arriving at the same city he loved. Kadir said this and somehow it did not feel like the tired cliché of our age. Why didn't it? I felt like I was drunk, somehow amazed at the profundity of the metaphor. Or maybe it wasn't the metaphor so much as how he so calmly assumed God's hosting presence, here, between us and all our differences. I could feel it. I remember laughing, and feeling subtle waves of heat all over my face and the back of my neck. But there had been no alcohol. I've heard Pentecostals describe this feeling. "Soaking in the presence." I looked across the table at Kadir, the still-healing scars on his lip, on his forearm.

"So," I said when Mustafa cleared the emptied coffee cups with another broken-nosed bow, causing me to wonder whether he had been honoring a holiness all along that I only now was sensing, "what's next, Kadir?" I asked this while stretching my arms out, feeling entirely at home.

He checked his cell phone, a text message.

"Come, my-*fhrend*." He stood up. "You join me. Eez time."

Time for what? It had to be near midnight.

"To work."

In the old white truck we rumbled back into New Haven, and the city was different. There were only red intersection lights, street sweepers, groaning garbage trucks, the occasional taxi, and homeless folks shuffling along the sidewalks. The high-Gothic architecture of the stone Ivy League dormitories looked menacing, like sealed fortresses against the night. At one stop-light, an enormous street sweeper hissed to a halt beside us. Its horn blared. We looked over and the large black man at the wheel waved.

"Was' goin' on, Kadir!"

"How are you, my-fhrend?" Kadir shouted back as they both rolled down their windows to greet one another. We passed the trash man stepping down out of his large night shift vehicle, an old Irish-looking guy, and he too waved at us with a bright smile as we drove by. Pakistani-looking men leaning against two taxis parked near an intersection both raised their heads when they saw our truck from a distance, and both pointed to Kadir as we neared. He was known among the nations. Even two homeless guys nodded and lifted their tired arms to salute Kadir under the streetlamps.

"Do you know all these people?" I asked.

"Oh yhes," he answered after the cab was silent for a moment, a simple fact. "They love me. At one time they are my customers. I help them. All races, my-fhrend. I help them, they help me. They eat my delishious pizza."

He told me about his friendships with the mayor, and a Jew-ish synagogue leader, how they'd helped him petition to get legal status in the United States. He was a legal resident alien in the city.

We pulled up to the Brick Oven, unloaded more wood from the truck bed, and headed in. Kadir invited me under the counter back into the kitchen where the night rush was just beginning. A bathtub-sized Hobart was twisting the dough, young Mexican guys with gel in their hair and white aprons greeted Kadir more like a friend than a boss, one spinning soft dough on his workstation like a DJ with a vinyl record and the other shuffling bubbling pies out of the glowing brick furnace. I remembered something Kadir had said earlier that night about how he usually hands off each business he starts to one of his employees. ("It eez gift. I prefer to live simply, my-fhrend. I like my truck. It eez enough.")

Kadir checked the order slips, answered the phone twice, and made quick work of a head of lettuce, three tomatoes, and other toppings with a heavy knife, telling me more stories as he hustled to make one of the fattest, most generous salads I'd ever seen. Before I knew it, he had added me as a "friend" to his Facebook account on the flour-dusted computer, shown me photos of his wife and children and hometown in Turkey ("We call it Anatolia"), and we were back in the truck with two large pizzas and salads fresh on the seat between us.

Our work was delivery.

Banquet to go.

We pulled up outside one of the castle-like doors on the dark dormitory row, and Kadir dialed with his large hands on his small cell phone.

"My-fhrend, it is me, Kadir. I have the pizza from the Brick Ohven."

A head emerged from a blue-lit window above, and I could hear the electronic trance music through the rolled-down window. The teenager came downstairs, handed over cash, and took the pizzas all without looking at Kadir, not seeing him. As if Kadir were invisible as the Spirit, like Duncan's invisible fly-fishing guide.

We pulled away, ready for Kadir to take me home. Then I realized I was not sure where my host Sam's house was in New Haven, unclear where I would be staying the night. "Don't worry," Kadir shifted the truck into the next gear. "You are with me." I trusted the stranger to find the way, happy to follow his lead wherever we'd go, be it more deliveries or to his place of prayer beyond the county line and outside my experience so far. We rumbled into the night.

WANTED VI

I KNOW I'M A MONSTER," RICHARD SAID AT HIS final sentencing for the murder of Mavis Browne, standing in red coveralls with chained wrists before her weary-faced family and attentive media representatives. He didn't say what he'd told me in the privacy of our visiting booth earlier that month: that he felt rotten about what had happened between him and "that nice old lady Mavis," that he thought about her every day, that he prayed for her and never for himself, that he didn't deserve his own prayers and how he cried. "I know you guys hate me," was what he said instead. "I hate myself for the things I've done."

These were the words printed on the front page of the newspaper the next day, in a side column below a picture of Barack Obama taking the Iowa primary. The judge took liberties to go above the twenty-two-year deal to which Richard thought he'd already agreed, slamming the door shut for a new total of thirty-four years in prison. In his remarks before closing the case and ridding the community of the young man before him, the black-robed official set a heavy hand on the block of paperwork on the high oak altar before him. He flipped a thumb through Richard's entire legal story thus far and made this public pronouncement, which made the caption on the front page: he said life amounted to "a commercial for how not to live your life."

Some others in the community agreed.

The local newspaper's website was full of reader comments: "I'm sick and tired of hearing people talk about the 'rights' of illegal Mexican trash like this, who don't belong in our community where we raise our kids. No one's safe until we get rid of these criminals, and the faster the better."

Someone who used the tag name Angry Citizen made the post. Many other comments in the extended, scroll-down area on the website agreed with this position. One commenter in the thread, though, who apparently knew this Ricardo Mejia—Richard's birth name used in the paper—pointed out that Richard was not "illegal," but actually born right here in Mount Vernon, at Samish County's central hospital. The comment went on to say that although his last name was admittedly Mexican, he was part native (Upper Skagit, to be exact) and part white as well. While this may not have been genealogically accurate, the message was interesting. He was one of us.

Angry Citizen did not reply. That person would not sit at the same table with such a one as Ricardo Mejia, share the same garment of region and identity. "Mejia should hang for this, if you ask me, or at least rot in prison."

Richard was in prison only one year before he started to deteriorate. He was shipped out to Walla Walla, Washington State's oldest prison in the most remote, farthest east, and driest corner of the state. When most people in Washington hear "Walla Walla," they think sweet onions, a variety shipped to grocery stores all over the country. When guys on the street hear "Walla Walla," they think *Oh shit*.

Washington is a death penalty state, and state executions happen only there in Walla Walla, inside what inmates call "the Walls." And other than Delaware, it is the only place in the United States where death by hanging is still "an option." Such traditional methods of disposal, though, are not the most cost-effective options. It costs millions less in legal fees to simply toss the convicted into these lockdown warehouses and throw away the key. But it's even *cheaper*—if an inmate is facing, say, thirty-four years, at an average of thirty thousand dollars a year to house an inmate—if Angry Citizen's wish comes true: that is, if an inmate rots and dies early in there. The problem goes away on its own.

At first Richard felt pain in his stomach. Inmates heard him moaning at night in the cell above them or next to them. As in Samish County Jail, they all knew Lil' Jokes. When they asked him in the morning whether he was all right, he said he was cool.

Then he wasn't cool.

He couldn't sit down. He couldn't swallow. He was burning inside. Guys in his neighboring cells heard him crying out for the floor nurse, and each time he'd come back from the medical wing without seeing a doctor, they said he looked even worse. He was given penicillin. Lots of it, from what the other inmates reported. The D.O.C. record, of course, tells a different story. But his adoptive mother, April, and friends and lawyers have their evidence. In Richard's medical files, penicillin was consistently listed as his only severe allergy. Soon his celly noted the rash, the red spots covering Richard's torso and creeping above the uniform's low neckline where he couldn't stop scratching. Then the constant blood in his constant stools.

"You should get that shit checked out," a new cellmate who was swapped in that week told him. But soon he too would witness what nine other inmates later confirmed and documented in misspelled, handwritten letters. That is, each time Richard banged on the bars and pleaded that he be taken to a real doctor, someone would come by and tell him again: there was nothing more to be done, the problem would go away on its own.

Then came Friday. *Just wait,* he was told, *the problem will take care of itself over the weekend.*

And it did. Richard was dead by Saturday night.

CALIMERO

I AM HAUNTED BY THE GHOSTS OF HUNTED THIEVES. Richard wasn't the first. Before I knew I wanted fellow recruiters like him for the banquet, I came across another thief, and another fellow messenger, nearly a hemisphere away.

This happened several years into my time with Tierra Nueva, when I made a lonely two-month journey south along the Pan-American Highway from Mexico City, through Central America, all the way down to Caracas, Venezuela. I traveled mainly by bus, with some hitchhiking, and a short flight over the cartel-controlled swamps of the Darién Gap. I was, in part, trying to make sense of my small world in the Skagit Valley: I wanted to trace the histories that had pushed north across several borders and converged in that fertile place. I would visit the remote Oaxacan villages, economic wastelands high in their chilly mountains from which most of the migrants I knew in the Skagit berry camps had fled. I would visit Guatemala City's gang ministries and walk the terraced fields of corn and beans and coffee blossoms in the mountains of Honduras where Tierra Nueva began, visiting several villages with the founding farmers who still reached out to the most marginalized families, helping me get to know the roots of the story into which I had been grafted. In Panama City I would meet Rachel's great aunt, see where my future mother-in-law grew up and where she met Rachel's Oklahoman father in the Canal Zone, where the market and might and military of the United States had together sliced a shortcut through the middle of their country. I also wanted to visit other small communities, bands of men and women who lived their lives how we had tried for one year in Oakland, hunting God and serving others in their nations' worst neighborhoods. These were groups I hoped could help me understand my own calling that was taking shape among young criminals. That's when I first met the ex–gang member chaplains in Guatemala and they took me into the near-underground prisons full of ink-covered young men my age. But it was in Caracas, Venezuela, that my long journey hit bottom, in the slums stacked across the hills around the capital.

I'd planned to rendezvous there with Bob to visit a team of missionaries who invited him to spend a week with them. They lived in one Lego-like cement block among thousands of makeshift others blanketing the horizon around the capital with their earthen red and roofs of rusting metal. This small team of American and German expats—they all belonged to a larger "order among the poor" in Cambodia, San Francisco, L.A., Guatemala, and East London's inner city—were neo-friars, like the wandering monks of medieval roads with no monastery of their own. At supper our first night, over chicken and rice and candlelight, I met the small crew. There were John and Birgit, husband and wife, urban missionary veterans who looked worn down to bones, muscle, and a survival kind of kindness. There were their three blond and friendly teenage kids; and two twenty-something novices. One was a young woman named Corrie who'd researched at Stanford before coming here, dyed her fair hair dark brown, intensely loved many abused women in this neighborhood, and who now was leaving in a month after three years here. The other novice was a younger guy my age named Ryan who wore a bandana over his hair, had wooden plugs in his earlobes, spoke perfect barrio slang, and lifted his nose at my weak Spanish at our first greeting that afternoon. I was inspired, but unsure whether I could live in a cinder-block world like this. Mainly I felt happy to be welcomed one more time out of my traveling solitude, around a table now with Bob and such gently radical people.

It was at this supper that I heard whispers of a local thief they called California.

They couldn't speak his real name—*Calimero,* the youngest son whispered even softer—because the barrio has ears, they said. And Calimero was a wanted man. Neighbors might suspect that the missionaries were harboring the outlaw if they heard his name moving in their home, or were implicated in his crimes, or, conversely, were part of the inevitable plots rumored to lynch him. (They don't hang people in the barrio, but they use that verb: *linchar.*) Whispers through the stacked maze of improvised society said that he and his buddies Bichito, or Little Bug, and Jeremy had a hit on them too. They were wanted for robbing at gunpoint so many sick and tired families trying to survive up and down this hill where city taxis had long ago refused to drive. *"Gente decente,"* John nodded. "That's the term they prefer. Decent people."

Calimero had robbed both Corrie and Ryan within the past few months. He came up behind Ryan in an alley with another *malandro* and they both pointed loaded handguns directly at his head. Ryan handed over the few *bolívares* he had on him, but since that day he had lost any remaining sense of peace when stepping outside their locked home on the corner. Calimero was unarmed the day he and Bichito grabbed Corrie's hand and demanded she give them the silver band on her finger. Rather pissed off, Corrie fought back and yelled eye to eye with her young aggressor that "no man will take what I've saved to give some day to the man I love." The two boys probably had never heard of a purity ring.

The story got better. John asked Ryan and Corrie, as we finished dinner, to tell Bob and me about when they heard Calimero was shot and together went to visit him in the hospital. He'd survived but was heavily sedated and had had no visitors. Just the two of them at his bedside. Corrie gave a short, moving account of how she held Calimero's fingers in what she realized was her ring hand, how it was a very different kind of touch from their last meeting. They weren't sure whether Calimero remembered them, or that visit. Ryan said he'd looked for him several times that last week, had spent three hours the day before we arrived walking up and down the steep, winding streets, talking with some of the *malandros* he'd started to befriend, like Bichito. No one knew where Calimero was. "It's hard to find someone who, for good reason, doesn't want to be found."

Ryan also said that he wanted to pay a visit to the barrio witch doctor, Señor O, a man high in the arts of brokering with spiritual juju. Most witch doctors in Caracas barrios practiced Santería, which I had read about during the long bus rides along Costa Rican highways in preparation for this visit. But Señor O was a *palero* and practiced Palo, which had a darker reputation, Ryan told me. He didn't know much about it other than those who practice it call on the spirits of the dead to do their bidding. "Most of the time to do *bad* stuff." Corrie described "the distinct sense," when she'd visited Señor O with John, "that despite his tiny size and peaceful, friendly demeanor, his crippled hands held many of the chains of evil that strangled the barrio in captivity."

Birgit forbade Ryan from visiting Señor O at this point, along with trying to find Calimero anymore. Ryan was the newest, after all, of the few young people under her care. And, she made clear in her pointed but warm German accent, building trust with their neighbors was hard enough without his poking at the local nests of curses and cross fire.

Barrio Pedro Camejo is not a lovely place. There is no green. Even the small potted plants that some *gente decente* hang on their balconies look wrong, out of place. The air smells of burned tires and trash. The jerry-rigged sewer lines back up frequently. If you want beauty, you look up, out of the place: the sky and sunsets are nice, as Caracas is not far from the coast of the Southern

Caribbean. Or you look out over the distant barrios from a balcony. The clashing colors and hard surfaces soften into an endless rusty patchwork that covers the muscled hills and valleys. Our second night there, after accompanying Corrie and Birgit to visit a half-blind woman with hip pain who lived in a small hovel with filthy kittens and who wouldn't let go of Corrie's hand in her lap while she told Birgit for the third time the story of how her husband died of cancer, I snapped a photograph through a chain-link fence: a child on top of a house, silhouetted between water storage containers, with a makeshift kite—string curving up to a trash bag held wide by knotted straws—rising against a pink and blue sky. Birgit told me promptly to put that camera away before anyone saw me with it.

Pedro Camejo felt like a cramped Wild West town, full of bandits and raw civilization—a teeming outpost on the rolling frontier outside Latin America's hopeful new socialism: Hugo Chávez's brightly colored billboards promising utopian progress stopped halfway up these hills. The promises didn't reach up here where the vultures circled through the day. It was a lawless place. And loud. Motorcycles growled up and down the cracked concrete corridors between houses, so loud that it felt like living inside an exhaust pipe. And the barrio's engine never turned off. Everyone's nerves were on edge, night and day, Ryan said, including his own.

One night he pointed out to me from their balcony "yard" how the young men on the roaring motorcycles below sometimes had their girlfriend on the back, with a baby and bag of food from the stores down the hill. But sometimes there was another young man seated behind the driver with a not-so-hidden pistol in hand. "That's how they do it," he said, "each revenge killing. *Bam bam*—and they're gone. No one catches them."

———————

It was late in the week of our visit there that something important happened. It began with something very Pentecostal. As in, *the* Pentecost—when a group of friends of a recently executed man, Jesus, were laying low in an upper room, afraid, with doors locked, and a spirit broke through the windows, lit something that looked like small flames atop each head, like human Bic lighters. This spirit then slipped out and left everyone not just spilling out into the streets laughing like drunks, but making everyone more generous in the days and weeks to come, ditching, for example, the idea of private property. In the midst of their laughter they spoke both musical and ugly sounds, which the various foreigners in the city heard and said they understood perfectly well, hearing, in their own tongues, about a God who wanted even them. The fire was leaping through barriers of syntax and culture and geography. And it made fishermen suddenly fearless and articulate in the face of enemies and religious interrogation during the hours and years that followed.

We were gathered together in the team's tiled common room for their morning time of silence, prayer, and discussion. I was playing guitar to close our time, right before lunch. It was simple stuff. Just one of those cheap guitars that refuse to stay in tune. And a song, "Peace Be to These Streets." It was my jail-altered version of a Taizé-style song—from that diverse community in the south of France where everyone sits on the floor and sings in a large candlelit room, very Ram Dass. *Walk here, Lord.*

Draw near, Lord. Pass through these streets today. Bring healing, forgiveness . . .

We were singing this when John started laughing. There was no reason to laugh. It was a song I never thought to be very funny. As we kept singing, he kept cracking up and didn't stop, like he'd heard a private joke. And it kept getting better. Or like he was drunk, already here at nine A.M.

This was when things came unglued.

Corrie popped open. She started weeping, and it got louder. Soon Ryan was on the ground in the fetal position. Birgit showed no signs of putting things back in order. The tiny team was not as they had been during all our mornings that week. Bob knew what to do, like he'd been waiting for it and knew how to host it: he put a silent hand of prayer on John's back, as if blowing on the heart of the small fire, where it had caught. I kept singing, feeling nothing, really, except confusion. I'd read about these kinds of things, where the Spirit crashes a quiet party and touches each person differently, but I didn't know my role in the melee.

After hammering out a few more songs while Bob tended to the others in turn, while laughter and sobs and crosscurrents of spontaneous prayer filled the tiled room, it became clear that the music wasn't necessary. I set down the guitar. It seemed like John was still listening to something hilarious, so I lay down next to him and tried to listen, as I had with Noe Solazo. While lying there, I saw in my mind's eye John waltzing down the cracked alleyways here—*Does this stiff dude,* I thought, *even know how to waltz?*—and handing fruit to everyone. Mangoes. Apples. Bananas. He looked absurd.

I turned my head and shared this image with John. "That's it!" he laughed, and nodded, there next to me, as if he were seeing something similar. "Yep . . . ." He started to hum, there on the ground, what I can only assume was an echo of the barrio waltz carrying him, something like the way I imagine Connor Harrison tried to sing along with what he heard when he fell to his knees in the Cambodian shower tub.

Aside from singing, this is one effect I've caught onto when a holy presence breaks in: when the unexpected rushes in, it is common to lose balance, to fall. Another effect is what happened to Ryan. I made my way over to where he was now kneeling on the floor, and he shook his head when I leaned in. "I don't know if I believe in any of that speaking in tongues shit," he said to me, "but for the last few minutes, all I keep thinking and kinda mumbling, without trying, is *shanti-shanti-shanti . . . shanti*" (the Sanskrit word for *peace*). "It's crazy." When he shook himself from that sound, he looked at me and whispered, "One other thing keeps going through my mind: let's go find Calimero."

That's the effect that most interests me. The outward-leaping love. The heat of pursuit.

Everyone else was mellowing out from whatever had happened, not surveilling us. "Let's go, then," I said.

Ryan first needed to get something from his room. "A gift," he said, "for someone who is used to only taking. That's what kept going through my mind on the floor. That Calimero should have the experience of something being simply given to him."

This desire had caught Ryan, spread to me, and it moved us out into the hot midday streets. If we were following the Spirit, then the Spirit was like Kadir and it knew those streets and everyone on them—including the wanted thief whom Ryan hadn't found after hours of walking and asking earlier that week. But now, this Spirit on Ryan led us right to the wanted thief in fewer than five minutes.

"He's right up there," Calimero's fellow *malandro* Jeremy said as he pointed us up the steep path. We'd almost run into Jeremy right outside the front door. "I'll show you." He spoke in the thick barrio slang only Ryan understood, and he led us there under the high noon sun.

I was struck by how small Calimero was. He'd slid out of an opening in a fence up ahead and now shyly smiled when he saw Ryan coming up the hill with Jeremy. He did not look like the criminals I knew in the United States: he had no tattoos, no large pants, no shaved head. He and Jeremy had small tank tops and skinny brown arms and beat-up sneakers with no socks. Both wore faded baseball caps over thick curly hair. Calimero stood with no swagger in a pair of tiny orange swim trunks, the kind of things you'd find at the bottom of a pile of donated clothes sent to developing countries. These *malandros* did not look like dangerous men but like frightened boys.

"I've been looking for you," Ryan said after we made basic introductions. By the look on Calimero's face, I got the sense he was not used to people looking for him who didn't want to harm him. But Ryan called him *compay,* like "bro" or "buddy," the same word he used when referring to me in the same sentence, telling the kid who'd robbed him at gunpoint how he'd been telling me, his *compay* from the States, all about this other local *compay* of his in the barrio. As Ryan said this, I too wanted to be Calimero's *compay*.

I don't remember his face very well. Or what he said. He spoke in the thick, Venezuelan barrio slang that Ryan had learned to fit into his ears and shape with his own tongue. I was very much on the outside of something between them. Ryan and Calimero had the kind of bond that exists between a thief and a victim, made less by words and more by fear and, now, forgiveness, one surprising the other in vulnerable places.

Ryan said he knew that lots of people in the barrio wanted to curse Calimero—but that we were here because we wanted to bless him. Was that okay? "Like," he shrugged and looked around, "okay to pray for you, out here?"

"*Claro que sí.*"

Calimero just stared at Ryan as Ryan placed a hand on his upper arm out in broad daylight. Ryan said—boldly, wonderfully boldly—that God sees him, how he's suffered, and wants to care for him. That's why He sent the two of us, Ryan added.

"And here, I have this thing I want to give you." Ryan held in his hand a small, rolled-up poster. It looked like a scrolled invitation, something an ancient messenger might bring from a distant kingdom. Calimero unrolled it there in the street. I stepped to his side to see what it was: layers of light and dark words, thousands, that made up—if you held it away from you—a face. The face looked familiar, like the Shroud of Turin, that ancient blood rag, which legend says wiped Christ's face as he died and so left a haunting portrait.

Calimero didn't say anything. Just tilted his head and gazed into the poster.

Then he rolled it up and said something I couldn't understand, motioned to both of us, and turned back to the fence. I looked to Ryan. "He says he wants to invite us in to show us where he lives, to put the poster on his wall."

We ducked through the hole in the boards, and a massive green ravine opened below us. This was the edge of the barrio. I could see, as we walked carefully down two switchbacks of a footpath, that this was where everyone dumped their trash. Plastic bottles and food slop and burned tires and Styrofoam and chip bags and soiled toilet paper all had been slowly spilling down this slope for some time. Both stench and fresh air pushed back and forth against this cliff. Here among unwanted things stood the young thief's home, his hideout shack.

We followed Calimero through a small door he'd made and locked with some pink twine, and ducked under the corrugated tin roof. It was an impressive shelter of salvaged parts, beams he'd collected now balanced in the hillside dirt as a frame, with rusted metal sheets nailed up. Save for a hammer on the ground, a stool, and a mat to sleep on, it was completely bare inside. The tin and cardboard floor was swept clean. No furniture. And it had only three walls. The fourth side of the shelter was either yet to be found or had blown off in a storm. And so we looked out across the great ravine where vultures rode the thermals.

We hung out there maybe twenty minutes. Maybe an hour. Calimero offered the single wooden stool to us. Ryan maintained that I was *his* guest still, so I took a seat and looked out on the view. I thought of the three-walled woodshed Thomas Merton turned into his solitary hermitage on the far outskirts of his Trappist monastery in rural Kentucky, overlooking the cornfields and thin forest. It was the monk's favorite place to go, hiding from the busy chapel, to know God. Calimero crossed his arms and looked around, adjusted his cap a few times, possibly shy about his home, about what to say, but clearly happy to have guests. He told us he lived here alone in this shack with another street kid. His parents died many years ago. He apologized for not having any food to offer us.

Ryan said we'd bring a meal to eat here together soon. I liked the idea of doing it that night, but in a few hours we were going away on a two-day retreat in the mountains with other Venezuelan service groups. Ryan said Calimero should come over to their home to eat, anytime he wanted—just knock on the door and ask for him.

Calimero said he would, he knew where Ryan lived.

Was he lonely here? we asked. He nodded. At night, he said, it was hard to sleep. He heard screams that collected in that ravine, with no protection against them. He then showed us where he slept, in a small space in the corner he'd set apart with an extra plywood wall. There was just a sooty blanket on the ground. Here, Calimero took out the poster from his back pocket, rolled it in reverse to flatten it, and pressed it over a single nail sticking out from the dividing wall. He smiled at it, his first work of art hung in his home, the trace of the face of God there with him, a nail in his head, between two sleeping thieves on a hillside. "Gracias," he told Ryan, now with eye contact, and patted him on the back as if it were the first time he'd tried such a thing. We took our leave some time after that. He told Ryan he'd stop by soon.

But that was the last time we saw him. Two days later, while we were on retreat, Calimero was found by vigilante justice and lynched—that is, stabbed seven times. When we got back from the retreat, neighbors told John and Birgit how a local store-owner's sons—*gente decente*—finally got the *malandro*. And good thing you gringos were gone that weekend, they said, because when the thief was dying and bleeding, dragging himself around this street corner here, he was trying to get to your front door.

It was only an afternoon, a few hours together in that shack. It was only one kid among thousands, one crowded hill among the endless rolling slums.

But it tore Ryan apart.

In the weeks that followed, he was unable to sleep. He crumbled. In his shared trauma and tenderness with this one wanted barrio thief, Ryan had touched something greater than this world had to offer. And the world killed it.

I found Ryan in his room minutes after he had gotten the news. I sat next to him and put my arm around him, but also rested a hand on his stomach as he trembled, not knowing why I did that. The excommunicated mystic Meister Eckhart wrote about God being birthed in us continually, similar to the way God snuck into our world through the womb of a suspect teen-ager. Whatever faith or hope or love was growing inside Ryan died with that night's news. I felt the stillborn beneath my hand. The motorcycles roared on outside the open balcony.

And they kept roaring in the months that followed. It was hard for Ryan to celebrate John's new joy that endured long after our visit, his holy fool laughter and refreshed motivation after years in the trenches. While a deep furnace was now lit within veterans John and Birgit, Ryan dropped into a rapid decline. He'd seen the darkness win. How cruelty reigns. It got to him. He saw his neighbors shutter their windows when the man next door made his wife scream every other night, fist after fist, often out in the street. When Ryan mustered the courage to confront this man, knocking on the iron grate, his neighbor came out of his house and pushed Ryan down a half flight of concrete steps. He told Ryan he was going to tear Ryan's face apart. When the landlord let Ryan know not to mess with that guy, he has a gun, Ryan didn't come home for three days, hiding at a friend's place two barrios away.

He and Corrie still worked with local children to make a colorful mural on the concrete walls that said *PAZ,* peace. But the gut punch had already hit with Calimero. The blows that followed were like kicks when he was already down. Like when he and Corrie got out of the barrio for one night, to eat at a nice restaurant in Caracas with a visitor in town to talk with them about living with trauma, and the restaurant was held up at gunpoint. Ryan forgets if any shots were fired. All he remembers is watching the gun, how close it was to their table.

He dropped the missionary gig, returned to his native Southwest in the States, and continued to fall apart. He felt like a failure, a quitter, a punk-ass dreamer who'd had his ass handed to him. He tried to bury himself, or arm himself, in some utopian community experiences in the desert, but these collectives were full of cynicism, mostly young people filling their evenings with empty sex and their daylight hours with desperate language of revolution. One girl in his class had an AK-47 tattooed up her back. Ryan moved back into his parents' house. He read Tolstoy's pacifist manifestos and hid his face behind a growing, unruly beard. He became a vegetarian, tutored the children of migrants crossing the Mexican border into Arizona, studied permaculture—any way to opt out of the world's violence and predatory order.

But he was alone, and sinking.

I wanted him to join us in the Northwest. Though he now counted himself among the fuckups, I wanted Ryan to join us. I persisted in recruiting him with the same glow in my bones that fires up when I meet guys in the dumps in jail, men who have lost faith in themselves, like I had, in their own ability to do good. I'd come to experience how God goes after not just the unwanted outcasts—calling them, inviting them out of the places we've dumped them—but also those of us who have dreamed big and been crushed, who have given up. Those who have seen the ones they love be mishandled, who have let hope and faith disarm them only to be thrown against a wall by cancer or divorce or corruption in their clergy.

I wanted Ryan because I wanted a friend. And I needed a fellow recruiter of *malandros,* what Lil' Jokes said he wanted to be. I knew, though, that Ryan wouldn't want to work for a religious organization again. So I tricked him. I persuaded him to visit us up in Washington for a week, a vacation from the desert. To see me and Bob, and maybe some September salmon home from distant oceans, laying new eggs in the clean shallows.

Just as I'd hoped, after one week here—I remember him dancing to loud salsa music with Ramón's and Evaristo's kids in our little roach-friendly kitchen—Ryan canceled his return flight. He moved into our apartment at Tierra Nueva. He shared a tiny room with Ramón, who now finally had a white friend who could understand, and fire back, his rapid Juárez Spanish. Ryan went to the jail with Bob and me, week after week. He took notes when inmates in the circle spoke about their dreams. At night, we'd sit outside my window on the fire escape. Ryan would ask Rachel about her grad school classes on early childhood development, attachment theory, the effects of trauma on children, and abnormal psychology. He asked Rachel and me, in our many months of engagement, about till-death-do-you-part fidelity, "how beautifully unnatural" it was. His beard shrank, his hair shed the bandana, most of the wooden earplugs came out.

Ryan—like Teddy and Juan before him—needed the green Skagit landscape to heal his traumatized nerves, to smooth civilian reentry. He spent a season volunteering on a friend's organic farm, picking purple bush beans off the spindly stems, kneeling in the dark soil under white clouds sailing across the blue sky. Most Saturdays over the next two years, he would disappear into the cool forest, walking among the mossy and towering pillars. Bent sword ferns littered the canopy floor. It was a place disarmed.

He began to pray again, at first for others, like the weeping men in the middle of the circle in the jail multipurpose room.

Then for Ramón's daughter Rosie when she screamed at night, holding her as she slowly woke from nightmares of being left alone in dark parking lots. But more often Ryan laughed with Ramón late into the night, just on the other side of the thin plywood wall separating our low-ceilinged bedrooms.

Sometimes I thought about Calimero's shack. Were more young people finding refuge there? And did they whisper to each other from both sides of that thin plywood wall, where the poster maybe still hung, the invitation to the banquet still posted? Here, many miles north, nearly a hemisphere away, I sometimes heard my housemates whisper to me, or to each other, on the other side of our bedroom wall, "Ey *güey*, you awake?" "*Simón.*" "I can't sleep. Could you—could you pray for me?" And many nights I fell asleep, or woke, to the sound of Ryan and Ramón's cackling back and forth, one-upping dirty jokes in their mix of Caracas-Juárez slang that I could barely understand. Their laughter nonetheless made me betray my eavesdropping and laugh loudly on my side of the wall, which startled them into silence for a moment before laughing all the more. The prophet Isaiah describes the angels he glimpsed in God's presence—seraphim, or fiery ones, on either side of the heavenly throne—calling back and forth, something he heard as *holy, holy, holy.* Most of those nights I think I was hearing the same.

WANTED VII

I WAS APPLYING TO SEMINARIES THE WEEK RICHARD was dying. He and I had exchanged two letters in the weeks just before his end. I'd suggested he write his life story when he was back in jail, and his first letter from prison told me he'd started—that he had more than three hundred handwritten pages so far. He did not tell me, though, how he was itching by day or crying out at night. He also didn't tell me he was in the process of withdrawing his guilty plea, just waiting to take care of those medical issues before coming back to Samish County Jail to reopen his case with a proper lawyer. Instead, he asked me how Rachel and I were doing.

"So what you mean you going to seminary? are you happy?" his letter asked.

> *Will you stil write me or what, will you become a monk?*
> *You know I got mad respect for how you rep' the shit*
> *outta Jesus' gang. But what, now no more G.B. (God*

*Banging) for you? I don't understan, you already know ev-
erything you need to know, will you teach them something?*

While most inmates contemplate the mystery of their own
actions, or stew over the motives of their enemies and the system
in general, Richard was busy trying to figure out the reasons for
my behavior.

> *sometimes I don't know why you do what you do. don't you
> want more in life or would you do something else if you
> could? you can do so much more and have whatever you
> want in life, but no, you want to help people that can't be
> helped like me. . . .*

It was as if the nurse's response to "people like him" made
more sense: there was nothing more to be done. So it was my
interest in him that confused him. Farther down the page, he
asked two questions back-to-back. "Why do you love God?
Why do you love people like me and the homies?" They were
the same question.

In his last days, in these paper conversations, it was as if we
were back in our one-on-one pastor visits. But the roles were
curiously reversed.

> *It is about time I ask your ass something, que no? I remem-
> ber when you would ask something and you always wrote
> what I siad like it ment something to you. for me it showed
> that you loved me and that is why I love you as a bro*

homie. not cuz of god but cuz you showed me love. Well Im
going to go cuz Im going on . . .

Why don't you ever say Love Chris? Whats 'Laters'?
Wow . . .

Love Me
Lil' Jokes

Richard came limping back to his cell after his last visit to the medical wing of the penitentiary. He told the inmate in the cell next to his that the medical staff had called not the nearby hospital as he'd hoped, but the prison's superintendent instead.

"Obviously somebody somewhere knew what was happening," this fellow inmate later wrote, "or what was going to happen." This same man, already embraced by Richard as a friend, had been passing to Richard, through the bars, several bottles of his own generic anti-itch cream that he bought with his own commissary money to help soothe his neighbor's endless burning. "He personally told me that the Superintendent of the prison took the time to bring him a liability form to sign," but "luckily Jokes didn't sign it. If I were to send a kite [inmate request form] to the Super, I wouldn't get a response for weeks. Yet in this situation it was important enough for the Super to come down here into the Walls . . . to save his own ass." If this inmate's allegation is correct, then Richard refused to wipe their legal end for them as they dumped him like waste from their system.

It was slow. Still wincing in pain, he was passed out of the prison walls to St. Mary's Hospital in Walla Walla around dawn.

They take patients from the prison all the time, and so the doctors and nurses have the ethically and emotionally loaded job of fighting to save the lives of men they know to be convicted criminals. Men who had hurt, possibly even murdered or raped, another person. So: did they know that the tattooed young man being wheeled through their doors that morning (no doubt loud with foul language in his anguish), who showed signs of advanced internal gangrenous infection, still had thirty-four years to go on the public dime across town? Did they know he was convicted of murder in the first? For the death of an elderly woman? What they *did* know was that he was dying and was beyond their hospital's capabilities to save. He would need an emergency airlift to Spokane, and quick.

"It normally takes one hour to helicopter a patient from St. Mary's in Walla Walla to us here in Spokane," the doctor told Richard's surrogate mom April in the days that followed, after Richard had died on her operating table at Spokane's Sacred Heart Medical Center. The waiting doctor didn't know who was responsible for the unexplained twelve-hour delay after she had already okayed the transfer. She was rattled. "We could have saved him, easily."

———

"So I can't understand why you would want to go back to school so you can learn all there is about god's son." Richard wrote one last letter to me, stuck on this question there in his cell, possibly between hollering in pain through the bars to the nurse down the hall, though he said nothing of it in the letter. He never told me he was burning from the inside. "So I wanted to tell you, you know I believe in god and his son, but at times I feel like he don't give a fuck about me, so why should *I* give a fuck about me?"

Richard died facedown in the surgery room of Sacred Heart, much of his left hamstring and buttock removed along with his rectum and scrotum. At age twenty-six, he literally rotted to death in prison, from the inside out. But the final cause of death, the unnerved doctor had pointed out, was not the necrotizing fasciitis (flesh-eating disease), nor the unreported internal trauma from which the bacteria grew. No, Richard finally flatlined from two cardiac arrests he suffered during the surgery attempts after sundown. His heart, literally, could take no more.

SAINT CHRISTOPHER
ON A KAWASAKI

I HATE MOTORCYCLES. NEARLY EVERY TIME I'M SIT-
ting at a café or outside at a restaurant, someone rips the
sonic fabric of the air as they zoom by with an expensive rocket
pinched between their legs. There's the high-pitched, surgical
zing of Japanese models that slash through your brain like a
Skilsaw as they pass. And there's the customized Harley exhaust
rumbles that feel like twelve boulder-muscled and tattooed arms
rushing you and socking you in the ears and stomach while you
try to sip your coffee. Each time I want to throw a rock at their
tires. Maybe send the sadist flying, launched from the eardrum-
and-soul-sawing machine, liberated into the sky while the bike
explodes below. Then the rest of us can go back to enjoying the
afternoon sunshine and chirping birds.

I'm also just scared to death of riding one.

So on my latest trip to learn in the slums of Guatemala City—for research, for inspiration, for escape—when my friend, nearing-mentor, and host for the week named Shorty, a stocky and muscle-bound former gang member, zipped up his imitation leather jacket and handed me a heavy white motorcycle helmet, I swallowed and felt that rock lodge in my throat.

"There's no car," he announced. "This is all we got, homeboy." He nodded at a royal blue Kawasaki Ninja waiting under a lone streetlight on the corner where we stood at ten P.M. "It's the only way you're getting home, *güero*." That's what he calls me each time I'm here—*güero*, or whiteboy.

Home—for that night, and for the week I'd be there—was the "rehab" household Shorty had started way out on the edge of town. Over the years, he had filled it with lives he believed God called him to take in from the streets: tattoo-faced gang youth, abused orphans, stumbling old drunks, crack-addled hit men for hire, and other urban throwaways who had lost their families (and some their very minds) in the storm of the streets. The way they'd all sat down around a broken table for dinner the last time I was here, how their clear eyes smiled at me and welcomed me to sit on one of the small plastic stools at the table among them, had loomed in my mind for two whole years. It was a glimpse of something I've wanted in my own life, what Richard had helped us imagine around the jailhouse enactment of the banquet: to create a home, a table, where the unwanted from the cracks and dumpsters of society are gathered together for a taste of heaven.

That image in my memory, of Shorty's table, had become a kind of religious icon for me. I had tried to re-create it back in the Pacific Northwest: inviting men I met in the jail and on the streets to come and share life in my apartment in that funky old Victorian building when they got out. But the icon hung not on my wall; it was fading in my memory. And so I had returned to Guatemala City, traveled more than a thousand miles on several jets, like a modern pilgrim, just to spend more time in that hidden house. To once again touch—and briefly inhabit—the image.

But there was a problem. Between the bed they had prepared for me at the rehab household and where I stood now, there lay a treacherous city, and a motorcycle was my only way across it. I considered turning back.

I looked over my shoulder.

Shorty and I had just climbed a winding ad hoc maze of concrete and chicken wire steps, up out of a massive ravine in the heart of Guatemala's capital city where an estimated five hundred thousand souls still managed to survive. They call it La Limonada, the largest urban slum in all of Central America. Gangs proliferated in the gully behind me. Businesses—even some law enforcement now, unless clad in riot helmets—refused to descend into that community. It was what they called a *zona roja*. A red zone.

"Wait here while I swing it around," Shorty said while firing up the engine.

When I'd followed Shorty hours earlier down into the dense labyrinth of improvised shelters, the sun was setting. At first the wash of orange-red light made one narrow passageway look like an old Italian villa alive with all the ragged laundry hanging in the sunset, lines crossing between the windows just above with vibrant veils of color, filtering the cooling air with that sweet and pungent all-purpose soap I've smelled everywhere in Central America. But then we took a sharp turn, down curved steps with gang graffiti emblazoned across the stucco walls, and suddenly we were deep in the corridors of an urban inferno, each tight corner either black in shadow or ablaze with the sunset's reddening light. The air was thick and hot, smelling of urine, burned tortillas, and bad marijuana. But Shorty walked with ease, a cheery gangster-swagger, how Richard walked across the multipurpose room to invite the other homies like Danny and Oscar to the party. In this way, Shorty walked ahead of me like Richard's ghost, an incarnation of what Lil' Jokes had been becoming before he was thrown away—a recruiter for the heavenly banquet.

Shorty had hummed under his breath like a man out on a Friday night going to visit his girl, his beloved. He was a Guatemalan John of the Cross in the slums: *In the happy night . . . O night more lovely than the dawn, O night that joined Beloved with lover.* His hair was gelled carefully, his XXL striped polo shirt clean like his baggy (and hemmed-short) jeans, both creased according to strict codes of Los Angeles *pachuco*-style ironing zeal. These he learned after riding atop Mexican trains and crawling through Arizonan deserts alone at age twelve to flee Guatemala's civil wars, surviving on the streets of L.A., commanding his own gang by age fourteen. How he was found by love, a strung-out addict on the streets, how he surrendered to it on the point of throwing himself away—"God, you don't want a piece of trash like me," he'd mumbled on the ledge of a high building before weeping, "but if you want trash, then I'm yours"—and how he crossed back over to Guatemala . . . that's another story.

I'd followed Shorty deeper into the slum. I'd walked in the wake of his sweet cologne, and this fragrance, and the sound of his voice greeting old ladies in small doorways seemed to transform the cramped space around us all. Sullen young men waiting in the dark intersections two feet wide smiled when Shorty came through. They exchanged familiar handshakes and banter with slang I did not understand as I stood close behind my low-statured guide.

Now, hours later, I considered clambering back down there for the night. The blue Japanese motorcycle up ahead made me more nervous than any shaved-head *marero* could, decked out in the same color. During past visits here, Shorty had taken me into several prisons, usually the gang-only sectors. I still felt safe. But not on motorcycles. Not at night. And definitely not in this city's raging currents of maniac traffic.

"How much you weigh, *güero*?" Shorty asked, and he handed me the round white helmet.

I told him I weighed around two hundred pounds. His eyebrows rose. He laughed nervously. We didn't need to state the obvious—that my long legs and six-foot-three frame with a massive round helmet would make for a comic burden swaying on the back of this aerodynamic craft at sixty miles per hour through traffic. That is, it would have been comic if it weren't also a life-threatening part of the physics equation at high speeds. And I knew they would be high speeds, remembering how Shorty had fired us through the capital in his lowered and battered Honda on previous visits.

"God told me to give that car away," he said while straddling the bike and sliding on a pair of clear, curved lenses—the kind of safety glasses you have to wear before turning on a belt saw in woodshop. "One day, God told me to bless another family with that car, homie. A family who really needed it, know what I'm sayin'? So I did that. And now I got *this*." He roared the throttle just slightly. "The Lord is *good,* man."

I hiked up my jeans and threw a long leg over the extended seat behind his back. My size-thirteen sneakers fumbled for the tiny chrome peg on which I would rest my life.

"And put on that helmet, dawg."

I pressed my large head into the snug casing. My vision was narrowed, half-blinded, by the visor.

"So I just hold on to you?" I asked, my breath warm inside the helmet as I loosely hugged Shorty from behind with both arms, stomach to back, the way I'd seen passengers do in movies.

"Whoooooa-hoaaa! Hold up there, homeboy!" He threw out his elbows, knocking off my hands, as if his life were already threatened, before we even took our feet off the ground. "I got real love for you, dawg, but I can't let you ride with me like that. This is a *macho* country here, Guatemala. You can get killed for that kinda shit."

He explained that I could reach one hand, and one hand only, *around* him and press it against his chest only for a second or two when we'd accelerate, so I wouldn't fly off the back of the bike. And then I should drop that same open palm down onto the body of the cycle to brace myself when he threw on the brakes. "And you gotta use all your strength, *vato*. I'm serious. Or else you're gonna crush my ass."

Shorty had experience in carrying others, both in the literal and figurative senses. And he had experience in being crushed by their weight.

So how, I wondered, would I hold on as we swerved through traffic? He told me before I asked: there was a tiny strap tight across the seat between us. I was to grip only this. Like a rodeo rider. That was where my other hand would be through the whole half-hour journey to the outer limits of the city—right between my legs, like a man about to wet himself.

With a wobbly lurch forward, our feet left the ground and we were flying. The grim ghetto walls fell away from us on both sides. The bike pulsed into higher and higher gears, emitting higher and higher pitches of sound that I used to experience as violent noise from a distance. But now, joined with the motorcycle, each loud gearshift registered differently within me. I felt my eyes and mouth open wide within the helmet. As the bike jumped forward with greater power and I saw the red dial on the dash surge from forty to sixty, I did not hear what felt like screams charging from my throat. I did not hear what could have been my own ecstatic laughter as the wind raced over us, slicing through the streets and leaning deeply around the corners. My ears were too full of the drone from the motor beneath us. I felt the motorcycle's cries rising through my bones, joints, and senses.

"*¡Agárrate, güero!*" Shorty shouted from his unprotected skull—*Hold on tight, whiteboy!*—and two diesel trucks closed in on us from both sides, red brake lights lighting up all around us. I leaned in and held my breath. We shot through the merging urban freighters, and their horns did not even blow in concern for us. I swore I could feel their rearview mirrors brush against my speed-inflated sleeves, rippling like a plaid cotton aura around my skin in the night.

————

Back home, I keep a real icon on a shelf above my desk. It is of Saint Christopher, my namesake. One of the oldest saints in the history of Eastern iconography, he is commonly known as the patron of safe travels. I'd learned the legend of this figure behind my name only two years earlier, from a homeless youth I met in San Francisco's Mission District. He needed a ride to L.A., and folks at the agency I was visiting told him I was headed that way with my sixteen-passenger church van full of colleagues like Ryan and ex-gang members like Ramón and Teddy on our tour of various gang ministries down the West Coast. This gutter punk wore double-stitched Carhartt pants that were almost as shiny as blacksmith's leather with soot and oil from a hundred nights under park bushes and by freeway on-ramps. His long, black, and matted hair stuck out from his trucker's hat with its deeply curved bill. Tattoos were his sleeves.

"No way!" he glowed when we first met. "My name's Chris, too! And this is my dog." A huge pit bull jumped up onto the bus's rear bench.

"What's its name?" an annoyed Teddy asked as the reeking animal crawled over his shoulder.

"That *is* his name," Chris said. *"My Dog."*

As we sailed down the dark Interstate 5, past miles of mono-crops and rest stops, Chris told me the legend of this martyr from the third century who had become the patron saint of travelers. According to tradition, he was a wild man, tall and strong, who lived by the side of a river and helped travelers cross to the other bank. One day, so the story goes, a child came to the riverside and asked for his help. The boy was all alone, like an orphan. The man hoisted him to his shoulders, and when they reached the middle of the charging river, the child felt heavier than anyone else the man had borne over the water before. He felt as though he were "carrying the weight of the world" on his back. When they finally arrived safely on the other side of the river, the man had one of those legend-like epiphanies: this small child now facing him had been Christ in disguise all along. And just as suddenly, the child disappeared. This is how the man became known in Greek as *Christophoros,* or Christ Bearer.

When our dirty bus parked alongside the star-paved curbs of Hollywood late that night, Chris thanked us and said he needed to make a call at a pay phone for a friend to pick him up. He and My Dog disappeared into the city's moving lights, and we never saw them again.

I have since recognized this saint he told me about—the bent-over figure with a staff in his hand and the river's waves up to his knees, a child on his back who is radiating holy light—on many small necklaces worn by the Roman Catholic migrants in our foggy agricultural Skagit Valley. These people have left their homes in Mexico and crossed the treacherous U.S.–Mexico border to pluck a new life from the north, one plastic bucket of pennies-a-pound blueberries at a time. San Cristobal is the tiny *santo* kissed on their sweaty fabric pendants and tucked back into T-shirts as these families cross impossible distances and barriers, from one life to another, uncertain whether they will make it alive.

The painted woodblock of Saint Christopher above my desk has become a symbol for me and my emerging vocation. I live alongside a large salmon-laden river in the Northwest, and like my namesake, I am tall, though not very wild. As a jail chaplain and pastoral worker among young gang members, I have found my work in accompanying these North American orphans through turbulent legal and existential transitions. I walk with them through their criminal and immigration courts, through airport security, through drug and alcohol treatment programs, through relapses, job interviews, university classes, drivers' tests, broken hearts, emergency rooms and shotgun wounds, maternity wards, parenting classes, fly-casting lessons, cold river baptisms, and sometimes, finally, into a shared home to raise their children together with me and others.

The icon's imagery helps me see a simple narrative in all this: the men are crossing over from one life to another. Rivers, like the Rio Grande, are barriers. Dangerous ones. What strengths I can offer—like my education and privilege as a tall, white male with no criminal record—enable me to navigate the lawyers' offices, online credit-card-only portals, streams of paperwork, crosscurrents of collections agencies, court payments, and fees at every department. These all comprise an intimidating barrier to a vulnerable young man with tattoos secretly wanting a better future on the other side.

In the slightly bent Christopher figure, I see a shape for my ache as well: not just weariness from ferrying guys all across town in my car, but an invisible spiritual weight, another's anxious heart and restless dreams that temporarily have no footing, riding on and trusting my own flexing hope, barely fixed on what I see just ahead.

In this legend of the river-crosser, the border-crosser, there is a spiritual geography of transition. It is a metaphor I can hold like a map. It helps me see where we are: when I sense one of these guys in recovery suddenly cling to me in a choking relational grip through months of transition, and then when I sense an ease and his weight suddenly sliding off. I know we have crossed that river when we see each other face-to-face, on the same level, as friends, as members of the same community, the same household, and even my wedding party. And at this point we share the radiant sense that somewhere in the middle of those late nights and jail visits, the long drives to impossible court dates and laughter beside a river where we'd fish, the weight of terror we bore together for a moment was also filled with a mystical presence we did not understand at the time.

That is what I see in those traditional yellow circles looming behind the heads of the ferryman and child in the icon. Not crowns of saintly status, but the simple shape of intuited mystery. Those yellow circles are what have kept me going back and forth between the jail and our shared housing all these years. It is the curve of invisible ultra-presence that the human eye could not recognize at the time. It is the indefensible knowledge that the stuff of heaven I've always sought was, for a moment with this criminal youth riding on my metaphorical shoulders, heavy upon me.

In this legend, then, there is a shape to the hiddenness of God. A shape rather like a lonely kid wanting to be picked up on the side of the street.

I could hardly see now because I was squinting against the air speeding into my face. Through the blur of my watering eyes, I could barely make out the iridescent yellow lane markers, darting in and out of the tires beneath us. So I risked bringing my left hand up to close the visor on my helmet—just in time to see the nose of a taxi stick into our narrow path. I reached under Shorty's brake-squeezing arm to brace myself against the motorcycle's body with all my strength. He braked hard. The front of my round helmet rested against Shorty's shoulder, and my knees pressed in to squeeze the bike. Being carried like this is not a passive experience. It's not like sitting backseat or shotgun in a car. I was already sore, perched like this, pinching new muscles just to hang on. I had to watch the road as we leaned together, around the near collision and into the ascending full-circle on-ramp that washed us into the rush of a major highway.

"That was good!" I thought I heard Shorty yell, the back of his gelled, spiky-haired head turning slightly, possibly calling to me through the tumult.

I wondered whether he was afraid, whether he was as unsure as I was that we would make it unscathed to the house. Motorcycles didn't scare him, of course. He knew these streets from childhood. This was his daily commute. But he might have been having second thoughts about his ability to stay upright while carrying—in me—such an awkward burden.

The Kawasaki hushed to a soft rumble as we turned into a downtown district. It was after hours, and all the storefronts were boarded up. Guys on the corner glared at us. Heads in the alleyways turned and followed us as we passed. Shorty had told me about several anonymous threats made on his life during the past year. They could have been from gang leaders losing recruits, drug peddlers losing customers, prison officials losing secrets and scapegoats—he didn't know. He was a threat to them, a thief, every time he welcomed another trashed life into his home.

Shorty's whole body bent, looking back over his shoulder and down a small street. He was searching for someone; that is why we'd come through here on the way across town. *But we can't pick anyone up,* I thought. *There's no room on the bike to carry another.*

A car with a tinted windshield rolled slowly out of the alley beside us, its rear window halfway down. *"Agárrate, güero,"* Shorty said quietly. I held on, my hand pressed against his jacket and chest. He turned his wrist and we tore down the shadowed street faster than any car could even reach second gear.

––––––––

I thought of our destination, the rehab house out on the rim of the city. On my last visit almost exactly two years earlier, Shorty had dropped me off there for a few hours—with my now-fellow-comrade Ryan—while he took care of other business. "Just kick it with the homies there till I get back," he'd said as we pulled into his loud barrio, Canalitos, high on the outer hills of the capital. "They won't bite." He'd looked at me out of the corner of his eye and laughed.

Minutes later Ryan and I were standing in a cramped alley and knocking on the rehab's rusty metal Dutch door. It was something like the Rothko painting I'd stood before in college, like a portal. Light seeped out all around its edges. It smelled like a dog had been peeing on it. A fat gangster named Wilson with a soft voice and round tears tattooed below his eyes opened the top half with a loud creak. He gave us a nod and let us in. We spent the afternoon sitting among the laundry lines in the cement courtyard hearing the stories of each man living there. We heard how Wilson was in prison when Shorty visited him and offered a place to live here when he got out, hidden from the gangs. We heard how buzz-cut Taco couldn't inject enough heroin to erase the images in his mind of all the men and women he'd been paid in drugs to murder as a hit man, and how his sister knew Shorty was the only "pastor" who would accept her traumatized killer of an older brother. We heard how never-hurt-anyone Raul was tired of being lonely and asked whether he could move in to this curious house where he heard music and laughter in the evenings. We heard how several of the residents decided to take in the drunk old man in the plaza, Tomás, who now smiled and nodded shyly at his name while he set up plastic cups around the table in the spare courtyard for supper.

One quiet guy with an intense stare and red Converse high-tops around his bare ankles leaned against the wall and said nothing the whole time the others told their stories, looking like a bored intellectual. Then he casually interrupted, crossing the space between all of us while another was speaking, came directly at me to shake my hand, then Ryan's, and then turned back just as abruptly to his post in the doorway. Minutes later, he did it again, shaking my hand very seriously. Then a third time, always shaking my hand, as if I didn't understand how welcome I was the first time, his other hand patting my shoulder while he stared into my eyes. That's Hardy, they told us. *"No habla."* *He don't speak.* His mind was blown from years of huffing glue in the alleys all alone. It was clear everyone here looked out for Hardy, though he'd been a resident the longest. He'd probably never recover, they said with a smile, and he would never be kicked out. He was loved. He was family.

And there was Alejandro. He was a shifty teenager with what could be called a baby face—shiny, dimpled cheeks and long-lashed brown eyes that still seemed to sparkle. He grew up in La Limonada and his parents had recently asked Shorty to help their troubled son. Alejandro admitted to us that only days earlier he had been high on crack-laced weed, robbing bus drivers at gunpoint, shouting at the passengers and waving his shotgun over the families in their crowded seats.

Wilson later whispered to Ryan that it was Alejandro's seventeenth birthday that day. He was worried because Alejandro was feeling bad about himself, and he'd shared with Wilson his plans to slip back out to the streets and pull another shotgun on some bus for birthday money, maybe buy some new jeans or shoes, a gift for himself. Ryan had an idea: a few of the guys snuck out with us, escorted us down the dirt road to a store window, and bought two liters of Coca-Cola and some sweet bread from the bakery. We would all celebrate Alejandro together. Back at the rehab, guys hollered with bellowing congratulations to their young housemate. Hardy got so excited he unzipped his fly and took a leak against the inside of the front door, in a manner that seemed guilty but regular. Wilson pushed an un-marked CD into the old stereo and the others all sang along with the swelling track, something I'd heard on the polished religious radio stations. But it now sounded like nothing I'd heard before as the unlikely choir of society's unwanted men shouted with off-key passion into the warm evening, *"Me viste a mi cuando nadie me vió . . ."*

> *You saw me when nobody saw me*
> *You loved me when nobody loved me*
> *You gave me a name . . .*
> *I love You more than my life*

I heard a sharp whistle outside in the alley. Wilson unlocked the door and Shorty's stout, weight-lifter's frame was there, soon slapping handshakes that pulled each house member into different embraces, one at a time, each full of laughter and nicknames. It was the only time I saw Hardy smile as Shorty pulled him into a headlock and asked him whether he'd showered today: *"¿Te bañas, Hardy—o te baño?"*

He smiled at me across the group as if I were his best friend, English our own private language. "So wassup, *güero*? You keep these *vatos* in line or what?" He sat down like a father at the head of the table and offered thanks for the beans and rice Tomás served in neon plastic bowls before us. There, with a few warped candles on the table lighting up the scarred and smiling faces of old men, teenagers, Hardy, and fat gangsters with tears tattooed down their cheeks, all seated together, I sensed I was inside a living icon, or portrait. It was the kind of family that only something holy could make. It was the banqueting table Richard had helped us imagine, from the pages of the trashed New Testaments, now living flesh and bone. The good and the bad, Guatemala City's throwaways, were invited from the streets and prisons to partake of a heavenly joy in this cinder-block hilltop house. I didn't want to leave. Apparently, neither did Alejandro. He never left for the streets that night.

The next day we all piled into Shorty's Honda—seven of us— to play soccer at the city's main complex of courts. Alejandro was on my team, and he was the best. Shorty took off and returned half an hour later, ferrying another crew of guys across town from La Limonada to our games, eight bodies weighing his overloaded sedan into a lowrider.

I missed that car now, on this return visit. On the motorcycle, I felt the road getting rougher. We sped off of the smooth municipal streets and up the steep hill toward Canalitos. There were no streetlights, and only our trembling single headlight searched the cracked asphalt racing under us. We hit crude pot-holes. We leaned deeply into the curves, around blind hairpin turns that cut into the hill's exposed side. Suddenly a pickup truck's bright lights swung around the corner at us. Shorty veered to the right, close to the edge of a drop-off. For a moment I wasn't sure I could hold on, my grip on the strap between my legs weak and numb. I was slipping, in more ways than one. As the high-speed thrill of the ride slowed on this hill, I began to slide back into the despair that I'd come to Guatemala to flee.

That is, I had just learned, less than an hour earlier, that not everyone Shorty carries over the currents of chaos makes it to the other side. Back in La Limonada's ravine-slum, Shorty had taken me to the one-room home of an older couple. Their youngest son had recently been gunned down by enemies, the father told me. We'd stood beneath the corrugated metal awning behind their house, and the passing hour of tropical rain was loud against it. The mother was sweeping, pushing the dust into the darkness where their patio dropped off and the sewage-filled gully running through the basin of the slum's ravine roared with new street water. She stood silent with the broom in the rain and wiped her eyes. He was not quite nineteen, the father continued. His birthday would have been this last week.

I thought of Alejandro's birthday, the cola and sweet bread and song two years earlier during my last visit. Then I did the math, and the world seemed sadly smaller. "Was your son's name," I asked, "Alejandro?"

Shorty told me the story after we left, as we climbed up the winding steps toward the waiting Kawasaki. Enemies had been after Alejandro. He'd been slipping back into old patterns after getting clean at the rehab house and moving back to La Limonada with his family. On the way to the soccer courts one day, a car pulled up alongside their crammed Honda at full speed, and two firearms emerged from the windows. Shorty said he threw on the brakes and peeled into a back alley, like a chase scene from a movie. "We got away that time." Then weeks later, Shorty said, Alejandro and friends called him for another ride to the courts. But Shorty had given the Honda away by then, he himself bumming rides at that point. "I told him to walk, I'd meet them there." So the boys walked—up out of La Limonada and across two *zonas* of streets to get to the courts.

But Alejandro didn't make it to the other side that day. "Those other homeboys, they saw him walking. They blasted him, bro."

Shorty had been carrying me at high speeds this night through those same violent streets. The streets—they are today's equivalent of the turbulent waters roiling around Saint Christopher's legs, the menacing gray curls in the wooden icon above my desk. The streets can swallow you.

Not everyone makes it across.

The motorcycle groaned in a low gear now, still turning switchbacks up the hill. Clinging to Shorty's back on the Kawasaki, I felt like a child, an orphan in this foreign country. I was feeling what it is like to be carried across a spiritual transition.

I came here because I had recently reached an impasse in my own work up north. As a pastor, a shepherd, I had lost too many. They'd been assaulted and had rotted behind bars. They'd been dropped over the Mexican border by forces much stronger than me. Guys I'd known for years but who had been just out of my reach had been turning from drive-by shootings in rival neighborhoods to more direct forms of suicide: syringes of crystal meth in their neck veins, Russian roulette with loaded Glocks to their temples, wild shots at state marshals in broad daylight because the return fire was better trained than their rival's retaliation—nearly guaranteed to hit the target. As they'd drowned in the despair of the streets, rotted in prison, I'd felt myself starting to sink as well, thinking, *My work is useless; I'm chasing illusions, fantasies of what could be, beautiful or not.* I'd returned to Guatemala because I suspected Shorty could carry me to some grounded hope on the other side of all these currents of death. To that house where I might be reminded why I continued doing this with my life, and decide whether I wanted to bother continuing in the years ahead.

And I'd wanted to see Alejandro.

All this heaviness had fallen away when I first climbed onto the bike and we pushed off, the bad news forgotten in the thrilling blur of speed through the streets. But now, climbing up out of the city so slowly, trying not to fall backward off the bike on this steep hill, my heart grew heavier. The despair weighed more profoundly on me than ever. I wanted to go home. *This trip was a bad idea,* I thought.

But I couldn't turn back now. I could only hang on to Shorty. By this point I was unable to keep myself from holding him with both my arms. This must be what the homies feel. Shorty did not shrug me off or say a thing as I maintained this tight embrace the rest of the climb up the black hillside.

———————

We eventually pulled into the quiet hilltop barrio of Canalitos. The city's asphalt receded behind us like water from a steep riverbank. Here, the smoothed dirt roads with a few homemade speed bumps made the bike rise and drop beneath us. We turned into the small plaza bathed in the light of streetlamps, and I saw our shadow run alongside us for the first time. In sharp silhouette against the empty soccer courts, I saw a tall figure riding high, clinging to the back of a short figure hunched forward. It was a reversal of the Saint Christopher icon, now framed in cracked concrete. I was normally the one carrying another. But now I was feeling what it was like to be carried through my own chaos and despair, trying to hold on tight. Now I had to trust someone so different from me with my life, neither of my feet touching the ground.

We were almost home. I began to relax. I thought of stretching my arms out, flying-style through the easy streets with all their windows and doors sealed up, not high in the sky but close to the ground, like a large white trumpeter swan swooping the barrio night. But I didn't. I kept them around my carrier, and no longer for safety. I leaned in, as if I could extend the ride, maybe loop around the sleeping neighborhood a while longer. I was no longer eager to get to the rehab house, its table or beds or laughter. I was at home where I sat, in need and carried on someone else's back, not quite there.

The plaza on our right fell away, and very suddenly I found myself facing our full reflection in the dark glass of a storefront window. The oversized round helmet was where my head should have been, shining brilliantly under the yellow streetlights like a mock halo. It was Shorty's. He had insisted I wear it.

DONACIO'S TABLE

THE TABLE WAS IN THE DUSTY BUS DEPOT PART of town, in the ugly industrial rim of Guatemala City. It was back behind a fleet of red and chrome buses being renewed with buckets of soapy water slopped over their bullet-riddled fenders. I stepped over the bus yard's chain and squinted through the low sun.

I was nervous.

The man I had come here to meet, the man sitting alone at the crude wooden table in the shade up ahead beyond the buses, the man who just whistled at me sharply, had been waiting for me all afternoon. And this man, Donacio, was not someone you kept waiting.

Like Shorty—who had just dropped me off here and driven away—he was a "rehabilitated," tough, tattooed ex-gang member who had experienced U.S. prisons and deportation, who had been both a perpetrator and a victim of extreme evil. And like

Shorty, he had felt the call to go back into the shadows, the prisons, with the same love that found him in those places. He felt at home in terrain far beyond where most missionaries dare to go. When he and other such chaplains who preached in gangster slang first took me with them into the crowded prison corridors a few years back, I had found a resurrected form of Richard Mejia. But unlike Shorty and Richard, Donacio was not quick to smile, to let me know we're okay. And on this day, I was not sure whether we were okay.

———

I sat down opposite Donacio at the large table. It appeared to be where employees of the small bus line took their lunches. An old woman was slapping tortillas in the nailed-together shed adjacent to us, one gas burner glowing blue in her dark kitchen. Donacio was just finishing up; he leaned on his elbows over the remains of a plate of rice, beans, and fried chicken legs. He sucked last bits off a small greasy bone and dropped it in his plastic plate, all without taking his eyes off me.

I hardly recognized Donacio since the last time I'd seen him. His head was no longer shaved gangster style. Instead, he had trim, gelled-back hair. He was wearing khakis and a striped, fitted dress shirt with long sleeves and French cuffs that covered the fully tattooed barrel arms so apparent on past visits. He looked like he'd turned into a businessman.

During this trip, I'd heard rumors that Donacio hadn't been visiting the prisons for a while, that something had gone wrong and he'd lost permission from the government administration. (Or possibly the gangs inside the armed walls had cut him off; they, after all, have the ultimate say.) Some said he was in danger, maybe had a price on his head. He had distanced himself from the other chaplains and the now-expanding nonprofit ministry organizations of which he was once a founding and central figure.

Shorty had warned me when he dropped me off, just minutes ago: Donacio had changed. I wasn't sure what he'd meant. So, I assumed, even one of my heroes had fallen away. Rumors among other former comrades in the city hinted that Donacio had been swept away not by the chaos of the streets, but by money, the rat race. He had an upwardly mobile hustle going on. A new distance had grown up between him and the others, including me: he'd hardly returned my texts during this trip, and the warmth was gone from his voice when we talked on the phone. I came out here because I wanted to cross this divide between the chaplains, between us, before returning home.

I apologized to Donacio for being so late.

He didn't answer me, but checked the time on the cell phone that rested on the table between us.

I was late because I'd spent the morning with two of the other chaplains in a prison full of Mara Salvatrucha (MS-13) gang members, young men with torsos and foreheads covered in macabre webs of fading ink, some of Guatemala's highest-profile young killers. We'd played basketball and read the Bible together in a caged courtyard. The chain-link roof was so low that none of my jump shots reached the hoop. The hot sun above cast the fencing's gridded shadow over our Bible pages.

I was eager to visit that prison because I'd been there three years earlier, in that same cramped courtyard. I'd brought Bob with me, insisting he meet this crew of chaplains in the same volatile country that first had radicalized him decades earlier. So, inside this MS-13 compound, Bob did what he does best: he led a discussion with the circle of inmates over a Gospel text, where Jesus calls Matthew the tax collector. "Who are the tax collectors in today's society, here in Guatemala?" Bob had asked in Spanish. The young men laughed nervously. Gangs like the Mara Salvatrucha are notorious for their extortion rings, threatening to burn down businesses and often opening fire on city buses for not paying the "protection taxes" to the regional gang. Their laughter said it all: there we were, sitting in the den of Guatemala's tax collectors and thieves.

The Gospel text in our hands described Jesus calling a notorious tax collector to be his key disciple. "Follow me," Jesus says to Matthew in broad daylight. But in the next sentence Jesus is over at Matthew's house, eating with more "sinners."

"So," Bob asked the lounging crowd among the laundry yard's ad hoc hammocks and cheap plastic seats, "who followed whom?"

It was hard for them to say out loud: Jesus follows the tax collector. He doesn't bring them to temple, to church. He doesn't have a building. He follows the ones he calls deeper into their worlds, and disappears, for a while, with them.

Afterward, Bob asked whether one of the inmates could show him to a toilet. A high-up leader named Spider, an oversized totem of scars and bodily calligraphy, personally escorted Bob back into the private halls of improvised "cells" whose walls were made of plywood or hanging, faded blankets. Aside from the toilet, Spider also showed Bob his own personal cell. Only in this privacy did Spider ask for prayer. Bob offered him a gift, what he had in his backpack throughout this trip: a CD of contemplative flute music. The gang leader put the disc in his small plastic player. The flute and soft synthesizer soundtrack lilted through the dark air while Bob laid gentle hands on Spider's scarred heft and blessed him.

Then, hours after we left, Spider called our hosting chaplain. The chaplain emailed us that night how this *ranflero*, or head of the gang, had stammered to describe a rather significant mystical experience that had taken place throughout his mind and body during Bob's prayer. Something had made contact, a touch that made this noted villain feel treasured.

But two weeks later Spider and three other men were abducted from their cells in the middle of the night by tear-gas-hucking militiamen with masks. The four inmates were taken to a different prison and assaulted by the other inmates as soon as they stepped off the bus. Spider and the others were quickly decapitated, their bodies burned, their bloody and tattoo-masked heads used as soccer balls and then lined up along the barbed-wire fence for the media vans and cameras. (Guatemalan news web pages don't censor such things, so I saw Spider's lifeless head among the others from the safety of my laptop in Washington.) It was an act of public catharsis and sensational political theater. The message was clear: this government administration was cracking down on gangs.

The chaplains later forwarded to us what they had learned: it was a setup job. The attacking inmates at the second prison were paid by the officers to dispose of the new arrivals. But the money came from outside. The city's bus drivers' union had put together a large sum for the prison administration to "take the heads off" of the gang networks. This was the bus union's reprisal for years of gang extortion: teenagers like Alejandro daily mounting their buses and threatening—and sometimes massacring—their drivers, and passengers, with loaded shotguns.

Our encounter with Spider was just a glimpse into the ongoing civil war where these prison chaplains labored daily to communicate the gospel. You eat together with a notorious sinner, let flute music fill your ears with a new song, and then a darker human justice intervenes and sticks the guy's head on a fence. A spiritual pattern emerged for me, regardless of the country: if you treat those you find in the dumpster like treasures, like Calimero, they could be snatched back and disposed of more permanently.

———

I broke the awkward silence and asked Donacio whether he still visited the gang prisons.

"Naw, man. I gotta work." He picked up a dusty smartphone and pointed to the bus yard around him. "Gotta pay the bills to survive. Take care of my family."

Donacio picked at his teeth, then set his light hazel eyes on me.

"You know what *you* need? What all these Christians and pastors need? A *real* job."

Donacio said he didn't work with the missionaries anymore, the well-networked organizations with money. "We see too much money flowing. Too much money . . . and people aren't doing what they said they'd do." He paused and stared at me across the table.

Two days earlier I'd made plans to meet with Donacio this morning, and he'd set aside much of his day to take me around the city, show me what he had been up to since my last visit. But I'd called him at the last minute and rescheduled so I could visit Spider's old prison instead.

"On the streets," he stared even harder at me, "you get killed for that."

I swallowed.

"*¡Seño!*" he called to the old woman in the hut. "*Una Coca más, por favor.*" He motioned for her to set the chilled bottle of cola on my side of the table.

"Christians, man," Donacio shook his head and laughed. "They talk big God stuff. But it's just *makin' money.*" He sucked the gristle off the last chicken bone.

I was feeling defensive. No missionary I knew who was connected to these street and prison projects in Guatemala was in it for the money. No one was getting rich, nor passing any baskets at large gatherings. And further, I don't like being lumped in with the sort of Christian religion I thought I'd fled years ago.

Maybe, then, Donacio was talking about the local mega churches. Like the famous City of God, where sixty thousand of Guatemala's wealthiest conservative Christians drive in from the gated suburbs in the hills around the capital to hear TV-radio evangelist Cash Luna preach the prosperity gospel in a billion-dollar stadium-plex perched in view of Central America's sprawling urban slums.

Or maybe Donacio *was* talking about me. After all, I'd begun to write grants and make small appeals to sustain our small "gang ministry" in Washington. And a big part of the funds so far go to my small salary as a pastoral worker. I see such fundraising as both natural and necessary, but maybe this was what Donacio was referring to when he said Christians "use the poor, the gangs, to get money for themselves."

"That's why I left Refugio Joven," he continued, knowing I'd be asking what he'd been up to since I had last seen him two years ago. Refugio Joven, or Youth Refuge, was the government-funded NGO where he was working when we'd last said goodbye, where he worked a desk job connecting youth leaving the gang life with employers who would give a tatted *pandillero* a chance. He offered job skills training and brokered tattoo removal services. "Just money. That's all it was about there. They didn't give a shit about the homies if a USAID grant came up short one year, making their paychecks a little lower. *Fuck 'em,* was their attitude. I left cuz I wasn't seeing no love."

I grew irritated with Donacio. I "wasn't seeing no love" in this embittered man across the table from me, apparently stuck with a job he didn't want in this lonely bus depot outside of town, styling his hair out and buying slick shirts, turning his own back on the homies when organizations couldn't pay *his* bills for loving the lost. I felt the tension between us at the table.

But I remembered I'd come here to listen. To learn. I'd funded this latest trip with a research grant I'd written about how these men from the streets whom I'd met—like Richard

Mejia and Ramón and Neaners, Shorty and Donacio—see what church insiders don't, and about how we the well-meaning whiteys need to learn from them, and let them lead.

So I bit my tongue. And something began to happen.

The seats at the table around me began to fill.

A beefy guy with engine grease on his hands, no older than twenty-two, slid into a seat next to Donacio. He slid with him a cracked bowl full of canned-tuna ceviche, from the woman cooking under the lean-to near us, and began to eat hungrily.

"This is Fermin," Donacio said. The young man lifted his head and nodded at me, having heard only his name. (Donacio preferred to continue in English with me, both to brief me on a sensitive backstory and to enjoy the taste of his years in Houston now back on his bilingual tongue.)

He told me he first helped Fermin through Refugio Joven but then went beyond the organization's protocol to help the young man in trouble with his gang life. Only now did I notice the long, distorted sections of skin on Fermin's thick arms— whole swaths of incriminating tattoos had been partially removed both professionally and home-style, with peroxide. Donacio said he took a personal, pastoral interest in Fermin, helping him start a clandestine sewing shop where other guys leaving the gangs could find honest work to support themselves . . . and not be found by their former comrades and enemies.

"Sewing makes enough to support them?" I asked.

Donacio shook his head. "He's got three jobs. His second one is here in the bus yard, with me."

"What *is* your job?" I finally asked.

"I'm a consultant," he smiled. "I know gangs. And gangs are the number one problem for any bus company in Guatemala." He told me he educates the drivers about things like which routes require added security, how to tell whether a kid leaping on board with a weapon is only bluffing, and how to best coordinate with honest law enforcement. Drivers call him on one of the two cell phones sitting by his elbow on the table: to be a negotiator between regional gang leaders and the bus company's management. "Sometimes we gotta pay. I decide if it's worth it."

Three more young guys took a seat. They rolled their tortillas like edible spoons and shoveled them into the heaps of simple lime-and-radish-soaked tuna. I realized this was the perfect job for Donacio. Not only did he have a unique skill set to serve this small bus line, and not only was he himself paid instead of looking for international donations, but now, instead of trying to persuade small employers to give these guys a chance, he *was* the employer. I turned and saw several young men standing on buckets, wiping down the last buses rolling in.

"We're supporting eight homies now. Helping them go to school. Fermin here"—Fermin looked up—"after he finishes his meal, he's off to his night classes. A few more credits and he's off to *university*, man. A formerly violent dude like Fermin! You believe that?" Fermin's mouth was still full. He nodded and smiled at his name again.

Two more guys sat down beside me, just having clocked out from a day's work. One of them was not an ex-gang youth, but a middle-aged man with a few white hairs. He was one of the bus drivers.

"And these guys are the victims," Donacio lifted his head at this man, as if curating the curious tableau of fellowship assembling around us. "The victims of the gangs we've been working with all these years. I see both sides here. These guys, the *choferes*, they're not bad people, man. They just drive the buses—and they get killed. Check out this guy's neck."

He pointed over my shoulder. "*Paco—muéstrele al gringo lo que le hicieron, por fa.*" Show the gringo what they did to you.

The gentleman behind me lifted his chin with a smile and I saw a long, waxy scar spanning his collarbone and neck, up to one ear.

"Some fool pulled a machete on him. You believe that?"

Donacio seemed on a roll, the would-be professor in him rising as he saw me racing to scribble in my notebook, now out on the table.

"That's the last one," he said and pointed behind me. I turned to see another *chofer* approach the table on crutches. One leg, below the knee, was missing. "*Bombazos,*" Donacio whispered, then nodded when I turned back in disbelief. Shotgun blasts— what each *chofer* feared when someone like Alejandro climbed aboard with a bandana covering his face and a sawed-off locked and loaded.

I could not yet assimilate the scars, the crutches, the stories, or Donacio's intense eyes, all closing in around me now. So I looked down to my notes and tried to piece this all together. Donacio, I gathered, was not as alone as I'd thought.

"When you say, *We're supporting eight guys,*" I asked, "who is *we?*"

He told me he and his wife. And Fermin, who helped pay for other guys' needs from his own earnings. Fermin also led a discipleship, or training, group, Donacio said, that met twice a week in the hidden sewing shop. He told me about ten other guys. These new disciples being adopted out of the streets and gang networks had become Donacio's "we." There was no "us" (a professional ministry class) or "them" (the gang youth who receive help). No, Donacio was building his "ministry team" out of the ranks of the gangs. Not out of seminaries or local churches or international volunteers.

I told him he spoke less like they were a mission organization and more like they were a family. A *growing* family.

Donacio's face seemed to light up when I said this. He wiped his hands with a napkin, swallowed, and snapped his fingers across the plate at me. "That's *it*. Family." He leaned forward, licked his fingertips, and looked around the table.

"Jesus is with us, bro," I heard him say while I wrote some of this down. "That's all we need."

For a moment I thought that sounded like a self-protective remark, a we-don't-need-anyone-else attitude covering years of hurt and frustration with the church. But as I looked up and saw Donacio's eyes celebrating the full table of ex-gang members and bus drivers, former enemies passing and pulling apart tortillas among themselves, victims and perpetrators quietly working and ending their day together, I heard Donacio's words as a kind of priestly proclamation. The kind of thing a minister says at the culmination of the mass from the other side of the altar, announcing the Lord's presence in the breaking of the bread. It was what Jesus himself promised his crew as they ate together the night he was arrested, before he himself was torn apart the next day.

I now realized that a lifetime of training under the eucharistic ritual in places of worship had barely prepared me for this moment: to recognize right before my eyes, in this bus yard, the feast of an alternative kingdom already among us. The good and the bad were seated here together at the banquet—the banquet Richard helped us imagine. I was witnessing a table being set before these bus drivers in the presence of their enemies. The lions sitting down with the lambs. The wall of hostility torn down. Or rather, the bullet-laden walls of the red buses between these two street classes were being mended and washed, the doors restored and left wide open, even as we ate.

I have often preached—usually at tables of friends back home who've come to see me as the token pastor, their only religious friend—that on the night before his death, Jesus relocated the center of sacred communion from the altar to the common table, from the temple to wherever we sit and eat. Jesus pushed the act of atonement outward: from the house of worship and the hands of priests to the outskirts of town where he gave himself, hidden among the dust and criminals at the end of the day.

I had preached this, but still I was slow to see it here at the lunch table, incarnate before me.

Indeed, this meal was so peaceful, so mundane, that it had taken me half an hour to realize what had snuck up around me. I was witnessing one of the most authentic signs of reconciliation in this city, one of the most beautiful accomplishments of gang ministry I had ever been near. This was beyond what I'd hoped to find in my return to Spider's prison that morning.

And there were no documentary cameras filming. No media flashes for the papers. No mission committee planned this special outreach meal or hired pastors to bring opposite sides to the table for one hopeful, press-friendly afternoon.

Rather, we were all here because this unpolished rogue, Donacio, had been faithful to his call. Or, as a former gang member, he was loyal to carry out the mission of his barrio—Christ's barrio. He would do this whether he had ministry support and recognition or not.

I thought Donacio had given up since he had moved off the radar of career ministry. But I was wrong. He had walked with guys like Fermin beyond the NGO's social service boundaries, keeping him close and helping him develop as if he were blood family. Now Fermin was reaching and leading others. Some of those others were here with Fermin and Donacio, here with the wounded bus drivers at the table. The homies were here because they worked all day with the *choferes*, repairing and cleaning these buses they drove. The drivers laughed at ease with the youngsters because the tattooed bodies around them were genuinely transformed.

I wanted to celebrate all this, call attention as an outsider to the glory of what I was witnessing among them. I grabbed my Coca-Cola bottle and asked Donacio whether I could say a few words.

"Naw man," he shook his head uncomfortably. "That'd be awkward."

Donacio had ditched his cooperation with the established church, and he resisted my itch here to ceremonialize it, to raise my voice.

I'm still learning to keep silent, not always report the rogue presence when I glimpse it, bump into it. This is difficult. Sometimes I'm able to look the other way. Other times, the only thing to say is the haunting, priestly claim that Donacio used—with an under-the-radar hush and a wink—while looking over the table he'd helped gather, there in the unlikeliest of places: *Jesus is with us.*

FIRE IN THE HOLE

S INCE I WAS A SMALL BOY, I HAVE OFTEN TRIED TO
imagine what it would be like to be locked in a small cell,
entirely alone for months and years. I'd make a nest of blankets
in my closet and slide the door shut. See what happens. People
change in a solitary cell.

Some have been criminals. In such prison cells they often lose
their minds. Like the documented case of Robert Felton. At one
point during this man's fourteen years in prolonged isolation in
a Virginia prison he began ripping apart his mattress, stuffing it
into his pillowcase, knocking out the light fixture for sparking
wires, and then setting his cell ablaze. He did this so often the
walls turned black.

Some have been saints. Like John of the Cross, who spent
nine months imprisoned (and occasionally tortured) in a
cramped dirt-floor cell outside Toledo, Spain, during the
sixteenth century. He found a different spark in his cell: a flame

of passion and unity with God there in the darkness. He fell in love. The poetry he composed in that space to "the Beloved," including what later became his *Dark Night of the Soul,* was so explosive that when his reduced frame eventually slipped out a tiny window for the open fields, the spiritual canticles he'd composed on smuggled parchment went on to ignite a mystical awakening across the continent.

I thought about all this when I last visited my friend Neaners in the maximum-security prison's solitary confinement wing. He had been changing. He had been a criminal most his life and was now, possibly, becoming a kind of saint. Recently, he introduced himself in a letter to a church this way: "My real name's José Israel Garcia. I've always gone by Neaners. But in here they call me Huesos, or Bones, cuz I'm so skinny. I'm twenty-nine, in a cell, tatted up in the face and arms, doing nine and a half years for blasting my ex-homeboy." But now, he wrote to them, he wants to do what I do. When he gets out, he wants to work alongside us at Tierra Nueva in the Skagit Valley. "Know what I hunger for, homie?" he'd written me around that time. "This might trip you out, but I'm serious. I wanna be a pastor."

As we'd written letters all these years, he'd learned about what Ramón was doing with us, about Shorty and Donacio in Guatemala, and he wanted in. Like Richard, Neaners had started to feel himself wanted by God. He too was eager to join the mission of recruiting more of the unwanted to the banquet. But after Richard's early death, his insides rotting and burning while in a prison's segregation wing, and after seeing what happened to Calimero in Caracas, then to Spider in the Guatemalan prison system, and to many others like Edgar who had been

barely touched by the desire of God before the system disposed
of them, I'd started to worry whether my friend Neaners would
be taken out too, whether he'd make it out alive.

———————

I'd driven four hours to see him on a summer day. It was the
time of year when strawberries grow red and round and sweet
under their green leaves in the Skagit fields, when the sky opens
up to a high blue vault again, when the muddy Chevy Astro
vans full of the families from southern Mexico return to our
valley from California along I-5 and the winter-chilled cabins
in the labor camps are filled with the warmth of sweat, crowded
and exhausted bodies, playing children, and blue flame burners
under blackened pans of handmade tortillas. It was on a Saturday, a day I normally would have taken my old fly rod up a local
river. Summer steelhead would have been returning from the
sea and laying their orange eggs among the stones, like tiny orbs
of fire under the clear and shallow snowmelt. But something
else was happening, in a solitary confinement cell many miles
away, something I wanted to connect with even more, something that does not happen every year with the regular rhythm
of sea-run trout.

At the time, Neaners was detained in a prison out on the
Olympic Peninsula, the farthest northwest thumb of our state
that reaches away from the nation and into the cold Pacific with
miles of rainforest, jagged glaciers, and violent coastlines. I'd
sped off I-5 and down remote two-lane roads, beyond the cities
and thinner green forests, and four hours later finally pulled into
a clearing. Ahead of me slouched the grim prison compound,

double-wreathed in razor wire. This is the place where hundreds of unwanted people are dumped, busloads arriving every week. The transfer station prison. Here they are evaluated, first-timers stamped with a number, and, within weeks, sorted and sent to the several human warehouses across the state.

And Neaners—the leader of a Mexican gang who had first dubbed me their pastor, who first called me *carnal,* or brother, first called me out into the night of my valley to shepherd his flock and to interrupt his gang meetings, to break into that mossy and padlocked trailer for his orange box of personal treasure, to find him in seedy motels and talk and pray with him while the town slept—he'd been living in this prison world, shipped between these warehouses, all the years I'd been learning how to pastor his homies on the outs. Even his "ex-homeboy," whose foot he "blasted" when a sawed-off shotgun they were loading for a drive-by shooting accidentally fired, blowing the ex-homeboy's ex-big-toe through the floor of the trailer's kitchen. The hole was still there last time I checked.

And now Neaners was in the hole.

—————

I'd slowed my car beneath the first sniper tower and waited for the security camera by my open window to look me over. The intercom voice asked me why I was there, and I'd named one of the souls locked deep within those walls: *José Israel Garcia, number 816-567.* Inside the bare lobby, I'd left my keys and wallet in a locker, passed through a metal detector, submitted to two pat-downs, let the officer inspect the small digital voice recorder I'd gotten special permission to bring for this visit, waited for a gate to automatically groan open, handed over the last thing on my person—my ID—to a uniformed man behind a glass window, and waited for a second gate to groan wide. I'd walked through the loud room of tables where men in all-khaki clothes and shoes with Velcro rather than laces sat with their mothers and children and girlfriends and ate chips and drank soda and played Candy Land and squeezed each other's hands for their few hours together. I'd waited all by myself for a third gate to open at the end of the loud room, and now finally stood facing the long empty corridor to the isolation wing. The gate slammed shut behind me.

It was silent. The walls were white. The floor was squeaky clean beneath my shoes. Through the double-paned windows to my left, I saw three more layers of spiraling, hurricane wire fences between the bleak yard on this side and an evergreen forest on the other. Though it was summer outside, it was cold in here. There was no smell, nothing for the senses to fix upon. That, in itself, I imagined, could induce madness. This was a sterile environment, nothing like the vibrant alleys or even the teeming prisons I'd been visiting in Latin America, nothing like the lush Skagit Valley where I lived. Here, life is not encouraged to thrive.

Early in Neaners's time in solitary confinement—prisons often use the Intensive Management Unit (IMU) to quarantine gang leaders and to punish any involvement in gangs' violent politics—he mailed me a diagram he'd sketched of his ten-by-seven cell. Small arrows he'd drawn pointed to where in the small rectangle he slept, where he did jumping jacks, where he took "bird baths" between the stainless steel sink and toilet combo, where he sat at the tiny "desk" slab and prayed and wrote and drew that very drawing. After Rachel and I got married, and moved to Montana for a year, then moved back to the Skagit Valley, I kept this solitary cell diagram pinned to our refrigerators with a magnet—right next to the blueprint he'd also drawn of the farm he imagines building with others at Tierra Nueva when he gets out, a place where other "unwanted, unloved" young people can learn to plant flowers and vegetables together, sing together. The drawings of the cell and the farm, side by side, speak to me.

I'm interested in how one thing can be used for another purpose. Like a Molotov cocktail: take a liquor bottle usually used for its subduing powers, empty it, fill it with a different substance, fuel, add fire, and when it breaks it becomes a bomb, a tool for subversion. This creative reuse ethic is the imagination behind all sacrament. Take this ordinary bread, this cheap juice or wine, this broken marriage, unglorious things, lift them to a mystery we can never fully understand, and you might have the substance of heaven disguised in crude form, something charged with possibility to toss into a mean world. It's how things that don't belong in one place—like a bomb in a disarmed town— can suddenly appear. Prisoners, people in captivity, understand this instinctually. They know how to make a tattoo gun out of a tape cassette player, a guitar string, a hollowed pen, and some burned chess pieces. Or hard liquor out of grape juice, dirty socks, and patience. They understand transubstantiation.

So as I walked down the corridor toward the isolation wing, I thought about Neaners's solitary confinement cell, the drawing on my fridge, the simple, cruel design. There were many of these down at the far end of this corridor. Solitary confinement is the greatest threat leveled at prisoners in our nation, the cross of our age looming against the growing prison horizon, what happens if you go against the regime. You will be left absolutely alone. Across state lines, it has different names. You can "catch another program in IMU," be "put in Ad-Seg" (Administrative Segregation), or "get tossed in the SHU" (Security or Special Housing Unit). But whatever it's called, the hole is the deepest pit at the bottom of our system. I wondered, then, how Neaners had undergone what seemed like such a beautiful transformation in such an ugly place. Could the hole itself become something other, be repurposed? Could these cells themselves be hollowed of their punitive power, filled with another more potent substance, lit with a divine fire, and so become something subversive deep within the human disposal system?

I have no desire to romanticize these cells that have been called both hellholes and human rights violations. I'm even hesitant to use the world *romanticize*. But over the course of Neaners's many months in one of them, as we wrote back and forth, it sounded as if a kind of romance had broken into even a hellhole.

During his first few months in solitary confinement, Neaners's letters were hard for me to read—because of both their legibility and their emotional content. His loopy handwriting on blue-lined paper described pulse-racing anxiety attacks that pressed his hands against the white cinder-block walls. "I get those in a daily way," he wrote early on, "so I gotta be careful that I don't get too excited or too down. What sucks more is if I take a nap, I will get an anxiety after I wake up. So I get up at 6 am and won't let myself go to bed till 11:30pm or midnight. I hardly sleep anymore. I'm afraid to look out my cell door window because then reality sinks in that I'm caged in a lil' cell." In his single hour outside the cement box each morning, he could make overpriced phone calls and get his exercise by doing pull-ups or walking in circles in a bare, kitchen-sized space—which they still call a "yard"—while guards watched. "Sometimes it feels like these guards pick and choose who to fuck with," he wrote. "They can put us in the hole for years, it seems, just on hearsay. Allegations from another inmate. I'm serious. Like that guy you told me about in the documentary"—Robert Felton, the man who torched his pillowcase—"who'd been in the hole for fourteen years. How you said they kept him in there for more and more infractions, and how before he was locked up in the first place he only had nonviolent offenses."

We kept writing back and forth. Soon he began to name the pain. "Sometimes I get so fucking lonely, it hurts."

There is an old saying passed down from the early Christian monks who fled to the desert and locked themselves in small rooms. Abba Moses told his monkish comrades, "Your cell will teach you everything."

But that cannot be true.

It can't be the cell itself that transforms and instructs a soul. This is why: an estimated eighty thousand lives in the United States are currently wasting away in solitary prison cells now labeled "administrative segregation." This is not a new development. Our nation's corrections industry began with what some could argue to be a naïve and literal application of Abba Moses's theory. That is, nonviolent Quakers in Pennsylvania believed that criminals need not be hanged or flayed for every offense. Rather, they thought, some time alone, apart from society's corruption, with ample silence to pray, might restore the men. Restore them to themselves, to God, and eventually to their community. And so began their houses of penitence, or "penitentiaries." Despite some of its spiritual intentions, however, the experiment did not go as planned. The formula didn't work. It was not like a solitary retreat. Men were not restored. They went mad. The Quakers eventually shut down their Eastern State Penitentiary decades later, but by that time hundreds of these prisons were being built across the land. Rampant mental breakdown was, and has been, the ongoing result of this American isolation solution. When the men cannot leave whenever they want, as monks can, psychological deterioration is often what their cells teach them.

So this is my question: if it's not the cell itself, as Abba Moses said, then what *does* turn a cruel and tortuous existence of isolation into one of spiritual transformation? The whole Molotov cocktail question. I can't help but wonder about this, in an age where such painful places are multiplying in our country. Not only does our nation incarcerate more of its own people per capita than any other, and not only are we building new prisons at a rate that's quadrupled while the crime rate has hardly increased since the seventies, but our use of prolonged isolation to handle inmates within those prisons is steadily growing. Activism and legislation are important means of resistance. But as a chaplain, I am interested in that elusive spark that saints have found in captivity, some mystery that can slip beneath the doors of suffocating solitude and light the human heart like a prayer candle.

As I walked the corridor alone, I remembered the first time I'd walked down this sterile passage to the IMU wing—with Neaners's five-year-old daughter Adelita at my side. In pigtails, red tights, and patent leather shoes, Adelita had reached her hand up to hold mine as we went deeper into the prison. Her small presence at my side had taken the chill out of these halls as we'd walked—even skipped, which she had suggested with wide eyes. The balding guard in heavy boots pacing toward us from the other end of the hall, who in past visits had only mumbled scornfully at me, now bent over—as we halted our skipping—and removed his glasses to ask Adelita her name and compliment the red ribbons in her hair. His bristly moustache had widened into a smile. Once inside the tiny visiting cloister at the end of the hall, she'd looked through the scratched glass. That was the day she sang "You Are My Sunshine." To this day, when I read the mystics who talk about "visitations," I cannot help but think of this. Neaners told me in letters that, before that visit, he hadn't cried in more than fifteen years.

Those early monks who went out to the desert famously cherished tears as a sign of God's presence. "First pray for the gift of tears," wrote Evagrius the Solitary, "so that through sorrowing you may tame what is savage in your soul." It was not misery that made Neaners crack and tear, but mercy. It is God's kindness, Saint Paul wrote in a prison letter, that leads you to repentance.

In the months that followed, Neaners began to really weep. "I feel now that I have let down my guard," he wrote, "and am trying to put down all my hardcore attitude and let go of hurtful emotions, I'm real fucken sensitive. Like a child, bro. A baby who you yell at and who cries. I cry for everything, bro. It's beautiful."

It sounded like the cell had been emptied of its intended punitive power, since Neaners was allowing himself to become increasingly vulnerable in there. "You know these anxiety attacks I get, this loneliness, the times I feel betrayed or just lost, I'm starting to let it all open me more to God. If it's yelling at him, or cussing him out or just asking questions, it's coming from my heart and I'm not holding shit in anymore."

Neaners started to sound less alone. He was reading as well. But not the trash romances and Dean Koontz thrillers that guys consume to "kill time." Deep within the pages of an old Bible he'd checked out of the library cart that rolls by the open cell slots once a week, Neaners found a companion in the prophet Jeremiah. "This Jeremiah is *sick,*" he wrote. "It's crazy how long he kept faith in jails, in a damn well. He's a strong *vato.* Like us." A modern criminal in a sterile prison cell found a connection with this ancient prophet. Jeremiah's cries helped give shape and direction to Neaners's anguish. That must be why monks for centuries have risen early to sing in unison with the words of the prophets and psalmists, forming their mouths and hours around this tradition of anguish and intimacy aimed toward heaven.

"I wanna read more of his story because it says in my Bible that they called him 'the weeping prophet.' Not like a crybaby, but he cries of all the shit going on around his *gente*. That's like me now that I'm letting my guard down. I've seen so much, and after all these years I can't stop crying. It's kind of like where he says *Oh that my head were waters, and my eyes a fountain of tears*." Jeremiah helped Neaners trust these tears that he'd been avoiding his whole life. "Almost every day now, something makes me tear up, for deeper reasons than I understand. I used to stop it. All my life. But now I just let it flow. It's beautiful, bro." His letters contained the word *beautiful* so often, you'd think he was falling in love.

"It's just so fucken beautiful to know I'm God's babyboy."

Such tears, I've considered, could constitute a kind of spiritual kerosene along which the invisible fire runs. If so, his cell was now being filled with a new, spiritually potent substance, a Molotov cocktail waiting to be lit.

Maybe it already had.

———

In the first stanza of Jeremiah's Lamentations, it says, "From on high He sent fire into my bones." Neaners's letters became more passionate. He used more pages, filled fatter envelopes that arrived with their prison stamps in my mailbox. I kept them in a small cardboard box, then a large moving box, many of my favorite passages like this one underlined in red: "Homie, I'm just soaking and letting God's love marinate in my blood. What trips me out *hard* is I don't even try. It just all comes to me. Like a waterfall, a crystal clear waterfall, fallin down some rough, ragged rocks, splashin down to a beautiful clear blue lake."

"Check this," another one of them began,

> *all the clecha [gang term for training, skills, wisdom] I have, from grinding the streets for jale [drug sales], to gang-banging, to playing women and so on, I'm not going to use it for the bad reasons anymore, but I can use it still for good causes, for God's work. Like helping youngsters before they start gangbanging. Or helping educate ignorant fools who only see us as flaws on society. Or supporting other homies in the changes they're trying to make out of the street life, but who feel stuck. You feel me, babyboy?*

Neaners went on to quote Jesus's parable about a treasure buried in a field, the kingdom of heaven hidden in what looks like a worthless patch of dirt. "Treasures don't gotta be diamonds and pearls. Sometimes treasures lie within us. And that's my treasure. It's not to be used in a wrong way like I did for years. It's got some big value on the streets, don't get me wrong. But when used for good, it's *more* valuable."

The criminal behavior in his life, all that society understandably wants to cut off and dispose of by locking him in this prison cell—it had been found valuable now, by an unauthorized presence in there with him. He and his street skills were wanted. His

letters were dispatches of a mystical rebellion against the criminal justice system: some spirit was breaking into this prison cell
and, in true dumpster-diving fashion, stealing what had been
thrown away, what the powerful had discarded, prizing it as
treasure. The material of this felon's life, locked in dumpster cell
IMU N-C-7, way outside of town, was not being incinerated as
trash but being recovered and made pure.

"Damn," he wrote on the very next line, lit up by his sudden
gleam of insight, "this *clecha* is just flowing thru my veins!"

———

I finally arrived at the bay of visiting cloisters at the end of the
corridor. Numbers were stenciled above each heavy door. Neaners was waiting for me behind one of them. I looked through
the small window of door number seven (the one they assigned
to our visit that day) through wire-laced glass: no one there, an
empty booth. I opened the door and sat down. I waited fifteen
minutes. Then I stepped out and decided to check if they'd sent
Neaners to the wrong booth. (I'd learned to accept these errors,
though the corrections system never acknowledges its mistakes.)
I peeked into each tiny window down the row. Through the
last one, I saw Neaners slowly pacing on the other side of the
large cell's glass divider. He was wearing an XXL jumpsuit of
bleach white, one long strip of Velcro down the middle. There
was cursive script inked across his shaved hairline, letters and
numbers and tears down his cheeks, a narrow moustache and
a new, longer goatee covering the 666 below his lip. He looked
like a vision from the Book of Revelation. He wore small, black-
rimmed reading glasses I'd never seen before. Neaners saw me

through the window and smiled, tossed up that marked chin and threw his inked arms open wide. *"Wassup!"* he mouthed and kept smiling with a clarity and warmth I hadn't expected. He looked fully alive, eager to receive me.

As I opened the door, I felt more like I was coming home to an old friend, not making a prison visit. I waved and took my seat inside my half of the sealed room, on my side of the shatter-proof glass, and took the black receiver off its mount. But when the door clicked shut behind me, my throat locked and my pulse quickened. I was locked in a public bathroom behind a fast food Del Taco joint as a boy, and so to this day I can still get claustro-phobic in spaces like these. I spun around and turned the metal handle, opening and closing my door again, just to make sure I could get out if I wanted to.

"You okay, babyboy?" I heard Neaners's voice thin and elec-tric through the black receiver sitting on the small counter.

"Yeah, I'm cool."

Reassured, I took my seat. Neaners was still smiling. He nor-mally stares down, fidgeting, anxious during the first half hour of our visits, quick to speak then quick to change the topic, his thoughts fluttering like a moth against the glass after weeks or months without normal conversation. But on this day there was a peace about him. He seemed more whole, more present. I told him so.

"I've come a long way." He rested his chin on his knuckles on the counter between us. "It's not just how I conduct myself during visits. I still trip when I think that two or three years ago, I wasn't even giving a fuck about my daughters or *who* I was playing or manipulating." He seemed as interested in his change as me. "It's weird to say this," his eyebrows pressed inward as if he were preparing to finish a difficult sentence, "but this solitude has really brought me . . . closer to . . ." his eyes looked up and around the cell, ". . . *Jesus.*" He whispered the name. *"La neta,* man. I'm serious. I can really *listen* in here. I mean, I'm not even trippin' now on whether they make me stay in the hole another month or not. That's crazy, cuz I used to fucking lose my *mind* alone in the hole."

"I remember those days," I said.

"But now I can't keep up with all the letters I been writing, people I gotta get back to. Fred. Adria. Zach. Holly . . . ," he counted them on his long, inked fingers. "All the people you've put me in contact with."

While I was in Montana, I'd asked Neaners whether I could copy portions of his letters about Jeremiah and anxiety attacks and loneliness and prayer into emails and, with his permission, send them out to a select group of friends and supporters of mine scattered across the country. He loved the idea. "Just don't censor my shit. Or make it sound too white." I introduced his reflections to these friends as something "like Thomas Merton's *Thoughts in Solitude*—with tattoos and a felony record." Many of the email recipients wrote back after the first few installments and asked for Neaners's prison address. They wanted to write him, contact the author. It started with a young woman who was jobless after going to seminary. Unspeakable trauma and ritual abuse in her childhood had manifested in chronic physical pain during her late twenties, leaving her house-ridden and lonely, a different kind of solitary confinement. She eventually became Neaners's longest-running pen pal to this day, other than myself. Others wrote as well. A gay priest, a farmer and author, a Pentecostal pastor, an atheist, a divorcée, a painter, some of my old friends from Oakland and Berkeley, a lesbian couple now alienated from the church, as well as several suburban mothers—including my own, now in Colorado—who lead women's home groups and bible studies and who daily pray for him.

"And the guy," he counted more fingers, "who wrote that book you sent me—Brad, right? And your mom. I call her Mama Hoke. She's *cool,* bro!" He laughed, and I could only imagine the conversations they were having. "But today I gotta get to Adria's last letter. It's a super long one. She gets into some deep, beautiful shit, homie."

Even for hermits, one of these friends wrote to remind me, the Christian life is always lived in communion with the church, the community of other believers. Hermits in their self-imposed cells still have a spiritual director, someone who can point them to scriptures and forms of prayer. That person need not be clergy. He or she can be a layperson—a "soul friend," some monasteries say. Even John of the Cross, while prisoner in his coffin-sized dungeon in Spain, kept an illicit correspondence with persecuted nuns in nearby Ávila.

———————

I reminded Neaners that one of the things I wanted to do today was record his voice. Something to send out to this growing community of his outside these walls. I pulled out the small digital recorder the prison counselors had to clear weeks before this visit. But while getting a sample of his direct voice, I wanted to talk about the visions he'd been having in the hole. *"Simón,"* he said and straightened his back.

Earlier that year Neaners had started seeing the small farm when he closed his eyes and prayed. It was a place, he said, where teenage boys in gangs and girls who ran away from home and sold themselves for drugs and inclusion could finally be together and be safe. They would grow vegetables, sink their fingers into the earth, and have "pigs and animals to take care of." I'd suspected that this was not a familiar desire for him, not nostalgia for some childhood dream. I now asked whether this was true as I pressed the record button.

"Oh hell no," he responded. "I don't even *like* animals! It's not cuz a that. See, when I was growing up, I would look out in my backyard and see some drunk motherfucker vomiting over there and this drug deal going down over here and that motherfucker screaming at his wife over here and some little baby crying on the sidewalk without any Pampers. . . . I grew up even before that in migrant housing, picking cucumbers, raspberries, blueberries, blackberries all day. . . . I woke up at the crack of dawn and did everything. It sucked. But I *wanted* to get out in the fields, because out there I wouldn't get abused."

He tilted his head.

"Maybe that's why I want a farm. Why I think I keep seeing it, keep thinking about it. Somewhere outside of the hood, out on the land, where homies can just kick it and feel safe. Where they don't gotta be posted up, ready for war, but just chill, in their sweats and *chanclas*. A place for pregnant teenage girls where they don't have to depend on a man who beats them or pimps them. A place where abandoned kids can come and be loved, and also learn responsibility. I don't want to force work on them. I'm not gonna say, 'You gotta get up at six A.M. and go pick tomatoes *conmigo.*' No, they'll see me out there picking tomatoes and smelling roses and they'll want to do that, too."

I reminded him that this vision was already coming into being: other young staff at Tierra Nueva had started a small organic farm—in addition to the Underground Coffee roasting business and an artisan bread-baking shop. "There aren't roses, really," I told Neaners, "but there are tall stands of huge sunflowers."

"Siiiiick," he nodded his head happily.

"And there aren't tomatoes, but there's red chard and raspberries and kohlrabi. All sorts of crops. Like five different kinds of kale."

Neaners still nodded, but his face went blank. "Homie, I'm not gonna lie." He shook his head and smiled: "I have no idea what *kale* is!"

Four years into my time in the valley, I'd given myself full-time to the gang work and dropped the farm jobs. So for several years I hadn't thought about the fresh snap of harvesting chard, nor the deep purple of some varieties of kale in the long, misty rows where I'd knelt so many mornings. Instead, I'd fallen in love with all things broken and ugly. I'd grown bored with all the photogenic produce I knew I could always find for sale in perfect, chilled stacks at our local co-op. But in the same way that the Bible I thought I knew came surprisingly alive when I opened it with new reading partners in a jail, so my memories of these varied and hippie vegetables revived and struck me as rather magical as I imagined farming them with guys like Neaners. "Yeah, kale," I nodded. "It's badass."

We laughed. He rubbed his skinny forearms covered in dark murals of women and clowns and skulls and names of old girlfriends and deceased family members. "That's cool, homie," he said. "I'm lookin' forward to learnin' all about it."

I told him the guys and gals running the farm had even started looking into expanding, using permaculture methods, "right there at the new men's recovery house we might open next year." We'd been planning a beautiful and sustainable garden wrapping around the property, among the small apple orchard flanking the house, where men out of prison and off the streets' addictions could tune in to the quiet life of interdependent plants as part of their recovery. "That's our hope, at least," I said.

Neaners smiled, the permanent numbers and tears next to his eyes wrinkling behind the glasses frames. "Hope for Homies" was the name he'd recently given to his vision, this mission. He even wove me a prison crochet-style necklace with these words, using the blue threads from his underwear and white from his bedsheets.

"How are the homies doin' at Tierra Nueva, like Teddy and Ramón?"

I told him that since I had gotten married and moved out of the apartment in Tierra Nueva's old building—where I had lived for more than six years and where I had brought home several guys out of the gang to share life together—Ramón had taken over leadership in the home. He and Teddy and others were raising their children there, kids they'd worked to get out of the child protective services system. "It's amazing to see these judges' faces," I told Neaners, "who never expected to see tattoo-necked fathers reappear in court with a handful of legit reference letters, sober and with light in their eyes. When they see one of these guys fulfilling all their commitments, with a community of support in the audience behind them . . . well, judges aren't used to seeing that."

I told him how Evaristo was not only doing well, with his new legal papers, working with Teddy as welders and inspectors at the same company, but both had recently been approved as volunteer chaplains to go into juvenile hall with me. Our team of messengers, what Richard helped me imagine, was coming into being. The detention authorities broke with traditional policy to allow these volunteers to enter the facility with former gang affiliations, tattoos, and felony records. "Just last week Teddy was doing raps with kids," I said. "He got them singing and sharing their own rhymes."

That day in juvenile hall eight shy teenagers in orange jumpsuits and pink booties had shuffled into the rec room—young gang recruits, a girl with bleached hair dyed three different colors—and sat with Teddy, Evaristo, and me around small, bolted-down tables. We'd discussed a few lines from one of Paul's prison letters in the New Testament: *Fan into flame the gifts that are within you.* "We talked about campfires," I continued telling Neaners, "though only two of them had ever been camping. But then one kid said something that stuck with me. He said, *Yeah, if you don't keep the fire alive, everything around you grows darker and colder.*"

"So," Neaners asked, "how do you fan the flame—I mean, like the verse says?"

"That was our question." I told him Teddy's answer was that he served others. Teddy told the kids how he'd recently asked me if there was a place he could "help feed the homeless or something," because he missed feeling closer to God. I'd said that's why I still go to the jail all these years: *Whooosh,* fire of love reignites. It rushes through me.

"Yeah," Neaners snapped his fingers, "that's what I been feeling. Love for the homies and love for our jefe—like, at the same time. I mean, I'm pretty sure I'm not the only one with a fucked-up life, you know? I'm pretty sure there's people who had it worse, and I want to help them." Like Jeremiah and the other prophets, Neaners was receiving a greater imagination, the pathos of God glowing within him, an urgent desire for all the young men and women locked up in prison, seen as useless to society and wasting away in the projects.

This was the mark of the fire.

I recently found an online video interview of Bernard McGinn, a leading scholar in the studies of mysticism. He has spent his life examining noted lives like Julian of Norwich and Meister Eckhart, as well as the more marginal Beguine communities of laywomen in medieval Germany who sought direct contact with God, living at the medieval city's outer limits and serving the hungry and the criminals, reading the Bible in low, common language together. In the video, the white-haired and frail McGinn sat in his small office cell, encased with books. He said he believed that the work of the Spirit was still very active today. Not everyone has visions and ecstasies, he said, "but often just a very, very deep sense of God's presence in their lives . . . that transforms them . . . changes them. Makes them better people." This might have been his most plain speech on record about his life's work. "The test is love of God and love of neighbor. And as that gets deeper and deeper and deeper, that's the sign that God is really present. All the great mystics teach that."

"I don't gotta wait until I get out," Neaners smiled. He leaned forward. "That's why I'm gettin' started in here already."

"Getting started in here already?" I repeated.

He said he couldn't see the other men in solitary cells around him, many of them in gangs as well. But he had found a way to connect with them. His vision was already taking shape.

"Here, check this out." Neaners began to draw this shape in the palm of his hand with a small floppy pen the prisons issue so inmates can't stab themselves or others. He pressed this hand to the glass between us so I could see. "This here is the whole IMU unit, see?" The crude blueprint of the unit's layout looked like a cul-de-sac, his local community of solitary neighbors. "See, this is Monster's—I mean Hector's—house, right here, next to mine. There's Sicko over here . . . Lil' Rob here . . ." He guided me through his parish in the palm of his tattooed hand. "It's not exactly a farm, but I'm bringing some of the most unloved and unwanted motherfuckers in the state together, and we're kickin' it, eatin' together."

I was confused. "How exactly do you do that—you know, with the walls and locked doors and all?"

He lowered his voice even more now. "We go fishing."

Fishing?

Neaners explained in rapid Spanish, just in case our booth was actively tapped, how inmates make long "lines" out of the material available in their cells: elastic they carefully harvest from the lining of their boxer shorts, threads from their sheets and socks. They cast these lines through the cracks under their cell doors and across the empty space between locked rooms. For hooks they used twisted paper or plastic comb bits tied to the ends. With enough patience and persistence, the lines met and grabbed hold of each other. Then the lines became one and could move in either direction. "You know that verse about how we walk by faith, not by sight? That's how I pray, babyboy." He snapped his fingers. "And that's how I'm starting our work in here."

Fishing like this, he said, is usually used for passing drugs, or gang politics inside little folded notes, names of people to punish. "But I'm usin' it to break bread together, to share what I got."

Break bread? What kind of food could be fished between the locked and separate cells? What could slip through the cracks?

"Fireballs," he said, shaping a small circle with his thumb and index finger.

Fireballs?

"You know, the red candy."

Oh. I laughed.

As kids my friends and I would dare each other to put an entire Atomic Fireball candy in our mouths and see whether we could bear the surprisingly intense burn of cinnamon longer than the last kid, whose eyes would eventually water. We'd squeeze our eyes shut before spitting it back into our sticky hands. Whereas some candies only boast an extreme experience, the vintage Atomic Fireball truly delivers.

"Well, I crush it up into powder in its little packet," he pounded a fist into one palm, "until it's totally flat, see?" He lifted it in his fingers, an invisible sample. These he patiently fed to the others in the hole, blindly. It takes days, he told me, to reach each lonely inmate in the unit, make sure no one is left out. "It's a *mission*." That's why he'd been asking me to put more money on his account, he said—to help support his small "ministry."

He now pressed a standard commissary list against the glass, an order form for various junk food items available at high markup to inmates. "I know it's not organic vegetables an' shit yet. But you don't understand what it means to a guy in here, who has nothing, who has no one to visit him, no one who writes him or cares for him, like I got goin' on with you all. These homies got *no one*. Sometimes, late at night, I can hear 'em cryin' a lil'. So when a fireball slides under his door, it's not just candy, babyboy. That's *love* sliding into his cell. They can see it. Eat it, taste it. You know what I mean?"

Neaners was describing what priests call sacrament. I imagined the crushed candy in its wrapper: flat, pink, processed. A new kind of communion wafer. Body of Christ in the hole. And I imagined a young inmate in this sector, enduring the boring, lonesome hours in such a cell—then a tiny cinnamon packet slides under his door, tied to both his line and another's. He opens it, empties its contents onto his tongue. Love, here in the hole, tastes like sweet fire.

I felt something myself as Neaners told me this story. Deep inside our society's dumpster, something had actually transformed this felon's cell, his story, and now even his commissary into something completely other, holy. It was overflowing. The fire was spreading into the other cells. Neaners was enacting a priestly role, reaching people no chaplain could reach, creating fellowship in the world's most finely engineered isolation system. I'd been learning how the banquet Richard imagined was happening out in the world, in hidden places like Shorty's rehab and Donacio's bus yard. But now my friend Neaners was preparing a kind of table I'd never imagined, one that defied even prison walls. I would never see it with my own eyes, but he had given me the vision. He was taking them all fishing, calming their raw nerves.

And as with the early church's activities, this gathering had a cost. They could catch another six to twelve months in the hole if a heavy boot were to step on one of the fireballs skittering across the nighttime floor. Here, communion was contraband. Jesus's disciples were hiding from the authorities behind locked doors when something like tongues of flame appeared over their heads. Soon they were speaking of love in new languages and spreading across the ancient world to share it with cultures the established Temple could never reach. This Pentecost, like the burning bush that caught Moses far outside Egypt, was not a flame meant only for inner illumination. These were matches, pilot flames. Beginnings of larger movements that burned through mighty nations.

"It all starts with a fireball, babyboy." Neaners glowed with excitement. He told me about an inmate who had recently transferred to this unit from another prison, out in Walla

Walla. "Last night he was whispering to me through the cracks under our doors, like how we do." This newly arrived man told Neaners that dozens of inmates on the other side of the state—inside "The Walls" where Lil' Jokes languished—they had caught word of "what the homie Huesos was doing." How he was sharing what he had with others in solitary confinement, talking about something called "hope" for homies. This new arrival whispered through the nighttime unit that Neaners's fireball movement was catching on in the other IMU sectors, as well.

Neaners nodded and smiled at me, letting me know I was implicated in all this. "We're gonna hurt 'em, babyboy," he said. "We're gonna hurt 'em with *love*. Just watch."

Saint John of the Cross wrote something similar: "The effect of love is to wound, that it may enkindle with love and cause delight. . . . Love is ever throwing out sparks."

A guard tapped on the small window behind Neaners. "Wrap it up."

"How long we got?" Neaners turned in his huge white jumpsuit and hollered back.

The young guard in dark blue fatigues and a matching baseball cap held his fingers up to the window: five minutes.

Neaners asked whether I was "cool doing a little prayer together."

I was.

"Dear God," he whispered through the crackling intercom between us.

Then it was silent for a moment.

I thought the electronics had shorted out again, as they had during other visits. I looked up and he was pressing his thumb and index finger into the place tears might come out.

"Thank you for blessing me 'n shit. I never had nothing, but you've made things work out. You gave me this friendship. You brought my daughters back into my life. You opened up my heart. Open me up more, Lord. I know I ain't perfect. Open my eyes. Help me see what I need to see, grasp what I need to grasp. Just keep these friends by me, supporting me, embracing me. God, you heard my cries in my cell 'n shit, you've heard me cry for a better life, a better *jaina* and a new family, to be part of my kids' lives. Thank you for hearing me . . ."

His voice cracked and broke us both.

Maybe it was all the anxiety and hope and risk that I'd kept contained inside myself over the years of our correspondence. The years of our dreams on lined-paper letters that had filled me with excitement the way the Gospels and New Testament letters had first done. The years I'd fought temptation to give up on Neaners's case—when it became harder to hope each time guys like Richard or Michael or Calimero or Alejandro or Spider all died, each time guys like Dirty relapsed and went back to prison, each time crushing the fragile flame inside me that wanted to still believe in God, in any of this.

Or maybe I was crying because this—here, with Neaners— was what I'd always wanted, the culmination of my pursuit through the night, the jail portal, crawling into padlocked trailers and into locked-down lives: that is, friends outside the church who can help me find the heavenly banquet, who will dream with me through the barriers that stand between this world and what is still possible, friends who want more than this world, who will accompany me through my own rebellion and despair and foul language, who will pray with me.

But as we prayed, one hand each pressed against opposite sides of the glass, we did not know that in just a few months, after being released from solitary and returning to the general population, Neaners would be typing a poem to his daughters in the computer lab when one inmate from a rival gang—normally housed in a separate wing of the prison—was leaked into the room to trigger a fight. I did not yet know that staff do this sometimes because buses are arriving every week with new bodies, and the system needs to free up more units, more space, so the prison needs to throw more guys in the hole. I did not know that in order to justify this, there needs to be an incident, an infraction. So they make one happen: any kind of a fight means everyone involved, victim or not, goes to the hole. Before Neaners would know what was happening that day in the computer lab, alarms would be sounding. One second he would be typing this to his daughters: *I wish I could wash away all of your pains, Carry your burdens and cover you when it rains.* And the next he would be swinging to defend himself, chairs kicked aside, a guard's boot on his shoulder, hands wrenched behind his back. He would be thrown into the hole with mace still stinging in his eyes, and no food, phone, or shower for two days.

As Neaners prayed with me that day in our IMU visit, he did not know that when he'd be back in the hole this second time, he would be denied his mental health meds for weeks without being tapered off under a physician's supervision. Or how, when he would grow shaky and impatient while asking to see the doctor—*"Please!"*—an officer would threaten him with another nine months in the hole for his "attitude." Letters would be delayed in the months to come, mine, his, as well as the growing circle of pen pals and support. Some letters would simply disappear in the system. We did not know how lines of relationship could be cut this easily. The fires catching within inmates' dreams, like the high fructose ones running between their cells, could still be stamped out.

As Neaners prayed with me that day during the IMU visit, I didn't know how all this would affect my life. I didn't know how, given his record in the past, this incident would cost him close to two years of his good time, keeping him in prison that much longer. Or how, since Rachel and I would arrange our lives around Neaners's first release date, preparing to receive him into our home to share life together before working with the farm or living with other men in transformation, building a foundation for his daughters, this news would change everything for us, for many months. I did not yet know that when you seriously connect your future to someone in prison and to their uncertain future, you get jerked around together. People change in a solitary cell, and the solitary cell changes the people who want them.

I did not know that even now, when writing this two years later, with Neaners's release date only months away, I would still be biting my nails in prayer for my friend to make it out. I would still have his hand-crocheted-out-of-sock-and-sheet-threads "Hope for Homies" pendant hanging from my car's rearview mirror, and younger homies getting into my car, leaning the passenger seat way too far back, would touch it, always ask me about it.

I did not know that on some days, either in hope or melancholy, I would put two or three Atomic Fireballs on the counter at the gas station checkout and spend minutes in the parking lot trying to stomp one flat against the curb, never able to crush it thin enough to slide under any door, but nevertheless emptying its contents onto my tongue and closing my eyes while sitting behind the wheel as my car warmed up in the winter rain. *Fan into flame the gift that is within you,* we'd read with the kids in juvie. "Or else," the kid had said, "everything around you gets cold and dark."

I knew none of this as Neaners prayed that day, his voice scratchy through the intercom on his side of the glass and into the receiver at my ear.

What I *did* know—and what I still know now—is that there was more going on than what I or anyone else could fully see. A banquet I had never imagined had broken into this padlocked dumpster. And it could be continuing still, deep in places I would never expect. What else could be happening that we will never hear of, nor see? "We walk by faith, not by sight," Neaners often said. "That's us."

"I thank you God," Neaners wrapped up and wiped his nose, "from the bottom of my heart. Amen."

When I opened my eyes, my own cheeks were wet. I felt an overwhelming burn of gratitude for our friendship, for my life. We both let our hands drop from the glass.

The heavy iron slot in the door behind Neaners clapped open. He stood, reached his hands behind him through the opening and said good-bye to me, still smiling, while the officer snapped shiny handcuffs around his wrists. Then, as he pulled his hands back into the cell and the door popped open, Neaners's face changed back to a stony mask just before the officer escorted him away.

I was left in the small cell alone. And I felt something warm shimmer up my spine and almost hurt beneath my scalp.

Love is ever throwing out sparks.

WANTED VIII

I CONDUCTED FOUR SMALL FUNERAL SERVICES FOR Richard inside the county jail. One for each small bible study group. I knew there were just as many people behind bars who knew him as out in the community, and they deserved a memorial service just the same. I had opened the floor for any memories of Richard, foul or fond, the men wanted to share. At first there was only silence. Some wept.

"I have a story." An Asian guy raised his hand while wiping his eyes with the other. "When we were locked up together—for six months, I remember it, last time I was arrested—Lil' Jokes always called me China Man Stan." He laughed and wiped his nose with his sleeve. "But I didn't mind."

Stan explained how one night before that arrest, at a house party in town, he'd seen Richard dart out the apartment door, forgetting a duffel bag Richard had entered the party with, which Stan knew was loaded with drugs. So Stan ran out the

door with the bag and knocked on Richard's window as the car
pulled out of its parking spot.

"Man, Jokes looked surprised and asked me why I didn't
'fucking take it,' you know, for myself. I told him if it were my
bag, *I'd* want someone to return it to *me*. Man, he just shook his
head and said 'I won't forget this.' Then he sped off.

"So sure enough, I got locked up again, and Jokes was running the pod by the time I got here. But this time, when everyone started harassing me like usual because I got no one in my
race to back me up, Jokes would shout 'Anyone who fucks with
China Man Stan, I'll kick their fucking ass!' He'd yell that from
the crack under his door when we were all on lockdown, before
meal time, just to let everyone know."

Stan's voice quavered now, his throat pinched by either grief
or laughter or both.

"Then he'd yell *I LOVE YOU CHINA MAN STAN!*'
all loud in the pod, he didn't care. And I'm Vietnamese, you
know, so I'd yell back from my lower tier cell: 'But I'm not even
Chinese!'"

I felt Richard's presence return in this story, his mix of bold
affection and gross error.

"Shit like that," Stan concluded with a shrug. "That's why I
and everyone else loved him."

The next day, I walked through the doors of our local funeral
home for the "real" memorial. I found a seat in a crowd of men
and women who loved Richard, all in one room for maybe the
first time: skinny young Chicano gang members in oversized

T-shirts; girlfriends with hair pulled back and small children behind their legs; gray-haired patriarchs of the large families of ill repute in our valley, their brows and mouths creased deep and early with scorn. I recognized more than half the faces from my years working in the jail. These were Richard's friends. He had no key family members to make the usual decisions involved in organizing a funeral, so the local Catholic church had charitably sent a priest and deaconess to fill the podium. These clerics had never met Richard, and maybe the only thing they had heard about him was from the newspapers about the high-speed chase and capture three years before. Or from the front page only a year earlier, when he was finally convicted of murder in the first degree of an aging woman.

The priest and deaconess, possibly mindful of what Thumper's father told him, *If you can't say somethin' nice . . . ,* filled forty-five minutes of Richard's open-casket memorial service by repeating the rosary into a microphone, English then Spanish, over and over again. I had assumed there would be an open mic for friends and family, as we had done in the jail, and so I had prepared a few words. But here in the funeral home, the rosaries droned on. I understand such traditions are meaningful to millions, but these were not practicing Catholic families in the room. I couldn't recognize any participation in the crowd around me as Richard's casket gaped open for another hour. This monotonous repetition uttered by two appointees at the podium felt like a final institutional lid sealed over his memory. I grew anxious and angry in my seat.

I couldn't sit by and watch this. Even his memory was being thrown away. I needed to do something, lift my voice. This was not like Donacio's table, where the right thing was already happening and I need only bear witness, not make it awkward. Here, it was already painfully awkward. But I didn't want to overstep my place, be seen as a troublemaker.

What would Richard want? I wondered. *What would he do if he were here?* In the banquet parable we'd read together in jail, I'd argued that Jesus's host is pained by the man who refuses to identify with his other guests, the man who remains safe and silent when asked why he is there at all.

The priest wrapped up by saying they would now begin one more final "blessing."

I excused myself past the others in the row who tucked in their knees for me and walked down the aisle before a hundred silent mourners, my heart knocking in my chest. I awkwardly approached the priest, while everyone watched, and whispered to him that I was Richard's pastor and that I would now speak. He took his hand off the foam-hooded microphone, shrugged as if he didn't really care one way or the other, and stepped aside.

Looking out from the podium at the people who knew Richard, it was evident that they had expected nothing more. They were used to nothing good being said about their friend. They sat as numb and still as Richard in the satin-lined box beside me, his hands crossed over his chest.

"Richard would have hated this," I finally said.

Hanging heads stirred.

"I . . . I think he would have interrupted all this."

I paused. The room was heavy.

"I think that because . . . when I first met Richard, I was trying to lead a bible study in the jail, and he interrupted *me.*"

With this my whole body relaxed. I could look up and smile, pleased by how this memory of Richard even now interrupted my own anxiety or sense of self-importance at the microphone. I told everyone there how Richard had confronted me. "*No,* bro. How 'bout you check *this* out." I leaned over the podium toward them with a pointed finger, imitating Richard's first words to me, now feeling his face rising in mine.

The whole room exhaled in laughter, just as relieved as the inmates were that day that somebody had spoken up and turned the tables on customary religious protocol. This was the Richard they remembered and loved. Their peer who did what it took to be seen, heard, and known.

"Tired of the babble of functionaries," I said from the podium, "Richard wanted to talk. He wanted to talk about him—what he'd seen and done and heard.

"He even told me in one of his last letters that he'd hand-written more than three hundred pages of his life story so far. April said he was always working on it. And I just heard today that it was mysteriously missing from the boxes of his personal property the prison mailed home this week."

I said I was used to working with men in jail and on the streets who won't open up their stories like that—in person or on paper—for months, maybe years. They have been through so much pain, so much hurt, so much shame and disappointment, gotten so used to having the details of their lives used against them by prosecutors and loved ones alike, that they have every reason to lock up their hearts and hide the keys. "And not just inmates," I added. "Most of us yearn to be fully known and loved, yet we hide and wait for someone to knock, maybe repeatedly, to ask for our hearts. We move slowly and make safe, subtle gestures to hint at our desires for friendship." Both the priest in the front row and the XXXL-clad gangster seated just behind him were still listening. "But Richard was different."

Richard, I said, was not afraid to raise his voice and get in my face. He approached relationships the same way he knocked on Mavis Browne's door that terrible afternoon: *I don't have time to waste. You have what I need. Will you help me? Will you let me in?*

I told the memorial audience how Richard, after cutting me off, asked me to visit him. How he'd immediately opened his door to me. "His address at the time, of course, was the county jail. But that didn't keep him from inviting me over to 'kick it' with him, there in the visitation rooms, as many evenings as I could." I saw several young women and mustachioed young men smile and wipe their eyes at the Richard they recognized, with whom they had "kicked it" many times, and with whom we were now kicking it, together, one last time. It was the kind of gathering he always wanted to assemble. But this time it was not the banquet of free drugs that brought us here. It was him.

I told them how Richard and I would talk late into the night during those visits, how most of his questions boiled down to whether God wanted him as much as he wanted to be wanted. "Richard was the first man in the jail who ever asked me to mail him photocopies from the pages of my theology books," I told the congregation. "I think he wanted written proof of good news. Wanted it in print. Like insurance against the day someone might deny him."

Either way, I said, Richard found a way into my heart. His loss, along with his final letters from prison, had broken my heart, and maybe that's how a greater love enters. In this way, I said, our house thief of a friend had taught me more than he meant to about "breaking and entering."

I said "Thank you" and stepped away from the podium.

I whispered "I love you" over Richard, as I never did in our letters, and took my seat.

Sitting in the silence that remained, before the priest dismissed us all, I remembered one last thing with the whole story of the banquet parable: Richard was also, despite his gangster claims to not comply with party attire, really the first and only guy in that jail who had eagerly taken on a new garment, who'd slid his arms into my goofy coat that was not his style. Even if the temporal authorities would not let him keep it on; even if it was just for a moment, together at a small table inside a jail before he would eventually, literally, be bound hand and foot by the law and left weeping, gnashing his teeth in the pre-dawn prison darkness; and even if the kingdom of heaven that gives such celebration garments to the good and the bad alike is not the kingdom running the world as we know it, Richard had taught me that we could still act it out together. We could imagine it, feel it, for one hour at a time, the way he'd break into those strangers' living rooms and make himself at home, feet up and smiling. Just to pretend.

That's how Jesus said his kingdom would come, anyway—like a thief.

EPILOGUE

LATE ONE NIGHT I WAS VISITING RICHARD ONE-on-one through the glass at the county jail. This was before he was shipped off to prison and rotted alone, but after the no-touch policy had moved us out of the small visiting rooms where we'd begun our friendship. I was scribbling down in my small notebook things he said, connections that occurred to me as he spoke, with the black phone pinched between my ear and shoulder. I noticed his silence, waiting for me to finish transcribing.

"What are you gonna do with all that, what you write down?"

I told him it was mainly for my own education as a young chaplain. To make me a better minister. "As a student I learned how to take notes," I said. "And now you're one of my professors." Judging by his change of posture, I could tell Richard rather liked this arrangement. Most of the time, though, I told him, I just loved what he said. I take note of beauty.

"So you gonna write a book on all us homies one day, or what?"

I shrugged and confessed that it was a pipe dream I'd always had, to write one day. "But don't worry," I assured, "if I ever write for the public and want to use something you've shared with me, I'll change your name, disguise you in some way."

His eyes narrowed.

"And I'll have you read it over and approve anything before it goes out. I mean, I know this stuff, all you tell me, is sensitive material."

Richard looked offended.

"I got nothing to hide," he cocked his head to the side. "I'm a bad guy, Chris. A criminal. Big fucking surprise. That's all most people know about people like me. They throw us away, and we're forgotten, like we never even existed. So why would I want to be disguised? They never even see us. But you—" his finger pointed through the glass "—*you* see us. So I'm telling you: You *better* write a book about me, Chris! You tell the world everything you know about me."

I wrote this down too.

"And you better not change my name, motherfucker!"

When I looked up he was grinning, grinning at me through the thick glass. Faint in the glare, just beside Richard's face, I saw my own reflection, smiling now as well. We were looking at each other, of course, but for a glowing moment I saw a portrait—the only one I have—of the two of us.

APPENDIX

Tierra Nueva

TIERRA NUEVA (NEW EARTH) IS A CHRISTIAN ministry located in Burlington, Washington, that seeks to share the good news of God's freedom in Jesus Christ with people on the margins—immigrant, inmates, ex-offenders, the homeless—and mainstream people through its various ministries. We are dedicated to proclaiming with the oppressed the Good News of God's reign (on earth as it is in heaven) for our mutual liberation, healing, empowerment, and total salvation.

Tierra Nueva began in 1982 as God brought Bob and Gracie Ekblad to work and learn alongside poor campesinos in Minas de Oro, Honduras. Seeking to address the poverty that underlay the regional wars and conflicts in Central America, Bob and Gracie learned and taught sustainable farming practices, nutrition, and preventative health. As they read the scriptures alongside their Honduran neighbors—many of whom were excluded from the local churches—they began to discover Good News for themselves.

After pursuing graduate studies in theology in Montpellier, France, Bob and Gracie moved to the Skagit Valley in Washington State in 1994, a valley with rich agriculture that attracts a large number of migrant farmworkers from Mexico and Central America. Here, they established Tierra Nueva del Norte and began to do legal advocacy and accompaniment of migrant workers and chaplaincy in the local county jail. These two ministries continue to be the anchors of Tierra Nueva, along with theological training through The People's Seminary for mainstream people wanting to work with people from the margins.

Since 1994 many people have been attracted to the ways they discover the Good News of Jesus through the work of Tierra Nueva and have come to stay. Along with their passion and energy, they have helped birth new ministries such as our Gang Initiative, New Earth Recovery, and New Earth Works, which includes Underground Coffee, seeking creative ways to see God's kingdom come on earth as it is in heaven.

Find us at www.tierra-nueva.org.

ACKNOWLEDGMENTS

I FIND THAT WHEN I AM GRATEFUL, AND ACTUALLY express it, I am a happier man. So it is with pleasure that I begin. (I will try to keep my thanks to those directly connected with the creation of this book.)

To my childhood friend—and high school English teacher's son—Ryan Murphy. Many Christmases ago we sat on your floor late at night and confessed that we had each begun to write during the hours when others slept. Thank you for helping me indulge this dream as I drew from yours. Thank you for combing over every word of every draft of every story-then-chapter of what eventually became this book. You helped write this, and I'd be a sham if I didn't name you first.

To Neaners, José Israel Garcia, my brother. Thank you for calling me a pastor when I didn't like the word and for sharing everything you have with me—through more pages of letters than this book can ever put into print—over the past nine years. May these new pages help welcome you home from solitude, babyboy, and open locked doors for you.

To Juanito Garcia, who always told me, in red scrubs, over the lawyer's table, or through the glass, to one day write what I was scribbling in my jail journal (even before Jokes did). You forced me to sing with you in those rooms and time and again you gave me authority, gave me my voice, to speak from the jail. When I stayed too late many nights during our visits, thank you for almost always telling me to go home and tell Rachel I love her.

To all the homies who have shared prayer with me over the years, as well as fishing, hard-pew court hours, car-ride confessions, tears that few others get to see, arguments, awkward texts and phone calls, and the chance to feel God's nearness with you: thank you for your trust. I wish I could have written a chapter for all of you. Evaristo Solano, Felipe Muñoz, Juan Ventura, Juan Luna, Ramón Loa-Mejia, Alfredo Luna, Israel Arreola, Gustavo Vargas, Juan Manrique, Joey Lozano, Angel Martinez, Amy Stanek, Alejandro Sanchez, Daniel and Anthony Siañez, Salvador Mendoza, Slim and Robert Mejia, Ricky Aguilar, Matthew Vasquez, Maribel Beltran, Juan Rosales, Tomás "Rico" Milano, and many more. Thank you for your grace with my errors and unintended harm, for the honor of sharing the hardest and holiest parts of your lives with me.

I am grateful to April Soria for trusting me with more of Richard's story and to Jessie Wing, Carrie Wilkinson, and Paul Wright (with *Prison Legal News and the Human Rights Defense*

Center) for all your work fighting against the human dumpster system.

To Fred Bahnson, my literary angel, advocate, and friend. You opened doors for me I never could have reached—magazine editors, your own agent—and walked me through each new step of the writing life, from the creative, to the emotional, to the legal. You did for me what I aim to do with guys I accompany through the system. And, as with many of my locked-up friends, you did it almost all through letters and phone calls. Thank you.

Mom and Dad, you have believed in me more than most kids, I've learned, ever get to experience. Mom, thank you for staying up and reading stories to me long after the preachers had gone to bed. And Dad, thank you for sharpening my theological and political edge over the heated dinner table debates when I was young. We can look back now with thanks, and turn that table into Eucharist. Your increasing tears in recent years have helped me to welcome them with other men who are even harder than the two of us.

To my big sister, Stephenie. Thank you for letting me cultivate a habit of calling you and reading entire pages of this book over the phone as you drove to your veterinary clients on cold Colorado roads. Thanks for helping me get unstuck by reading in this way, and then letting me hang up the phone abruptly to get back to work. You rock.

Grandmother Hoke, you prayed all through my childhood for me to be a pastor, and I hated it. Now I am grateful for such a calling. And for how you've prayed for me, for Rachel, "every morning, every night before bed," as you assure me, as well as for these guys you'll never get to meet. Thank you for how you've invested in me, supported this expression of church and mission, my education and desire to write. Ultimately, I'm amazed at how you've modeled a life of loving others "to the fullest," as the homies say—that is, unto death. You put the chaplain to shame in your retirement community with how well you visit and love the lonely, even with the two mites of life you have left in you. I'm only now seeing what a heritage you've given me.

Bob Ekblad. I thanked you on the first page and I'll thank you again. You opened the doors to your holy of holies—the county jail—for me, a stranger at the time. You taught me how to see the Bible superimposed over the world today, and vice versa. Thank you for modeling a tangible way to follow Jesus in this age. I have you to thank for putting my hands to this work, even though this work breaks my heart over and over.

I am grateful for my fellow dreamers at Tierra Nueva, both past and present, who have made the work—and the labor to see and understand—less lonely: Ryan Mathis, Mike Neelley, Roger Capron, Troy Terpstra, Gracie Ekblad, Rocio Robles, Amy and Alan Muia, Nick and Elizabeth Turman-Bryant, Bethany Dearborn (and the Dearborn family, who let me use their cabin for some writing escapes), Emily John-Martin, Holly Braun, Ryann Lachowitz, Salvio and Victoria Hernandez, Art and Lisa McKinnon, Paul Foth, Zach Joy, Omy Roberts, Julio Montalvo, Elisa LeDesky, Amanda Jordan, Anne Park, Jonathan Knutzen, and Larry Rogers.

My warmest thanks to James Alison, theologian and friend, whose interpretation of the scriptures sustained me through my darkest days of college. Your book, *On Being Liked,* with its title, helped me understand, years later, my friend Richard's tragic life pursuit to be *wanted.* Those pages I photocopied and mailed to him were from my old copy of your *Raising Abel.*

I am indebted to the practical mysticism taught by our friend just over the Canadian border, Brad Jersak. Your simple exercises for listening prayer have opened up intimate portals between my heart, God's, and others'. I forget how dry my faith would be if it weren't for your dare—and instruction—to really listen.

Thanks to David James Duncan, for modeling a sacramentally immersed and joyful way of writing and for welcoming the guys and me into your world of rivers and play. Thanks to Leo, Steve, and Brett for your ongoing work in sustaining the Liam Wood Fly Fishers and River Guardians school at WWU.

Thanks to Greg Wolfe for shepherding a flock around "art, faith, and mystery" in this land for twenty-five years—and for founding the Seattle Pacific University MFA program, where I could forestall divinity school by exegeting my own memory and encounters through literature. Thank you to my two mentors in the degree: Paula Huston, for caring for me as a weary young pastoral worker, and Lauren Winner, for forcing me to admit I am also a writer, so I can't half-ass it.

My "congregation" doesn't tithe to pay my check. So work like this only happens with missionary-style financial support-raising. Thank you to the handful of families who have chosen to tithe in this direction, from afar, and sustain my role in this community along with the money it takes to care for the unwanted: Martha Hoke, Randy and Donna Golden, Walter and Darlene Hansen, Steve and Eloise Hoke, Rick and Chris Armstrong, Ian and Heather Armstrong, Dan and Karina Whitmarsh, Myra and Dan Perrine, Bob Lee, Lilana Teabo, Paula Huston, Jonathan and Sharon Weldon, Stephenie Hoke, the Hunt Family, Mount Vernon Presbyterian Church, the NPS PC(USA) Community Blessing Grant, and the Louisville Institute Pastoral Study Project grant.

And to the staff at the jail. Thank you for your ongoing patience to buzz us in, night after night, to bring the men out of their pods and into gatherings with us. Your trust, your welcome, your continued accommodation of our pastoral services in your facility is a privilege. One that has changed my life, and many more.

Thank you to my team of readers who tithed their Christmas holiday hours to scroll through this manuscript on their computers and help me see what I couldn't see on my own: Lacie and Holly Braun, Stephenie Hoke, Nick Webber, Cynthia Villegas, Amy Muia, Bryan Bliss, Doug Cardamone, Malora Christensen, Jon Hiskes, Hannah Notess, Fred Bahnson, and Ryan Murphy.

To Wendy Sherman, my tough and lovely agent. I'm so thankful for you. You believed in the half-baked three pages of a proposal I fired off to you on a desperate morning, helped me brush myself up, believe in the book myself, and go to market. Rachel and I are in your debt.

And Roger Freet, my editor at HarperOne. Thank you for saying yes to my proposal, for believing in these portraits, and for your enthusiasm to help post them in the wider world.

Rachel, my love. You've been my quiet strength all through this pursuit. You've seen my head in my hands more than anyone, from the work with the guys, as well as the writing. You helped me embrace this calling, even though you haven't always read what I write. But you've read *me* better than any interpreter I've ever had. I'd be happy to be read by you for the rest of my days.